ETHICS FOR CONTEMPORARY BUREAUCRATS

In the current United States (U.S.) context, we are facing a constitutional crisis with frequent government shutdowns and new debates surrounding immigration, climate change, budgeting practices, and the balance of power. With competing interests, unclear policy, and inconsistent leadership directives, the question becomes: How do contemporary bureaucrats make sense of this ethically turbulent environment? This collection provides a lens for viewing administrative decision-making and behavior from a constitutional basis, as contemporary bureaucrats navigate uncharted territory.

Ethics for Contemporary Bureaucrats is organized around three constitutional values: freedom, property, and social equity. These themes are based on emerging trends in public administration and balanced with traditional ethical models. Each chapter provides an overview of a contemporary ethical issue, identifies key actors, institutions, legal and legislative policy, and offers normative and practical recommendations to address the challenges the issue poses. Rooted in a respected and time-tested intellectual history, this volume speaks to bureaucrats in a modern era of governance. It is ideally suited to educate students, scholars, and public servants on constitutional values and legal precedent as a basis for ethics in the public sector.

Nicole M. Elias, PhD, is an assistant professor in the Department of Public Management at John Jay College of Criminal Justice, CUNY and Founding Co-Director of Women in the Public Sector. Her research focuses on social equity in public administration and policy, with an emphasis on ethics of administration, management of human resources in public organizations, and public policy impacts on different populations. She regularly collaborates with practitioners in government agencies and non-profit organizations. She is a research partner with the New York City Commission on Gender Equity. Dr. Elias held a research fellowship at the U.S. Equal Employment Opportunity Commission Office, U.S. Department of Defense Equal Opportunity Management Institute (DEOMI), and served as the Lead Faculty Advisor to the U.S. Office of Personnel Management on the 2016 Government-wide Inclusive Diversity Strategic Plan. Dr. Elias is the author of numerous journal articles, book chapters, government reports, and practitioner training modules on means of fostering greater representation and inclusion in public service.

Amanda M. Olejarski, PhD, is the Department Chair and MPA Director at West Chester University and teaches graduate and doctoral courses in public policy and administration. Her research has been published in *Public Administration Review, American Review of Public Administration, Administration & Society*, among others. She is the author of two books on ethical decision-making. Olejarski serves as Immediate Past President of the Keystone State ASPA Chapter, chair of NASPAA's Pi Alpha Alpha Committee, and managing editor of *Public Integrity*. Originally from New Jersey, she lives in King of Prussia, PA with her husband, sons, and rescue cats. She enjoys gardening and Wawa.

ETHICS FOR CONTEMPORARY BUREAUCRATS

Navigating Constitutional Crossroads

*Edited by Nicole M. Elias
and Amanda M. Olejarski*

Routledge
Taylor & Francis Group

NEW YORK AND LONDON

First published 2020
by Routledge
52 Vanderbilt Avenue, New York, NY 10017

and by Routledge
2 Park Square, Milton Park, Abingdon, Oxon, OX14 4RN

Routledge is an imprint of the Taylor & Francis Group, an informa business

Library of Congress Cataloging-in-Publication Data
A catalog record for this title has been requested

ISBN: 978-0-367-86208-4 (hbk)
ISBN: 978-0-367-86190-2 (pbk)
ISBN: 978-1-003-02036-3 (ebk)

Typeset in Bembo
by Lumina Datamatics Limited

This work is dedicated to Clorinda Rose, Mauro Robert, and Luca Nicholas.

—Nicole

This work is dedicated to both of my Ryans and Kevin.

—Amanda

CONTENTS

FIGURES

TABLES

EDITORS

Nicole M. Elias, PhD, is an assistant professor in the Department of Public Management at John Jay College of Criminal Justice, CUNY and Founding Co-Director of Women in the Public Sector. Her research focuses on social equity in public administration and policy, with an emphasis on ethics of administration, management of human resources in public organizations, and public policy impacts on different populations. She regularly collaborates with practitioners in government agencies and non-profit organizations. She is a research partner with the New York City Commission on Gender Equity. Dr. Elias held a research fellowship at the U.S. Equal Employment Opportunity Commission Office, U.S. Department of Defense Equal Opportunity Management Institute (DEOMI), and served as the Lead Faculty Advisor to the U.S. Office of Personnel Management on the 2016 Government-wide Inclusive Diversity Strategic Plan. Dr. Elias is the author of numerous journal articles, book chapters, government reports, and practitioner training modules on means of fostering greater representation and inclusion in public service.

Amanda M. Olejarski, PhD, is the Department Chair and MPA Director at West Chester University and teaches graduate and doctoral courses in public policy and administration. Her research has been published in *Public Administration Review, American Review of Public Administration, Administration & Society*, among others. She is the author of two books on ethical decision-making. Olejarski serves as Immediate Past President of the Keystone State ASPA Chapter, chair of NASPAA's Pi Alpha Alpha Committee, and managing editor of *Public Integrity*. Originally from New Jersey, she lives in King of Prussia, PA with her husband, sons, and rescue cats. She enjoys gardening and Wawa.

CONTRIBUTORS

Daniel Boden, PhD, is an assistant professor in the Department of Political Science and Public Administration at the University of Toledo. His professional experiences include management roles in the public, non-profit, and for-profit sectors. His research interests are interdisciplinary in nature and include the intersection of politics and history, higher education policy, and public organizations.

Larkin Dudley, PhD, is professor emerita in the Center for Public Administration and Policy in the College of Architecture and Urban Studies at Virginia Tech. She has been a member of the Virginia Tech community since 1991, where she has contributed significantly to research on citizen participation, governance, and organizational challenge. She has written more than 40 publications and directed numerous sponsored research projects. Dudley also served on the editorial board of the *International Journal of Organizational Theory and Behavior*; and she served in leadership positions for the Southeastern Conference on Public Administration, the American Society for Public Administration, and the National Association of Schools of Public Administration and Affairs. Dudley received her bachelor's and master's degrees from the University of Georgia and her PhD from Virginia Tech.

Brandy S. Faulkner, PhD, is a collegiate assistant professor in Virginia Tech's Department of Political Science. She is a multi-award winning professor, including the College of Liberal Arts and Human Sciences' Teaching Excellence Award, its Diversity Award, the university's Edward S. Diggs Scholar Award. Her teaching and research focuses on race and public policy, American constitutional law, and Pan-African political theory. She is committed to cultivating community-based approaches to problem solving and serves several state and national organizations dedicated to social justice as well as social, political, and economic change. She has been recognized by the university's Student African American Brotherhood, Black Student Alliance, and the Black Graduate Student Organization with the Black Faculty of the Year Award, the Community Pillar Award, and the Edward McPherson Achievement Award, respectively.

Susan W. Gates, PhD, is a former Presidential Management Intern. Susan Wharton Gates served for five years as a budget examiner at the Executive Office of the President, Office of Management and Budget. In 1990, she joined Freddie Mac as an economist. Over the course of a 19-year career, she worked in financial research, mortgage credit risk, and government relations. In 2004, she became vice president of public policy. Since leaving Freddie Mac in 2009, Susan founded Wharton Policy Group, LLC, which provides policy analysis with an eye to developing consensus solutions. She is the author of *Days of Slaughter: Inside the Fall of Freddie Mac and Why It Could Happen Again* (Johns Hopkins University Press, 2017), an insider account of how ideology and public policy contributed to the financial crisis. Susan teaches normative theory, public administration, and business ethics for Virginia Tech's Center for Public Administration and Policy and the Pamplin School of Business. She is also a capstone advisor for Georgetown University's Masters in Real Estate program. Susan received a bachelors of arts at the University of Delaware, a masters in public and international affairs from the University of Pittsburgh, and a PhD in public administration from Virginia Tech. In 2007, she completed the Advanced Management Program at the University of Pennsylvania's Wharton School of Business.

Susan T. Gooden, PhD, is interim dean and professor of the L. Douglas Wilder School of Government and Public Affairs at Virginia Commonwealth University. She is an internationally recognized expert on social equity. Gooden is an elected fellow of the congressionally chartered National Academy of Public Administration and is past president of the American Society for Public Administration.

Sara R. Jordan, PhD, is an assistant professor in the Center for Public Administration and Policy at Virginia Tech. She serves on the Executive Committee of the Global Initiative for Ethics of Autonomous and Intelligent Systems of the IEEE. Sara is the co-chair of the Editing Committee for the 2nd edition of *Ethically Aligned Design*, the chair of the Glossary Committee, and is the co-chair of the Standards Committee for the Society for Social Implications of Technology. Sara's research addresses issues of research ethics, data science and ethics, and data quality in collaborative research projects.

Kate Preston Keeney, PhD, is an assistant professor of Arts Management at the College of Charleston. Her research interests bridge arts and non-profit management with a specific focus on cultural policy, leadership, and organizations. She serves as a consulting editor for the *Journal of Arts Management, Law, and Society,* and as a board member for the South Carolina Arts Alliance. Serving previously as a practitioner, Keeney managed aspects of the construction of the $100 million Moss Arts Center at Virginia Tech and has worked as an arts manager at the Kennedy Center in Washington, DC as well as other major cultural institutions. She holds a PhD in Public Administration and Affairs from the Center for Public Administration and Policy at Virginia Tech (2014) and an MA in Arts Management from American University (2005).

Michael S. Keeney, PhD, is a career public servant having first served as an auditor for the West Virginia Legislature. Upon completion of his PhD from the Center for Public Administration and Policy at Virginia Tech in 2012, he was appointed Presidential Management Fellow with the U.S. federal government where he served as a budget analyst at the Federal Transit Administration and the Department of Veterans Affairs. He went back to Virginia Tech as a postdoctoral associate in the Office of the Senior Fellow for Resource Development where he researched regional economic development policy for university, state, and local leaders. Keeney continues his public service in higher education administration at The Citadel, in Charleston, SC where he has been Associate Athletic Director for Budget and Finance and now serves as the college's budget director. He holds a BA in political science *(magna)* from Marshall University (2004) and an MPA from West Virginia University (2006). In 2018, Keeney was named the Charleston CFO Council's *Rising Star* for Large Firms. Dr. Keeney has taught public policy and political science at Virginia Tech, The Citadel, and the College of Charleston.

Roy Kirby is the vice president of Broadband Programs for the Center for Innovative Technology (CIT) in Herndon, Virginia. CIT Broadband's mission is to accelerate Virginia's socio-economic growth through the application and use of broadband telecommunications. Prior to CIT, Mr. Kirby worked in local government administration and spent eight years teaching in the Public Affairs Department at Roanoke College. His specializations include local government administration, public policy, and ethics in politics and administration.

Sue M. Neal is a doctoral student at West Chester University studying public administration and GIS. She teaches courses in the Political Science Department at Arkansas State University. She received her MPA from Arkansas State University and has over 20 years of executive-level leadership experience in the non-profit sector. Neal serves as a research consultant in the field of animal welfare. She is the president and founding member of the WCU Graduate Students in Public Administration Network. Neal is a lifetime resident of Michigan where she shares her home with an assortment of rescue animals from cats to tortoises and more.

Michelle C. Pautz, PhD, is a professor of political science and assistant provost for the Common Academic Program at the University of Dayton. Her research largely focuses on two areas: the implementation of environmental regulation, particularly at the state level, and the portrayal of bureaucracy and bureaucrats in contemporary American cinema and its effects on audiences. She has published more than two dozen articles in journals ranging from *Administration & Society, Policy Studies Journal,* and *Review of Policy Research* to *Public Voices, PS: Political Science & Politics,* and *Journal of Political Science Education.* She has published seven books, including *Civil Servants on the Silver Screen: Hollywood's Depiction of Government and Bureaucrats, The Lilliputians of Environmental Regulation: The Perspective of State Regulators* (with Sara R. Rinfret), and *US Environmental Policy in Action* (now in its second edition, also with Sara R. Rinfret). She holds a PhD in public administration and a MPA from Virginia Tech and a BA in economics, political science, and public administration from Elon University.

Mike Potter, PhD, is an associate professor at Mississippi State University. He is editor-in-chief of the journal *Public Integrity,* coordinator for the Doctoral and Masters in Public Policy and Administration program, and Co-PI on a $2.7 million grant for the Department of the Army. Before joining MSU, he served as graduate director for the master of public administration at the University of Wyoming and as an assistant professor at Appalachian State University. In his professional career, he worked for the West Virginia State Legislature and the American Bankers Association. He completed his BA at West Virginia University and his MPA and PhD in public administration and public affairs from the Center for Public Administration and Policy at Virginia Tech. He has authored a monograph with Lexington Books and has published articles in *Administration & Society, Public Integrity,* the *International Journal of Public Administration, Global Virtue Ethics Review,* and *Public Administration Research.* He has also contributed several book chapters to edited volumes (published by ABC-CLIO and Benemerita Universidad Autonoma de Puebla Press). His research interests focus on ethics and regulatory policy.

Patrick S. Roberts, PhD, is an associate professor in the Center for Public Administration and Policy at Virginia Tech and a political scientist at the RAND Corporation. His research focuses on public management and the policy process, and he has substantive expertise in homeland security, intelligence and national security, disaster risk, and emergency management. His work helps organizations improve decision-making through collaborative and evidence-based processes and to navigate risk under conditions of uncertainty. Roberts is the author of *Disasters and the American State: How Politicians, Bureaucrats, and the Public Prepare for the Unexpected* (Cambridge, 2013). He served as a foreign policy advisor in the State Department's Bureau of International Security and Non-proliferation, funded by a Council on Foreign Relations Stanton International

Affairs fellowship. He has also been the Ghaemian Scholar-in-Residence at the University of Heidelberg Center for American Studies in Germany.

Gwendolyn Saffran has an MPA in public policy and administration from John Jay College of Criminal Justice and was a recipient of the Carl Schreiber Memorial Award. She works with Professor Elias in John Jay's public management department studying sex and gender in the public sector, with a particular focus on social equity and transgender and non-binary gender issues. She is also currently a Tow Policy Advocacy fellow through John Jay's Prisoner Reentry Institute at the Vera Institute of Justice, working in the Center on Sentencing and Corrections.

Henry Smart III, PhD, is a military veteran with over 15 years of service in the U.S. Marine Corps and the National Guard. Throughout his professional career, he has acquired additional knowledge and experience in contract management, non-profit management, public policy, and social and public administration. In May of 2018, he completed his PhD in public administration and public affairs at Virginia Tech. He currently holds a tenure-track position at John Jay College of Criminal Justice in the Department of Public Management. At John Jay College, Henry teaches undergraduate courses in the Criminal Justice Management program and graduate courses in the Master of Public Administration program. His teaching portfolio covers topics related to the policy process, policy analysis, the evaluation of criminal justice programs and the foundations of public administration. His current research examines colorism's influence on administrative decisions, narratives related to state and local policy agreement, and the intersection of presidential pork and disaster preparedness.

Camilla Stivers, PhD, taught public administration at Cleveland State University and The Evergreen State College, Olympia, Washington. She spent two decades as a non-profit administrator in community-based organizations. Among her published works are *Governance in Dark Times: Practical Philosophy for Public Service* (2008) and, with David G. Carnevale, *Knowledge and Power in Public Bureaucracies: From Pyramid to Circle* (2019).

Kathryn E. Webb Farley, PhD, is an assistant professor of public administration and Director of the MPA Program at Appalachian State University. Her research interests broadly center around different forms of public engagement in hybrid and public organizations, with a particular focus on philanthropy. Prior to joining the Appalachian State faculty, she served as a Presidential Management Fellow. Her early career was spent in hybrid and non-profit institutions including the Smithsonian. These experiences have shaped her research and teaching interests.

FOREWORD

The publication of this volume could not come at a more urgent time. Since Donald J. Trump assumed the American presidency in January, 2017, the sense of constitutional crisis afflicting our political system has grown in volume, though not always in critical precision.

Perhaps the best rationale for the "crisis" label came from Walter J. Shaub, former head of the federal Office of Government Ethics, shortly after he resigned in protest six months after Trump's inauguration. Although the focus of Shaub's job had been misuse of positional authority, such as conflict of interest, he remarked that his central concern going forward is what he calls "assault on the container," that is, on the basic structure of American government, as it was laid out in the U.S. Constitution, and on the accumulated expertise that makes it tick.

The term "constitutional crisis" soon became widely overused and misused and has weakened as a result. Not every misdeed qualifies as an assault on the constitutional container; therefore, greater clarity and critical acuity are warranted, even as conditions appear to worsen. The present volume goes a significant way in this direction, offering guidance to people inside and outside the container about how to sharpen our perspectives and, perhaps most important, how to conduct our public selves in service to the broadest public interest.

As the political theorist Hannah Arendt observed about what she called "dark times," there are two kinds of darkness with which human beings have to cope. One is the darkness of particular events, such as the ongoing mistreatment of refugees at our southern border. The other is the darkness that stems from loss of the "light of the public," the space in which people appear to one another to say what each believes to be the case, and in which we can debate, argue, and figure out how to go forward. I believe Shaub is sensing this deeper darkness when he points to the assault on the structural container of our politics. Not only are fundamental elements and norms of governance under threat, so is the ongoing public-spirited conversation, our only hope for finding a reasonable way forward in public space.

The importance of each of us being able to develop considered opinions and to articulate "what appears to me" has been nearly lost in the onslaught of fake news, trolling, misleading imagery, and out-and-out lying. There is no such thing as a "worthy opponent" anymore. Ordinary people don't believe the rhetoric they see online and on television, yet they don't believe there is such a thing as truth either. We are fast losing the art of what Arendt called "thinking," that is, questioning accepted generalizations and stereotypes, not in isolation, but by engaging in the world.

What role can an ethics volume play in strengthening our ability to think, to form considered opinions, and to restore the public conversation? What is "ethics" anyway?

There are three ways of defining ethics, it seems to me. First is the old "CYA" version ("cover your anatomy"), in which ethics is a code or a set of rules that you follow on the job or in your profession—no doubt important in an era when the most basic conflict-of-interest rules are violated daily by those in power, but demonstrably inadequate. Then there is the well known sense of ethics entailed in the exercise of discretion, applying laws, rules, and so on to particular administrative situations, which is the sense on which most volumes on administrative ethics concentrate. Again, undeniably important, but insufficient in a context that has called the most basic norms and precedents into question, or tossed them out the window.

The third, and I believe most basic, level of ethics is the sense in which the philosopher John Dewey understood it. He suggests that when you decide what to do, you are at the same time deciding who to be. Thus, ethics is a way or mode of life, the "platform" on which you stand to assess situations, act, and in the process show both yourself and the world who you are. It is at this level that Arendt's thinking, the "silent dialogue between me and myself," takes place. The social theorist Michel Foucault called it "a struggle for freedom within the confines of a historical situation." Perhaps Walter Shaub would agree that this form of ethics is what's necessary in order to save the governmental "container."

The great John Rohr saw ethical public administration as a matter of choosing one's constitutional master, that is, judging in the particular situation which branch of the government has the most compelling interests in need of reaffirming. Considered in the light of Arendt and Dewey, choosing one's constitutional master may not be too far from choosing who to be: in the situation at hand, am I a judger, thinking-assessing the crucial factors of the situation (i.e., the judiciary)? Am I a decider, choosing the appropriate move based on my judgment (i.e., the legislator)? Or am I an actor, moving forward to put my decision into effect (i.e., the executive)? Rohr argued that an ethical public administrator has to be able to do, or be, all three—and in the process, practice statecraft.

For Rohr, then, constitutional public administration is grounded—below particular laws, policies, rules, and codes—in the fundamental "orthodoxy" that is the great public conversation out of which the Constitution emerged, a balance among forces and perspectives lodged in what Arendt thought of as the promise inherent in common deliberation.

I do believe that the present volume serves that, most fundamental, promise—the promise of a republic, "if we can keep it."

Camilla Stivers
Levin College of Urban Affairs
Cleveland State University

ACKNOWLEDGMENTS

Thank you to my colleagues and mentors at John Jay College and Virginia Tech who provided advice, feedback, and encouragement throughout this project, especially Brian Cook and Maria D'Agostino. This work was truly fun thanks to Amanda Olejarski's dedication and spirit. Most of all, I want to thank my husband, Rob, and my family for their love and support.

—Nicole

I would like to thank my colleagues in the Department of Public Policy and Administration at West Chester University for their encouragement and also my students for reigniting my love of ethics. I am especially grateful to my college administration for supporting this project from the beginning. Thanks also to my long-time mentors for their sage advice, as always: Jim Garnett and John Morris. To my co-author, Nicole, thank you for all of it, #teammomsgetstuffdone. Most importantly, thank you to my husband, Ryan, and our sons, Ryan Jr. and Kevin, for all the snuggles and laughter.

—Amanda

The editors would like to acknowledge the invaluable help of Sue M. Neal in preparing this volume.

INTRODUCTION

The Constitutional Tradition in Public Administration Ethics

Larkin Dudley, Nicole M. Elias, and Amanda M. Olejarski

Introduction

In the current United States (U.S.) context, we are facing a constitutional crisis. Under the Trump Administration, the federal government has run counter to the framework and values of American governance embedded in the Constitution. Amidst competing interests, unclear policy, and inconsistent leadership directives, the question becomes: How do contemporary bureaucrats make sense of this ethically turbulent environment? This text provides a lens for viewing administrative decision-making and behavior from a constitutional basis as contemporary bureaucrats to navigate uncharted territory. The Constitution can be understood as a compass for public servants, yet recently, it goes largely ignored. We make a case for bringing the Constitution to the forefront of public service ethics. This collection builds on the constitutional approach, the "Blacksburg Manifesto" in *Refounding Public Administration*, and especially John Rohr's foundational ethics text, *Ethics for Bureaucrats: An Essay on Law and Values* (2nd ed., 1989). At the 30th anniversary of Rohr's work, our volume is a direct response to the constitutional crisis facing public servants who take the oath to uphold that very Constitution. *Ethics for Contemporary Bureaucrats: Navigating Constitutional Crossroads* provides readers with a foundation for understanding and applying the values embedded in the Constitution.

The primary aim of this work is to educate students, scholars, and public servants on constitutional values and legal precedent as a basis for ethics in the public sector. A simple online search reveals an unfortunate pervasiveness of constitutional crises. Pressing ethical concerns abound in mainstream media, ranging from immigration detention and obstruction of justice to background checks for gun purchases. This collection presents contemporary examples of legal and policy challenges that bureaucrats must manage. Rooted in a respected and time-tested intellectual history, this volume speaks to applies a constitutional framework to pressing contemporary ethical questions.

This book is organized around three constitutional values: freedom, property, and social equity.[1] These are based on emerging trends in public administration and balanced with traditional ethical models. Each chapter is structured similarly to do the following: (1) provide an overview of a contemporary ethical issue; (2) identify key actors, institutions, legal and legislative policy, and other relevant factors that shape this issue; and (3) offer normative and practical recommendations to address the challenges this ethical issue poses. The authors of each chapter examine new applications of freedom, property, and social equity as United States regime values that emerge from the seminal work of John Rohr. The authors' foundation is the constitutional approach to ethics emerging from the Center for Public Administration and Policy (CPAP) at Virginia Tech, also known as the "Blacksburg School."[2] The major tenets of constitutionalism are described below.

History of the Constitutional Approach to Ethics in Public Administration

In the spring of 1977, Gary L. Wamsley, founding director of CPAP, began the nearly three-year long process of bringing together faculty, including Phil Kronenberg, Charles T. Goodsell, James F. Wolf, Orion F. White, and John A. Rohr, who would become essential to the creation of the Center's distinctive normative approach.[3] In 1982, the founding faculty of Wamsley, Goodsell, Wolf, Rohr, and White sat on the floor at the Federal Executive Institute at a faculty retreat brainstorming ideas that ultimately became a document known as the Blacksburg Manifesto. Introduced during an informal panel at the American Society for Public Administration conference in 1983,[4] the Manifesto asserts boldly that the "founding" of public administration at the turn of the twentieth century was a misfounding that privileged the concept of public administration as a field of managerialism, or administrative science.

Wamsley, Goodsell, Kronenberg, Rohr, White, and Wolf along with Robert Bacher and Camilla Stivers, PhD graduate of the CPAP program, authored *Refounding Public Administration* (Wamsley et al., 1990), resulting in the codification of ideas that extended premises in the Manifesto and elaborated on a normative approach to public administration and policy. Building on themes of the founding faculty, new CPAP faculty and graduates six years later authored *Refounding Democratic Public Administration*, edited by Gary L. Wamsley and James E. Wolf (1996). Since then, scholars have critiqued and extended these ideas, including a recent edition of *Administration and Society* (Volume 50, Issue 5, 2018).

As part of the faculty of CPAP, John Rohr contributed to both the 1990 and 1996 refounding volumes. In *Refounding Public Administration* (Wamsley et al., 1990), Rohr lays out the constitutional case for public administration, and in *Refounding Democratic Public Administration* (Wamsley & Wolf, 1996), Rohr prompts readers to compare the strong state tradition of France with the U.S. in order to recognize the limitations of our own administrative perspectives. The first edition of the work upon which the chapters in this volume are built, *Ethics for Bureaucrats* (1982), was published just before the Manifesto. Rohr's arguments for a constitutional basis of public administration are central to understanding the refounding premises. Rohr further elaborated on the constitutional framework's rationale in the second edition of *Ethics for Bureaucrats* (Rohr, 1989), *To Run A Constitution* (Rohr, 1986), and multiple other books and articles.

The Need for a Refounding

In light of the negative perception of public administration during the political climate of the 1980s, the Manifesto and subsequent scholarship proclaimed that The Public Administration,[5] as a field, was founded on the ideal of science of administration. This basis was argued to be an unstable and unrealistic one, indeed, a misfounding. For the authors of the Blacksburg Manifesto, the misfounding led to questions of legitimacy for the field, and thus, contributed to bureaucrat bashing. As a beginning solution to regaining legitimacy, the Manifesto proposes a refounding based on the concepts of constitutionalism and governance, which would encourage recognition of the legitimate role of public administration in governing the United States.[6] Further, the Manifesto addresses administrative power and discretion. In response to the concern that administrators should not have a place in governing since they are not elected, Rohr enumerates 21 ways other than election, for holding office under the Constitution (Wamsley et al., 1990, p. 82).

The Blacksburg tradition reframes the administrative debate by replacing the question of whether there should be a role for public administration in governing with the question of what form public administration should take in governance (Wamsley et al., p. 35). The Public Administration should be grounded in an institutional approach in the sense that public administration is part of governing, not just management or administration. Governance, according to Wamsley et al. (p. 25), entails the use of "authority in providing systemic steering and direction." If The Public Administration and public administrators are to be involved in governing, then it becomes crucial for them to be understood as legitimate and to have a constitutional grounding. Several principles in the Blacksburg approach provide guidance on how that might occur.

Key Principles from the Refounding

Establishing a Constitutional Basis for Public Administration: According to Rohr (Wamsley et al., 1990, p. 80), The Public Administration's place is subordinate to all three branches of government. Rohr explains that The Public Administration acts as a balance wheel:

choosing which of its constitutional masters it will favor at a given time on a given issue in the continual struggle among the three branches as they act out the script of Federalist 51, wherein ambition counteracts ambition and "the interest of the man …[is] connected with the constitutional rights of the place" (p. 81).

Acting as a Constitutional Officer: In *Refounding Public Administration* (1990), Wamsley and co-authors elaborate the Manifesto's concept that public administrators are constitutional officers. As such, public administrators are seen as bound by oath to apply constitutional principles to the practice of public administration and derive legitimate authority from the debates of the American founding period as described more fully in Rohr's *To Run A Constitution* (1986). In fact, Rohr admonishes public administrators to lift their vision and see themselves as actors who "run a Constitution" (Wamsley et al., 1990, p. 81).

Minding the Public Interest: The public interest, a concept long maligned in academic theory, is revived by Goodsell in *Refounding Public Administration* (1990, pp. 96–113). Goodsell describes the public interest as a symbol, which may remain somewhat ambiguous, but can be discerned through a process of assessing six values underlying the concept: legality-morality, political representativeness, political consensus, concern for logic, concern for effects, and agenda awareness.

Structuring Agencies: Acceptance of what Wamsley calls an Agency perspective implies recognizing that agencies are "institutions that have grown up in executive branches at all levels and that are instruments of action in pursuit of the *public interest*" (Wamsley et al., p. 37). An Agency perspective should yield not only a greater appreciation of the institutional history of agencies, but also promote the understanding of agencies as repositories of specialized knowledge. Further, institutions hold some consensus on the public interest relevant to a particular function of society (Wamsley et al., p. 37). The culture of such an Agency would then be situated as essential in shaping dialogue among powerful stakeholders to consider a higher notion of the public interest and to define programmatically the public interest (Wamsley et al., p. 143). In turn, institutions nurture legitimate, reason-giving authority, foster active citizenship, act in the constitutionally created polycentric power of multiple principles, and uphold the Constitution (p. 151).

Adopting an Agential Perspective: Wamsley promotes the concept of the administrator as a "special citizen," or an agent who stands in place of and acts for other citizens to achieve a collective purpose while always being consciously responsible to other citizens and acting by their authority (Wamsley et al., 1990, p. 117). Adopting this perspective can serve as normative guidance to enact the Agency perspective described above.

Calling for a Committed Public Service: After describing three worlds in which public administrators exist in job, career, and vocation, Wolf and Bacher maintain that the richer concepts of career and vocation paradigms in public administration have weakened in relation to the concept of the job paradigm, where exchanging labor for money becomes the only basis for the relationship of government and its employees (Wamsley et al., p. 177). To strengthen the capacity of The Public Administration, there must be a renewed call for a committed public service. An emphasis on vocation and use of the agency perspective should be cultivated to renew ties between individual efforts and broader communities (pp. 179–180).

Creating Effective Authority and Effective Participation: White (Wamsley et al., 1990, p. 210) presents a framework in which he proposes fostering effective participation through democracy. This model is characterized by effective processes and will result in wise public action. He further argues that the "precondition of effective participation is maturity and the precondition of maturity is participation's opposite—authority" (p. 211). White suggests we parse out in public administration our consideration of both authority and participation in order to return our attention to the public interest, the primary symbol of the field (p. 240).

Encouraging Active Citizenship: According to Stivers (Wamsley et al., p. 246), the legitimate administrative state is one "inhabited by active citizens." Stivers explains this dynamic:

> Administrative legitimacy requires active accountability. Accountability, in turn, requires a shared framework for the interpretation of basic values, one that must be developed jointly by bureaucrats and citizens in real-world situations, rather than assumed (p. 246).

To support this call for active citizenship, Stivers argues that revisions to the code of professional behavior are needed (p. 269). These include personal reflexivity, or a deliberative process of becoming aware of one's positions in sub-communities and the implications for self and others of those positions; development of a critical stance toward administrative contexts, or the realization of being an agent who can make a difference; and finally, a commitment to giving reasons, which Stivers sees as the essence of public decision-making (p. 269).

Extensions of the Founding Works

Six years after the publication of *Refounding Public Administration*, new CPAP faculty and graduates extended the themes above in a volume, *Refounding Democratic Public Administration: Modern Paradoxes, Postmodern Challenges* (Wamsley & Wolf, 1996). One prominent theme of the second *Refounding* was the concern for legitimacy and the understanding of public administration within the constitutional order (see, for example, Richard T. Green, Lawrence Hubbell, Larkin Dudley, Joy A. Clay, John A. Rohr, Larry M. Lane) in Wamsley and Wolf (1996). Others wrestled with nuances surrounding the concept of the public interest (Thomas J. Barth, O. C. McSwite). Still others confronted the relationship between agency and public (Camilla Stivers, Lisa Weinberg, Linda F. Dennard), while some sought better understanding of the contexts in which administration occurs (James F. Wolf, John H. Little). Finally, Wamsley makes a case for a normative grounding in public administration theory to tie together the themes above (Gary L. Wamsley).

Since 1996, numerous scholars have applied, enhanced, and countered the premises above. Most recently, several scholars and practitioners associated with CPAP extended and critiqued ideas from the refounding works in a 50th anniversary issue of *Administration and Society*, "The Renovation and Reassertion of the Refounding" (Volume 50, Issue 5, 2018). This special issue built on the original works and made the constitutional themes and concepts more applicable to current public administration and practice (see the work of co-editors C. Newswander, Mattingly-Jordan, and Boden, and other authors, L. Newswander, Dudley, Webb-Farley, Gniady-Banford, Fairholm, and Gray).

Regime Values in a Contemporary Context

The development of the constitutional framework detailed above complements Rohr's arguments in *Ethics for Bureaucrats* (1989) which is the primary basis of this edited volume. Rohr holds that through their administrative discretion, bureaucrats who are not elected, participate in the governing of a democratic regime. Because bureaucrats govern through discretionary authority and are unelected, they are not beholden to the ballot box. Yet, Rohr explains that bureaucrats still have an ethical obligation to abide by the values that are held by the public in whose name they govern. He delineates those values as constitutional or regime values and explores the specific regime values of freedom, property, and equality as debated by the U.S. Supreme Court. Rohr demonstrates how Supreme Court opinions necessitate ethical reflection and serve as a foundation for understanding regime values in an evolving U.S. context. Thus, at this anniversary of Rohr's work, the authors in this volume critique, develop, and enrich these values by applying them to current ethical challenges in public administration.

Contents of the Book

This volume is divided into three sections, consistent with the regime value framework: freedom, property, and social equity. Freedom is the first regime value examined and opens with Michelle Pautz's chapter on the challenges political institutions face while attempting to protect the public from greenhouse gas emissions. In Chapter 2, Patrick Roberts explores ethical obligations of emergency managers. Then, in Chapter 3, Kate Preston Keeney and Michael S. Keeney assess needs-based budgeting as a way to combat historical budget bias. Closing this section, Susan Gates analyzes the dynamic relationship between freedom and fairness in the context of the 2008 U.S. housing market collapse.

Property as a regime value is the central focus of the second section of this volume and includes traditional notions of property, such as land, homes, and businesses, along with more contemporary conceptions of intellectual property, financial privacy, and higher education transparency as forms of property. In Chapter 5, Amanda M. Olejarski & Sue M. Neal study due process requirements in the U.S. Constitution through the example of eminent domain. Next, in Chapter 6, Sara Jordan highlights the philosophical underpinnings of intellectual property. In Chapter 7, Mike Potter argues that privacy in financial services is considered property under the regime values framework. In Chapter 8, Kathryn Webb Farley contextualizes fundraising in higher education as property, from the regime values lens of accountability, legitimacy, and transparency.

Social equity is the final regime value covered in this volume. In Chapter 9, Nicole M. Elias and Gwendolyn Saffran present a normative argument for adopting and implementing non-binary gender identity policies based on regime values. Susan T. Gooden and Brandy S. Faulkner examine the U.S. Supreme Court's 2013 landmark ruling in *Shelby v. Holder* to highlight the social equity implications of this landmark ruling for voting rights in Chapter 10. Henry Smart, in Chapter 11, advocates for an ethically alert bureaucracy by analyzing the use of administrative discretion in local policing. In Chapter 12, Daniel Boden and Chuck Kirby present a study of broadband access to highlight social equity regime values in practice.

Notes

1 "Social equity" replaces John Rohr's original term, "equality." Adopting this more contemporary understanding is motivated by social equity's emphasis on outcomes rather than sameness of treatment.

2 This school of thought originated at the Blacksburg campus, though CPAP is now operating from three campuses—Blacksburg, Alexandria, and Richmond, Virginia.

3 Other early faculty were not part of the development of the Center's initial normative approach because of either brevity of appointment or other intellectual orientations:

Linda Wolf, Adam Herbert, John Dickey, Thomas Roback, Phil Martin, and adjuncts, Ron Boster, Carole Neves.
4 The Manifesto concepts were first published in *Dialogue* by the Public Administration Theory Network in 1984 followed by revised versions in Ralph Clark Chandler (1987) and Larry B. Hill (1992), then was expanded into *Refounding Public Administration* (1990).
5 Capitalization in the Manifesto and *Refounding Public Administration* is used to denote the idealized version of public administration that the authors think should be, rather than referring to public administration as it may be. Herein, we follow that use of capitalization when referencing the Manifesto.
6 These sections are based upon *Refounding Public Administration* (1990) CPAP oral history, and *Refounding Democratic Public Administration* (1996) as well as a description of Blacksburg Manifesto in *the International Encyclopedia of Public Policy and Administration* by Karen Evans and Gary Wamsley.

References

The Renovation and Reassertian of the Refounding. *Administration and Society*. (1918). *51*(5), 627–747.
Rohr, J. A. (1982/1989). *Ethics for bureaucrats: Essay on law and values*. New York, NY: Marcel Dekker.
Rohr, J. A. (1986). *To run a constitution: The legitimacy of the administrative state*. London: University Press of Kansas.
Wamsley, G. L., Bacher, R. N., Goodsell, C. T., Kronnenberg, P. S., Rohr, J. A., Stivers, White, O.F., Wolf, J. F. (1990). *Refounding public administration*. Newberry Park, CA: Sage Publications.
Wamsley, G. L., & Wolf, J. R. (1996). *Refounding democratic public administration: Modern paradoxes, postmodern challenges*. Thousand Oaks, CA: Sage Publications.

PART I

Freedom: Calling Health, Safety, and Financial Security into Question

1

CIVIL SERVANTS ON THE FRONT-LINES OF GREENHOUSE GAS REGULATION

The Responsibilities of Public Administrators to Protect the Public in the Face of Recalcitrant Political Institutions[1]

Michelle C. Pautz

Introduction

While the topics of bureaucrat bashing and congressional gridlock hardly escape prominent conversation, the United States (U.S.) Supreme Court's 2014 decision in *Utility Air Regulatory Group v. Environmental Protection Agency* (573 U.S. ___) added climate change as another vehicle for misplaced ridicule of public administrators. And while energies are focused on the bureaucracy, the earth's climate continues to change, and concern mounts about the lasting effects of these changes. As civil servants in the U.S. Environmental Protection Agency (E.P.A.) endeavor to address climate change, they are increasingly finding themselves in a difficult situation. Such a predicament is not unknown to government agencies—indeed, it is easily argued that these agencies perennially find themselves in challenging circumstances—but, it is argued here that in the face of a recalcitrant Congress, a White House prone to erratic behavior, an increasingly restrictive Supreme Court, and political appointees that give little credence to the mission of the agency, the civil servants within the E.P.A. are left to pursue the public's interest regarding climate change.

In *Federalist 51*, James Madison notes that an "auxiliary precaution" is frequently needed when the best-case scenario is not available. Using the outline of this Madisonian argument, the contention here is that relying on the public administrators within the E.P.A. to determine and enforce greenhouse gas regulations to combat climate change is the best solution given the behavior of the three political branches of government concerning this public challenge. This argument fits well within the late Professor John Rohr's notion of the civil service acting as a "balance wheel" to ensure that the public's interest is ultimately pursued.

To make this argument, the 2014 *Utility Air Regulatory Group v. EPA* decision and the events leading up to it are explored, including the effects of the *Massachusetts v. EPA* decision in 2007 (549 U.S. 497). While the practical outcome of the *Utility Air Regulatory Group v. EPA* decision is generally viewed as a victory for the E.P.A. and its efforts to regulate greenhouse gas (G.H.G.) emissions, the language in the Supreme Court's (Court's) decision, authored by the late Justice Antonin Scalia, further degrades the work of the civil service and adds to the multitude of reasons why it is incumbent on the public administrators in the E.P.A. to act as that balance wheel—in keeping with the regime value of freedom. Accordingly, the argument begins by investigating the E.P.A.'s efforts to regulate G.H.G. emissions and its statutory authority under the Clean Air Act, initially passed in 1970. From there, the agency's efforts to regulate G.H.G. emissions even with a lack of direction from Congress are considered. Then the Supreme Court's rulings in the two aforementioned cases and the directions from this branch of government are explored. Ultimately, the E.P.A.'s public administrators find themselves in the precarious, but not unfamiliar, position of having to balance the competing demands of the political institutions, including their own politically appointed leaders, all while endeavoring to serve the public. The conclusion is reached that given the history of the issue and the increasingly urgent needs to address climate change, the public administrators in the E.P.A. are in the best position to make decisions about protecting the nation and the public from the harmful effects of G.H.G.s, and they should be given both more latitude and respect from the political branches, as it is arguably the only government entity trying to serve the public and not succumbing to other motivations.

Context of E.P.A. Action and the Clean Air Act

Before one can adequately assess E.P.A. efforts to regulate greenhouse gas emissions and potentially mitigate the adverse effects of climate change, the topic must first be contextualized alongside an examination of the E.P.A.'s existing mandate and statutory guidance. Created by President Richard Nixon's executive order in December 1970, the E.P.A. was charged with protecting human health and the environment by consolidating federal government efforts into a single agency. The birth of the E.P.A. coincided with the national environmental movement and was the manifestation of a nation's clear desire to protect the environment (cf. Rinfret & Pautz, 2019).

The values associated with environmental protection continue decades later and are demonstrated in public opinion polls. Americans continue to tell pollsters that environmental protection is important and more efforts are needed. A majority of Americans (56 percent), in a CBS News poll, indicate that the condition of the environment will be worse for the next generation, 29 percent think it will be about the same, and only 14 percent think it will be better

(CBS News Poll, as reported by Polling Report). Additionally, in a 2018 Gallup poll, when asked if the government is doing too much or too little to protect the environment, 9 percent of respondents said too much, 62 percent say too little, and 28 percent say about the right amount (Gallup, 2018, as reported by Polling Report). Despite the campaigns of various political candidates and interest groups, Americans are generally supportive of efforts to protect the environment and think the responsibility falls to the government to achieve those ends. While this support ebbs and flows given other national concerns and economic realities, the trends are fairly static historically and demonstrate that there is still widespread public support for environmental protection (cf. Rinfret & Pautz, 2019). Finally, it is worth noting that Americans' opinions about the E.P.A. itself are quite favorable; 62 percent of Americans have a favorable view of the agency, while only 30 percent have an unfavorable opinion (Pew Research Center, as quoted in Goodsell, 2014, p. 208).

With the focus on climate change and air pollution, the guiding legislation for the E.P.A. must also be considered. Although the Clean Air Act is typically thought of as being passed initially in 1970, it was actually a significant overhaul of the first federal air pollution legislation passed in 1963. The 1970 Clean Air Act (C.A.A.) was intended to identify and achieve healthy air quality throughout the nation. It was passed with widespread, bipartisan support, and it delegated authority to the E.P.A. to determine threats to air quality and regulate those threats as it deemed appropriate.[2] National uniform standards are called for under the C.A.A. for both stationary and mobile sources of air pollution. There have been two major sets of amendments, one passed in 1977 and the other in 1990, to the C.A.A., but the initial framework largely remains in place.

The central component of the C.A.A. are the National Ambient Air Quality Standards; pursuant to Section 108, the E.P.A. is charged with determining potential air pollutants and then concluding whether or not those pollutants "may reasonably be anticipated to endanger public health or welfare" (42 U.S.C. § 7401–7671). This determination is typically referred to as an "endangerment finding." This background provides the context from which to explore E.P.A. actions regulating G.H.G. emissions.

Greenhouse Gas Regulation and Litigation

The E.P.A.'s efforts to regulate G.H.G.s have a tumultuous history due in no small part to the fact that Congress has not given the E.P.A. clear direction in this area since the 1990 Amendments to the Clean Air Act were passed.[3] As a result, champions and opponents of G.H.G. regulation have placed the E.P.A. at the center of battles in other venues, notably within the White House and within federal courtrooms. In this section, that history is traced in an effort to demonstrate that while the E.P.A. may be routinely seen as a pawn, the civil servants within the E.P.A. should instead be thought of as a much needed balance wheel.

Massachusetts v. EPA

The origins of the 2007 decision in *Massachusetts v. EPA* begin at the end of the Bill Clinton administration. In 1999, nearly two dozen organizations petitioned the E.P.A. to engage in rule making to set standards for G.H.G. emissions for motor vehicles. The petitioners argued that under Section 202 of the C.A.A., the E.P.A. is mandated to determine what is an "air pollutant" and then regulate such pollutants in emissions from motor vehicles. In 2003, the E.P.A. denied the petition (68 *Federal Register* 52922). Later that year, numerous states, cities, and organizations filed suit with the U.S. Court of Appeals demanding a review of the E.P.A.'s denial. The United States Court of Appeals D.C. Circuit upheld the E.P.A.'s decision not to regulate G.H.G. emissions.

The case was appealed to the U.S. Supreme Court, and on April 2, 2007, the decision was announced. In a 5-4 decision, the Supreme Court ruled that the E.P.A. did have the authority to regulate G.H.G. emissions from motor vehicles pursuant to the C.A.A.. In the Court's opinion, authored by Justice John Paul Stevens, the Court said that the E.P.A. could regulate G.H.G. emissions if they were determined to pose a threat to human health or welfare. The decision did not require the E.P.A. to regulate G.H.G. emissions, but required the E.P.A. to make an endangerment finding, and if G.H.G.s were found to endanger the public, then regulation must follow. The Court noted that the "CAA's capacious definition of air pollutant" and that the "broad language" of the statute was designed to ensure its "flexibility" so the statute would not become obsolete (Adler, 2011, p. 426).

E.P.A. Action during the Intervening Years

During the remaining years of the Bush administration, the E.P.A. opted not to pursue G.H.G. emissions and declined to make an endangerment finding, despite mounting scientific evidence of the danger of excessive G.H.G. emissions. Adler (2011) reports that the E.P.A. did not pursue such regulations because the agency did not think it was sensible and preferred to pursue an international agreement (Adler, 2011, p. 427). Additionally, for the first time, the E.P.A. denied a request for a C.A.A. waiver sought by California to set standards for G.H.G. emissions for motor vehicles (73 *Federal Register* 12156; Klyza & Sousa, 2014, p. 296).

When Barack Obama became president, he directed the E.P.A. to move forward with G.H.G. emission regulations and ordered the E.P.A. to revisit its denial of California's waiver request. On December 15, 2009, in response to the 2007 Supreme Court decision, the E.P.A. announced an endangerment finding (74 *Federal Register* 66496). As a result of this finding, the E.P.A. would pursue regulating G.H.G. emissions from new cars and light duty trucks. The E.P.A., along with the National Highway Traffic Safety Administration, promulgated new fuel economy standards and G.H.G. emission requirements for new cars and trucks starting with the 2012–2016 model years on May 7, 2010 (75 *Federal Register* 25324).

While rule making was underway regarding fuel economy and G.H.G. emissions for vehicles, the E.P.A. was also tackling the challenge of G.H.G. emissions from stationary sources. Once the E.P.A. identifies an air pollutant under the C.A.A., the E.P.A. then has to consider the implications for other sources of pollution beyond mobile sources—notably stationary sources. More specifically, a consideration of pollution from stationary sources brings both the Prevention of Significant Deterioration program and the Title V permitting program into play. Under these programs, regulation of G.H.G. emissions would prove challenging because the Clean Air Act specifies the threshold for a "major source" of pollution to be any facility that emits, or has the potential to emit, 100 tons of one pollutant or 250 tons of multiple pollutants combined. This threshold has arguably worked for more traditional pollutants, but these figures are met very, very quickly with G.H.G. emissions, notably carbon dioxide. Accordingly, the E.P.A. proposed the so-called "tailoring rule" in late 2009, which would change these thresholds for G.H.G. emission regulation because of the dramatic rise in facilities that would be subject to regulation under existing thresholds and the regulatory burden that would ensue. The E.P.A. estimated that without modification to the threshold, the number of facilities that would require a Prevention of Significant Deterioration permit would rise from 280 to 81,598 and the number of facilities that would require a Title V permit would jump from 14,700 to around 6 million (75 *Federal Register* 31535–31536). After a multitude of public comments, the E.P.A. issued the final "Tailoring Rule" on June 3, 2010 (75 *Federal Register* 31514).

Utility Air Regulatory Group *v.* EPA

The essence of the controversy in the 2014 decision in *Utility Air Regulatory Group v. EPA* focuses on the E.P.A.'s actions to regulate G.H.G. emissions from stationary sources in addition to mobile sources, of which the latter was prompted by the *Massachusetts* decision. With its decision to regulate G.H.G. emissions from stationary sources, the E.P.A. modified the threshold that triggers regulations for air pollutants established by the Clean Air Act because the E.P.A. argued that the lower thresholds for more conventional air pollutants did not make sense for G.H.G. emissions. The petitioners in this case included a number of states and industry groups who challenged the rules on the grounds that the rules were improperly constructed and represented arbitrary and capricious action on the part of the E.P.A. through its interpretation of what the C.A.A. permitted the agency to do.

On June 23, 2014 the Supreme Court announced its decision. It ruled 7-2 that the E.P.A. could regulate G.H.G. emissions from already regulated stationary sources of air pollution, but it ruled 5-4 that the E.P.A. went too far in assuming that it could regulate all sources of air pollution. This somewhat complicated ruling means that the E.P.A. can regulate most, but not all, sources of G.H.G. emissions that it sought to regulate; or as Justice Antonin Scalia noted in his comments from the bench in announcing the decision "…that the EPA is getting almost everything it wanted in this case" (as quoted in Martinson, 2014). Stated differently, the Court said the E.P.A. could regulate G.H.G. emissions from facilities that are already regulated for other, more conventional air pollutants. However, facilities that would only be regulated due to their G.H.G. emissions could not be regulated, encompassing millions of smaller facilities such as schools or even some restaurants. And the Supreme Court rejected the E.P.A.'s determination that G.H.G. emissions regulations should apply to all stationary sources of pollution and the E.P.A.'s modification of the threshold for a "major source" as stipulated by the C.A.A.

In the immediate aftermath of the decision, while the E.P.A. could claim a win in terms of practical effects, the E.P.A. was subject to scathing rebuke from the Supreme Court. Although it has been many years since the decision was announced, the general trajectory of the E.P.A. in pursuing G.H.G. emissions remains to be seen.[4] Additionally, this decision does not tackle or even take issue with the E.P.A.'s endangerment finding that came in the wake of the *Massachusetts* decision. However, commentary immediately following the decision remarked on the stern language of the decision about the E.P.A.'s actions. Politico called it a "judicial tongue-lashing about overstretching its powers" (Martinson, 2014). And *The New York Times* noted that the "combative tone" of the ruling combined with the "rejection of one of the agency's principal rationales for the regulations…suggests that the road ahead may be rocky…" for the agency and its efforts to combat G.H.G. (Liptak, 2014). The *National Review* observed that the decision "…sharply limit[s] the EPA's discretion…to unilaterally rewrite pollution thresholds" (Keim, 2014). It is comments such as these that signal perhaps the more significant and lasting implications of this decision for the E.P.A. and the efforts of civil servants to serve the public interest.

The Trump Administration's Assault on Climate Change Action

Donald Trump quickly signaled that his administration's approach to climate change and the regulation of G.H.G. would be radically different from its predecessors. Related specifically to this dimension of environmental policy and regulation, Trump announced the withdrawal of the nation from the Paris Climate Agreement, began action to undo the Obama Clean Power Plan, halted the new fuel economy standards, and revoked California's waiver to implement more stringent air quality regulations. These steps have sparked numerous court challenges that are currently winding their way through the judicial system. For example, in a D.C. District Court challenge in 2017, the E.P.A. was rebuked for suspending an Obama era methane rule when it failed to follow procedure dictated by the Administrative Procedures Act (*Clean Air Council v. Pruitt* 862 F. 3d 1 [D.C. Circuit]). Additionally, Trump's appointments to key environmental positions, which include Andrew Wheeler as his second E.P.A. administrator (replacing the scandal plagued Scott Pruitt), who used to be an energy industry lobbyist and is reported to be a climate denier, are not indicative of an administration that seeks to advance the stated mission of the E.P.A. (Kormann, 2018). These actions are coupled with significant cuts to the E.P.A., both in terms of staffing and fiscal resources. Numerous press accounts have documented the massive exodus of career civil servants from the E.P.A. (cf. Dennis, Eilperin, & Tran, 2018).

The Resulting Problem[5]

The preceding discussion has focused on the E.P.A.'s efforts to address G.H.G. emissions and ostensibly serve the public's interest as the scientific evidence for global climate change and its connection to G.H.G. emissions are overwhelming (cf. Intergovernmental Panel on Climate Change [IPCC], 2018). Even though it has been some years since the *Utility Air Regulatory Group* decision, problems are still present from it. First, it is evident in both this more recent decision and from *Massachusetts v. EPA* that the C.A.A. is not suited to deal with G.H.G. regulation and climate change more broadly. This conclusion is widely supported by legal scholars, as well as from those groups on various sides of the debate over climate change (Adler, 2011; Percival, Schroeder, Miller, & Leape, 2009, pp. 501, 516; Walsh, Erman, & Luxton, 2010; see also Klyza & Sousa, 2014). It is hardly surprising that the nearly 50-year-old C.A.A. is ill-equipped to deal with environmental challenges in the twenty-first century. More specifically, a major issue with the statute is how it conceives of air pollutants and the resulting implications for what can and cannot be regulated, not to mention the procedural issues associated with regulation and the political landscape. Additionally, the statutory threshold established for those more conventional air pollutants is not necessarily the most appropriate scale for G.H.G. emissions. Despite significant revisions to the Clean Air Act in 1990, the statute still lacks the necessary updates to effectively deal with climate change and G.H.G. emission regulations. It is worth noting that 65 percent of the U.S. population has been born since the C.A.A. was originally passed (author's calculations based on data from Statista 2019).

In light of these issues that are largely due to the age of the statute and the progress in scientific and technical knowledge since its passage, the most obvious solution would be for Congress, as the representatives of the American people, to articulate a clear direction regarding climate change and G.H.G. emission regulation more specifically. However, it takes little reflection to conclude that Congress is unlikely to act on climate change legislation anytime soon—even with the shift in control of the House of Representatives to the Democrats after the 2018 midterm elections.

A brief review of legislative efforts in the Obama and Trump administrations provide little optimism that action might be taken. When the 111th Congress took office in 2009, there was widespread hope for climate legislation as the new president signaled support for it and the House of Representatives passed H.R. 2454, the American Clean Energy and Security Act of 2009, also referred to as the Waxman-Markey Bill for its authors, 219 to 212. This bill would have established a cap and trade system for G.H.G. emissions. But the bill never made it past committee in the Senate, thereby dashing hopes of major, comprehensive climate legislation.

In subsequent sessions of Congress, the picture is even bleaker. In the 112th Congress, over 100 bills were introduced dealing with climate change, including G.H.G. emissions, but none of consequence made it very far in the legislative process. Congress' inaction led the League of Conservation Voters in their annual scorecard of members of Congress to say that the House was "…the most anti-environmental House ever" (as quoted in "2012 National Environmental…"). In fact, according to Columbia University's Climate Legislation Tracker, numerous bills were introduced to undermine the work of the E.P.A. and even strip the E.P.A. of its existing powers regarding environmental protection, including the No More Excuses Energy Act of 2011, which, if passed, would have specifically excluded G.H.G.s from being defined as air pollutants by the E.P.A. Even the U.S. Government Accountability Office told Congress in its annual update of the High-Risk Series report that climate change is a real and growing threat to the country (McAuliff, 2013).

The story of the 113th Congress is similar. According to a Congressional Research Service report in early 2014, there have been various bills introduced in both chambers of Congress that pertain to climate change. Some bills propose various provisions to encourage or require adaptation action and a significant number include provisions to prohibit the government from taking steps to regulate G.H.G. emissions (Ramseur, 2014). No bills passed both chambers, but a few measures passed the House, including H.R. 3826, which would forbid the E.P.A. from issuing G.H.G. standards in particular industrial sectors. The 114th and 115th Congresses continue a similar story. At the start of the 116th Congress with Democrats taking control of the House of Representatives, it remains to be seen whether climate change legislation will pass the House. Even with the introduction of the "Green New Deal" resolution, which if passed has no legislative authority attached to it, it seems unlikely that meaningful climate change legislation will be a priority for House Democrats. And, of course, even if it does, the Republican controlled Senate is unlikely to have an appetite to take up any such legislation.

Congressional inaction on legislation related to G.H.G. emissions—or any other significant environmental issue—is likely for the foreseeable future for a host of reasons that are beyond the scope of this chapter.[6] By way of summary, a few highlights of the systemic reasons for this inaction include intensifying partisanship, attributable to the seemingly permanent presidential campaign cycle, and increased party polarization (cf. Rinfret & Pautz, 2019). And while the former might be a more cynical rationale, another simple factor is that environmental concerns are only one of many issues competing for the time and attention of lawmakers.

It is easy to conclude that the inability of the U.S. to take decisive action on climate change is the fault of Congress, but the problem is also attributable to the other end of Pennsylvania Avenue and recent presidential administrations. Although the impetus for rulemaking on G.H.G. emissions came from the Obama administration, its approach to climate change was far less discernible. In a widely read *Rolling Stone* article, environmental activist Bill McKibben explored the Obama administration's conflicting positions and actions (and inactions) on climate change (McKibben, 2013). Further, Klyza and Sousa (2014), among others, note that the actions on G.H.G. emissions advocated by the Obama White House are unlikely to achieve "the deep and rapid reductions in GHG emissions called for by most climate scientists" (p. 298). The Obama administration seemed to prefer to expend its political capital with congressional efforts in other policy arenas. And the Trump administration radically changed course·when it came to G.H.G. emissions, and the environment more broadly. During his campaign for president, Trump called climate change a "hoax" brought on by the Chinese. And upon entering the White House, Trump indicated that his administration would undue all the burdensome environmental regulations plaguing business.

Elected representatives in the Congress and the White House appear immune to the concerns and desires of the American people on climate change. Polling data reveal the growing worry Americans have over the changing climate and the increasing desire to see action. Sixty-nine percent of Americans are concerned about climate change (Quinnipiac University Poll, 2018). And 45 percent of respondents to a NBC News/Wall Street Journal poll in December 2018 say immediate action needs to be taken (NBC News/Wall Street Journal, 2018).

The unwillingness of Congress, as the people's representatives, to take action on climate change, and G.H.G. emissions more specifically, and the uneven support from the Obama White House and the radical departure from environmental protection from the Trump White House leave the civil service in want of an "auxiliary precaution," to borrow from James Madison. In *Federalist 51*, Madison outlines his argument in support of checks and balances on the political institutions of government to ensure that power is sufficiently controlled. According to Madison, the separation of powers is a critical mechanism for ensuring the integrity of government, but ensuring that separation would undoubtedly prove challenging. In Madison's ideal, the people would be "…the primary controul [sic] on the government" rather than needing the separation of powers among the political branches of government

(Madison, in Cooke, 1961, p. 349). Nevertheless, "…experience has taught mankind the necessity of auxiliary precautions" (Madison, in Cooke p. 349). In other words, reliance on the citizenry to ensure that the separation of powers is maintained for a virtuous government is the ideal; but through experience, one knows that human nature cannot always ensure this check on government. Accordingly, there must be other mechanisms in place to ensure this check on government, and Madison terms those mechanisms "auxiliary precautions."[7]

A Possible Solution

Consider now the structure of Madison's argument as a mechanism to make the case for governmental action regarding G.H.G. emissions.[8] Ideally, the people's representatives in Congress, as the nation's lawmakers, would take action and pass legislation directing the E.P.A. about what to do or not do regarding G.H.G. emissions and climate change; thus providing the needed clarification that the existing C.A.A. lacks for these civil servants. But for a myriad of reasons, Congress is not acting nor providing guidance to the administrative agencies, and the White House is increasingly acting in ways that are contrary to the mission of the E.P.A. and the stated purpose of the nation's environmental laws. Further, the appointed leadership of the agencies has demonstrated agendas that are antithetical to the work of the agencies. This avoidance, or shirking, of responsibilities leaves the E.P.A. trying its best to serve the public in the absence of clear direction from Congress, while endeavoring to fulfill its obligations to the public and uphold the oath its employees take to the U.S. Constitution[9] (cf. Rohr, 1986).[10]

Given the inability of Congress to tell the bureaucracy what actions, if any, to take regarding climate change and G.H.G. emissions and the dismantling of environmental protections by the White House, the ideal solution is not feasible. Instead, Americans are left looking for an auxiliary precaution, and the argument made here is that the next best alternative to the political institutions is for the civil servants at the E.P.A. to work within existing statutory frameworks—however imperfect—to deal with G.H.G. emissions and ultimately serve the public.[11] And with this latitude, the E.P.A. needs the appropriate amount of administrative discretion and should not be subjected to the bureaucrat-bashing rhetoric that continues to flow from the political institutions, including the Supreme Court.[12] To make this argument, the following rationale is offered: (1) agencies are more likely to serve the public interest than political institutions; (2) expertise typically resides within agencies, not the political institutions and its politically appointed leaders; and (3) agencies are better positioned to balance the political institutions and the competition among them.

Agencies Serve the Public Interest

Although the rampant bureaucrat bashing might leave one with the perception that civil servants are incompetent and ineffective, those misperceptions generally have little basis in reality (cf. Goodsell, 2004, 2014). In fact, agencies can often be in a better position to serve the public interest than political institutions because they are closer to the public, more representative of the public, and allow greater access and participation by the public.[13]

The first component of this argument is that the civil service is far more representative of the citizens than Congress. As Goodsell (2014) reminds, the members of the civil service are rather representative of the American population. Consider the federal civil service as an example. According to the U.S. Office of Personnel Management, the average age of a federal employee is 47.50 years, women represented 44 percent of the federal workforce, 67 percent of employees were white, with 18 percent African-American, 9 percent Latino, and 6 percent Asian (U.S. OPM, 2017). By contrast, the 116th Congress—reported to be one of the most diverse Congresses—is 78 percent white, 24 percent female, and the average age of a newly elected member is 49 years old (Ballotpedia, 2019; Bump, 2015; Dresilver, 2018; Sullivan, 2015). And, in comparison, as reported by the Census Bureau in 2013, the U.S. population was 63 percent white, with 13 percent African-American, and 17 percent Latino. Just over 50 percent of Americans are female (50.8 percent). And the median age was 36.8 years. Glancing at these statistics, it is easy to conclude that the civil service looks more like the population than Congress does.[14] Rohr (1986) argues that because the civil service is more representative of the population, it is better in tune with the public's actual desires and the public's interests simply because it is more like the public (see also, Goodsell, 2014; Long, 1952; Meier, 1975). It might be easy to assume that bureaucrats, however, are liberal leaning Americans given their work in the mammoth government; however, as Goodsell (2014) notes that although more empirical verification is needed, there is little substantiation of such assumptions. In regards to the specific topic of interest here—environmental protection—Konisky (2008) explored the environmental opinions of environmental regulators as compared to the public. He found that there was little difference in the general population's attitudes about environmental protection as compared to regulators (Konisky, 2008; see also Pautz & Rinfret, 2013 for a more in-depth profile of environmental regulators). A diverse workforce fosters different perspectives and experiences that enable the civil service to understand better the desires of the public, and especially because so many citizens are also civil servants. Goodsell (1990) maintains that the "…public bureaucracy is regarded here as the leading institutional embodiment and proponent of the public interest in American life" (p. 107). And Cook (1996) reminds that the very nature of the work of the civil service puts it in a better position to understand the daily experiences and desires of the nation's citizens.

The representative nature of the civil service and its ability to embody the interests of the American public enables government agencies to achieve the public interest, often more so than political institutions. More specifically,

Croley (2008) makes a convincing argument that agencies are better able to achieve the public interest than political institutions through regulation. During the development of regulations, rule making processes enable greater citizen participation and access than lawmaking in Congress affords citizens (Croley, 2008; Kerwin & Furlong, 2018). In terms of the work of regulators and administrative agencies more broadly, Croley notes that regulators are committed to the public interest and their behavior reflects the pursuit of the public interest (pp. 73-ff). And the rule making processes "allow agencies to identify socially desirable regulatory outcomes" and pursue them (Croley, 2008, p. 74). Of course, as Croley indeed points out, this does not imply that outcomes in pursuit of the public's interest always result, but that they can and often do.

These conclusions are echoed by Denhardt and Denhardt (2007) in their advocacy of serving rather than steering. Civil servants "have a central and important role in helping citizens to articulate the public interest, and…[that] should guide the behavior and decision making of public administrators" (Denhardt & Denhardt, 2007, pp. 77–78). By way of summary, civil servants are more representative of the nation than members of the political institutions and this reality helps enable civil servants to understand and serve the public's interest. Additionally, the civil service affords the public ample opportunities to participate in government as the public's interest is sought and pursued.

Expertise of the Civil Service

A second component of this argument that the civil service is well placed to serve the public regarding G.H.G. emissions regulation is that the experts in government are in the civil service, not necessarily in the political institutions of government. Consider the origins of the National Environmental Policy Act of 1970 and the 1972 Clean Water Act as demonstrative of this intention by Congress. Senator Edmund Muskie envisioned the National Environmental Policy Act to entrust the bureaucrats with the power and autonomy necessary to protect the nation's environment precisely because they were the experts (Milazzo, 2006, p. 132). Additionally, with the creation of the Clean Water Act, Congress, pushed by first-term Senator John Tunney (D-California), embraced a simple proposal: clean water was defined as a person's ability to swim in it. The stated objective was for the nation's waterways "to achieve a level of purity sufficient to allow body contact with all the nation's waters, without health hazard" (Milazzo, 2006, pp. 196–197). According to Milazzo (2006), Congress knew that a national "swimmable" standard was not precise even though it was politically salient; accordingly, it would require the experts at the E.P.A. to devise appropriate standards, and there were likely to be variations in those standards.[15] These examples provide evidence that at least in the environmental arena, Congress recognizes the expertise of the civil servants it is tasking with implementing the statutes it passes.

Civil servants provide their expertise and professionalism in service to the public. That expertise might be hydrology, economics, geology, or some other facet of environmental protection. In these areas of expertise, professional norms and standards also are a part of the work of these civil servants (cf. Green, Keller, & Wamsley, 1993). Although civil servants are not elected, and therefore accountability to the citizens is less visible and direct, civil servants are indirectly accountable to the citizens through elected representatives and the ample opportunities for public input and participation, including during rule making. Of course, the ideal solution would be for Congress and the president to take clear action on environmental issues and G.H.G. regulation more specifically, but they are unable or unwilling. Therefore, the duty falls to civil servants who pursue the public interest via rule making. Croley (2008) notes that in terms of regulatory actions, civil servants are well positioned to affect regulatory outcomes because of their ability to know and articulate the public interest (pp. 92–93). And the processes associated with regulation empower agencies to achieve what is "socially beneficial" (Croley, 2008, p. 267). Denhardt and Denhardt (2007) echo these sentiments in their discussions of how civil servants help foster dialogue with the citizens and assist them in defining shared values. These dimensions, coupled with the expertise of individual civil servants, help ensure the public's desires are pursued. Indeed, incorporating the public into the governing process and serving the public interest requires the subject matter expertise that civil servants are positioned to provide.

More broadly, strong administrative agencies are needed, particularly in these times. Luke (1991) notes that civil servants are increasingly called upon to take a longer-term focus and contend with an increasingly interconnected and interdependent public sector environment. As a result, Luke (1991) outlines the demands facing civil servants and calls for a shift from behavioral ethics to policy ethics. Recognizing these themes, Goodsell (2011) finds that through their expertise and their service to the public, these agencies often develop a "mission mystique" that enables them to serve those interests very effectively (Goodsell, 2006, 2011). Administrative agencies are given a charge to serve some facet of the public interest and, over time, adjustments may be necessary, but there is the presumption of tacit acknowledgment of the expertise of the agency and its efforts (Goodsell, 2006). Although Goodsell does not explore environmental protection agencies in his work, a parallel argument could be made that with the public's general support for environmental protection and conclusions that more should be done, the mission of the E.P.A. and the responsibilities it assumes may need adjustments.

In all of these efforts, it is incumbent on these experts to "…use their discretion to favor those policies that they think are most likely to promote the public interest" (Rohr 1986, p. 183). Leaving significant deference to the experts in the bureaucracy can be cause for concern, but there are several points that help allay those concerns. First, civil servants are usually considered experts in their field, and definitely more so than the lawmakers who write the laws the civil servants are tasked with implementing. Rohr (1986) also reminds us that federal civil servants take an oath to uphold the Constitution and civil servants are duty bound to honor those obligations in pursuit of the public's interest, rather than their own.[16] Further, civil servants have a place as constitutional actors, which needs to be recognized (Rohr, 2002, p. 164). This oath is not a mere formality, indeed, it "...justifies the administrator's claim to a certain professional autonomy" (Rohr, 1986, p. 187). And it is precisely this obligation that bounds expert public administrators' use of administrative discretion—as their actions should be tempered by constitutional principles (Rohr, 1986, p. 183). As Rohr (1986) goes on to argue, the use of discretion by public administrators is moderated by their judgment by both the constitutional needs of the time and the needs of citizens. It is "[t]he link between subordination to constitutional masters and freedom to choose among them [that] preserves both the instrumental character of Public Administration and the autonomy necessary for professionalism" (Rohr, 1986, p. 183). The integrity and commitment to the needs of the public arguably tempers civil servants' discretion.[17]

Agencies and Public Administrators as the "Balance Wheel"

Serving the public interest and the expertise of civil servants are essential in considering the role of agencies, such as the E.P.A., in serving as a "balance wheel" among the different political institutions. The debate surrounding G.H.G. emission regulation epitomizes the necessity of agencies, including the E.P.A., to be the needed balance wheel that John Rohr argued was essential. To begin, "...we are told that administrative agencies must be kept firmly under the thumb of elected officials. This is a formula for inaction that betrays the vigorous government the framers of the Constitution envisioned" (Rohr, 1986, p. xi). In his argument grounding public administration in the Constitution, Rohr (1986) effectively argues that the civil service does indeed serve a clear role that is constitutionally legitimized. Further, civil servants "...should lift their vision to see themselves as men and women who 'run a Constitution'" (Rohr, 1986, p. 182). To run a Constitution, civil servants utilize their expertise to serve the public interest. However, Rohr does not argue, nor does this chapter, that in the present example, the E.P.A. should act without impunity. Indeed, constitutional checks are vital as the civil service is beholden to political institutions.

However, political institutions do not always meet or fulfill their obligations to the public and often have different interpretations of the public's interest. It is understandable that there are differences among those institutions, but Rohr contends that it is incumbent on the public administration to work out those differences and help bring about a consensus (Rohr, 1986, 1990). Indeed, this role for public administration is part of its fundamental role in society and is part of the professionalism and autonomy required to meet its obligations to the citizenry (Rohr, 1986, p. 183). Stated differently, public administration serves the public by maintaining its autonomy in order to preserve its role as the expert professional. It is this role as the expert that enables public administration to be the arbitrator when differences invariably arise among the political institutions.

Additionally, as a champion of the civil servant, Rohr argues that not only does public administration serve as a balance wheel when differences arise among the political institutions, but also that from time to time, public administration must proactively choose among the institutions in order to ensure that the appropriate balance is struck and the public interest is served. More specifically, Rohr (1986) states:

> ... administrators should become active participants rather than feckless pawns in the constitutional struggle for control of the Public Administration. Rather than wait to be captured now by Congress, now by presidents, now by the courts, statesmanlike administrators might consider delivering their agencies for a time to a constitutional master of their own choosing. Which master the administrators would favor and for how long would depend on the administrators' judgment of which branch needs to be strengthened to maintain the correct constitutional balance and to achieve the appointed ends so elegantly stated in the Constitution's Preamble (p. 89).

Public administration is well suited to fulfill this role as a balance wheel because of its professionalism, expertise, and accountability structure to the public. This is not to imply that public administration is better than the political branches of government, but rather simply to point out its unique role in the administration—or the doing—of government. Moreover, the meritocratic nature of the civil service helps ensure that serving the public can be married with the expertise to make the best decisions possible in pursuit of those ends. Of course these are not perfect reasons, and there are concerns associated with the prominent role of civil servants, but these reasons are not inconsequential and do support a claim that public administration can and should have a prominent role in working for the public interest. Perhaps optimistically—especially regarding the specific case presented here—public administration may find a way even to bring together the political institutions and refocus on the public interest (Rohr, 1986, p. 184).

In the instance of G.H.G. regulation, the current White House demonstrates its opposition to efforts to combat climate change. Congress displays its inability to reach consensus on this issue (and many others) and routinely chooses not to act. And finally the Supreme Court indicated its approval of the actions of the E.P.A., but appears determined to berate the agency through its opinions and its growing rumblings to limit (perhaps) agency deference—and the much needed freedom to act in service to the public. Therefore, while the ideal solution would have the political institutions devise appropriate action in the public interest regarding G.H.G. emissions and climate change more broadly, the ideal is not likely for the foreseeable future. As Madison eloquently notes, when the ideal is not possible, an auxiliary precaution is required. And maybe that auxiliary precaution—civil servants—might just be able to bring together these political institutions.

Trials in Pursuit of a Solution

In the absence of the ideal solution in this situation, pursuit of an alternative path forward is necessary. After all, as these words are penned, untold amounts of G.H.G. emissions continue to find their way into the atmosphere and result in consequences for human health and welfare. It may be argued that the only government entity that is endeavoring to address the public interest in this matter is the much-despised bureaucracy.

Yet the pursuit of appropriate actions to address the consequences of unchecked G.H.G. emissions occurs while the E.P.A. and its civil servants are subjected to the verbal abuse leveled at them in the 2014 Supreme Court decision alongside other blistering commentary from the various political institutions, and the general public, as tendencies toward bureaucrat bashing are arguably one of Americans' favorite pastimes. Much of the assault on bureaucracy comes from the two most political institutions, the White House and Congress, yet with increasing concern, one may note the attacks coming from the Supreme Court. And the decision in *Utility Air Regulatory Group v. EPA* is particularly noteworthy in this regard. Consider some of the language from the Court's opinion, written by the late Justice Scalia.

The Court's opinion, while ultimately endorsing the majority of the E.P.A.'s actions, demonstrates the politicization of the Court that further alienates it from serving the public interest. First, at various points in the opinion, the Court undermines the expertise of the E.P.A. The Court notes that the E.P.A. merely "believes" G.H.G. are substances that contribute to "global climate change" (quotes original in reference to climate change) rather than acknowledging the expert opinion of scientists around the world and at home in the E.P.A. Further, the Court remarks that the E.P.A. "should have" known better when it took "a wrong interpretative turn." This language and its attacks are not inconsequential, as the Court would be hard-pressed to argue that it was the expert in matters of air pollution and its regulation. The civil servants that comprise the E.P.A. are the experts in environmental protection in the federal government, as the Court is comprised of experts in constitutional law. Just as the Court is afforded respect and reverence commensurate with its expertise, so should the E.P.A. and other government agencies for that matter.

This is not meant to demean the Court, but simply to point out that their expertise lies elsewhere. Yet it is beguiling that the same respect is not afforded to the expertise within the E.P.A.

In addition to questioning the agency's expertise, the E.P.A. is also portrayed by the Court to be power hungry. An often-quoted line from this particular decision reads: "We are not willing to stand on the dock and wave goodbye as EPA embarks on this multiyear voyage of discovery." This comment is in reference to the E.P.A.'s efforts to phase in what it perceived to be a less burdensome regulatory approach. Yet it would not be hard to find the Court taking issue with any agency's inability to move with "all deliberate speed." And, for good measure, the Court points out that "…it would be patently unreasonable—not to say outrageous—for EPA to insist on seizing expansive power." The E.P.A. is not the first, nor is it likely to be the last, agency that has been characterized as power hungry. By the E.P.A.'s own admission during G.H.G. emissions rule making, its actions are far from the best way to deal with these twenty-first century environmental problems. However, the statutory guidance given to the agency is older than the average federal civil servant (49 as compared to 46.8) (Goodsell, 2014, p. 81). Government agencies are frequently told to do more with less, and while that adage applies to the E.P.A., the qualification should be added that its tools and directions are outdated.

Finally, the Court appears to contribute to the ongoing bureaucrat bashing which is unproductive. Moreover, while arguably granting the E.P.A. a "win" in this decision, the Court's language and tenor serve to delegitimize a rightful constitutional actor in its efforts to serve the public. Undermining the legitimacy of a fellow constitutional actor is problematic as legitimacy is vital for administrative institutions to be effective in their tasks (Rohr, 1986, p. x). If the E.P.A. were to blast the Supreme Court in a similar manner, the E.P.A. would be rightly condemned for doing so. It may be argued that the E.P.A. should be subservient to the three political branches based on our constitutional structure, but the constitutional legitimacy and role of public administration has been duly established (cf. Rohr, 1986, 1990; Wamsley et al., 1990). Further, if the White House or Congress were to attack the Court, these branches would also be appropriately critiqued for their actions. Therefore, the question again arises as to why the bureaucracy—a duly established and essential component of the government—continues to face relentless critiques. While a discussion of those ongoing attacks has been well documented elsewhere, one must be reminded of the ill effects these attacks have on the efforts of the bureaucracy to serve the public interest.

Despite these admonishments, the civil servants within the E.P.A. are the auxiliary precaution amidst rising G.H.G. emissions. In its efforts to pursue regulation, the E.P.A. needs to be afforded ample discretion to achieve its ends of serving the public interest. Through expertise and practical experience protecting the nation's air quality for decades, the E.P.A. should be empowered to make regulatory decisions and take regulatory approaches it deems—after requisite procedural steps—appropriate to deal with G.H.G. emissions. In these actions, the E.P.A. is striving to meet its obligations to the public while its political counterparts are shirking that responsibility. Further, berating the civil servants in the E.P.A. in pursuit of these ends in the 2014 Supreme Court decision does little to serve the public and only continues to delegitimize the work of experts in the E.P.A.

Ultimately, the *Utility Air Regulatory Group* decision effectively allows the E.P.A. to continue down the path of regulating G.H.G. emissions with only minimal restraints, but what are the ramifications of the use of the bureaucracy as an auxiliary precaution in the face of inaction by the political institutions? Indeed, the ill effects of Congress and the White House shirking its responsibilities could prove significant. First, the elected leaders of the country continue to undermine the work of the bureaucracy and further erode its legitimacy in the public eye as the bureaucracy's actions, though constitutional, seem not to be. The American public routinely views the work of the administrative state skeptically, leaving it subjected to the criticism of the Supreme Court and even the leadership of the executive branch, as it decries the "deep state," does little to combat those questions of legitimacy. Further, the distrust in government by the American citizenry is exacerbated when the public perceives squabbling and shirking of responsibilities rather than decisive action. An inability for the government to function as intended does little to stem the erosion of trust in government. Third, and finally, the lack of acknowledgment and definitive guidance on the threat of climate change by the political institutions undermines the ongoing efforts of government agencies, such as the E.P.A., in their efforts to serve the public. It is worth remembering the arguments of Publius that a well-administered government would win the affection of its people. Action to combat G.H.G. emissions have not been demonstrative of a well-administered government as we have to resort to an auxiliary precaution. Much could be done to win the affection of the people.

Concluding Thoughts

Regardless of one's viewpoint on the role of government in environmental protection and the need to regulate G.H.G. emissions, the conclusion reached here is that among the governmental actors, the only actor that appears to be trying to serve the public interest is the civil service, not Congress or the White House. And the Supreme Court chastises the E.P.A. in its pursuit while ultimately granting it permission to proceed. Further, it is within this context that the E.P.A. will continue its work serving the public's interest while also enduring the bureaucrat bashing that will likely persist.

As Dobel (1995) effectively demonstrates, the E.P.A. has found itself in a similar situation before having to exude leadership in an era of divided government during the leadership of William Ruckelshaus. Ruckelshaus was the first administrator of the E.P.A. and stepped back into that role after the scandals that beset Anne Gorsuch Burford's leadership during the early 1980s. "Managers in these situations must compensate for the limits of executive or network support in divided times" (Dobel, 1995, p. 495). Thus, there is precedence for the E.P.A. to ensure the public is served in a fractured institutional environment. But even with this precedent, the situation that the E.P.A. finds itself in under Trump's appointees is unprecedented since the agency's political leadership is acting against the agency's mission. An argument can be made that it is more important than ever for the civil servants in the E.P.A. to remain focused and committed to serving the public interest. Denhardt and Denhardt (2015) argue for "...a more transcendent role [for civil servants] based on a commitment to the amelioration of societal problems and improving the quality of citizens' lives" (p. 83). Moreover, ensuring the experts at the E.P.A. have the discretion to follow the agency's mission and serve the public interest could help stymie the exodus of capable and long-serving administrators from the agency under the Trump administration. Undoubtedly, those civil servants would probably be the first to argue that its approach is far from ideal, but the ideal of clear congressional action is unlikely in the near future. Therefore, an auxiliary precaution must be pursued.

And while far from the ideal, the argument presented here is that allowing the E.P.A. to pursue G.H.G. emission regulation is a positive development and the agency should be given the latitude necessary. This argument can be and should be debated in various other contexts and at multiple layers of government as we strive to situate and legitimate public agencies in the broader governance structure in the U.S., particularly in this hyper-partisan political climate. While it is argued here that the E.P.A. is in the best position to serve the public interest regarding G.H.G. emissions regulation, this argument should be considered in other policy arenas, including financial regulation and national security concerns. Explorations of those topics, and others, will enrich the arguments around the position and role of the public service. Additionally, further study of the effects of the behavior of the political institutions toward the bureaucracy should be explored for their impact on the work of public administration. Bureaucrat bashing by citizens is likely to continue, especially if the political institutions do the same. Perhaps if we investigate more fully the bashing perpetuated by all three political institutions, we might begin to understand their effects on society and maybe begin to reflect on the implications for trust in government more generally. Ultimately, all members of the government would do well to remember Alexander Hamilton's words in *Federalist 68* that "the true test of a good government is its aptitude and tendency to produce a good administration."

Notes

1 The author wishes to thank the late Professor John Rohr, whose guidance on a much earlier version of this argument was extremely helpful. The author is also very appreciative of the insightful comments and suggestions of reviewers for *Public Integrity* as an earlier version of this chapter was published there in 2016. Portions of this chapter are reprinted with permission from Taylor & Francis Group as this chapter is adapted from a previously published article "Regulating greenhouse gas emissions: The Supreme Court, the environmental protection agency, Madison's 'Auxiliary Precautions,' and Rohr's 'Balance Wheel'." *Public Integrity, 18*, 2(Spring), 149–166.

2 It is important to stress that not only was the political context very dissimilar in 1970 when the modern Clean Air Act was passed, but the scientific and technical understanding of air pollution was also very different.

3 It should be noted that public discourse about climate change and the adverse effects of G.H.G. emissions began prior to the passage of the Clean Air Act Amendments (cf. Mann, 2012).

4 For instance, the E.P.A. issued its final Clean Power Plant rule in August 2015 further demonstrating its desire to combat climate change. But the Trump administration swiftly reversed course and is undoing these actions.

5 For example, the E.P.A. issued its final Clean Power Plant rule in August 2015 further demonstrating its desire to combat climate change.

6 For additional discussion of the reasons for legislative inaction in Congress, please see Klyza and Sousa (2014), Rinfret and Pautz (2019), and Kraft (2017).

7 It merits mentioning that James Madison would not have expected, nor probably welcomed, a scenario in which the administrative state might need to counteract the political institutions. But serving the public's interest was a paramount concern of his, as it was for his fellow Founders. Furthermore, while the Founders did not explicitly provide for the "fourth branch" in the Constitution, their acknowledgment of its significance is readily apparent in The Federalist Papers (Rohr, 1986).

8 The use of Madison's notion of an "auxiliary precaution" in this context is not the same context as Madison used it in Federalist 51; that being said, though, the structure provides a useful framework in other contexts.

9 This is not to argue, however, that members of the political institutions are shirking their constitutional oaths necessarily. Here, the focus is on the role and responsibilities of civil servants, particularly those with the E.P.A. As Rohr (1986) states, "[t]he oath justifies the administrator's claim to a certain professional autonomy... the concept of 'profession' necessarily implies some sort of independent judgment" (Rohr, 1986, p. 187).

10 It is worth noting that the challenges facing the E.P.A. in this instance are not uncommon for public administration. Eras of divided government—not just the current one—present significant challenges for management in the public sector (cf. Chubb & Peterson, 1989; Mayhew, 1990).

11 A significant portion of Americans fails to distinguish elected officials from bureaucrats when they demand government action on a particular issue. Therefore, it might be argued that Americans ultimately seek governmental action on an issue from whichever entity of government is willing and/or able.

12 It is readily acknowledged, however, that the likelihood bureaucrat bashing will subside is very slight. Nevertheless, this should not stifle normative arguments to the contrary.

13 This is not to argue that agencies in all contexts always serve the public interest in practice, as there are examples throughout history of agencies erring in their pursuit

of the public interest. Instead, the argument here is that agencies can often be in a better position to serve the public interest than political institutions.

14 These observations are not intended to make a normative argument over whether or not Congress should resemble the American population; indeed, Americans elect their members of Congress, so ostensibly it is up to voters to determine the demographics of Congress. This discussion merely points out that the Congress is not representative of the American population.

15 The often quoted "fishable" standard to the Clean Water Act was added later that year, pushed as well by Senator Tunney. •

16 It is worth noting that this oath is also taken by Supreme Court justices, federal judges, members of Congress, and the president.

17 Worries about the exercise of administrative discretion by the civil servants in the E.P.A. should be dampened with the recall that, as with other executive agencies, the president, with confirmation from the Senate, appoints the head of the agency. This political appointment helps serve as a further check on administrative power.

References

2012 National Environmental Scorecard Ranks Members of Congress on Green Issues. (2013, February 21). *The Huffington Post.* Retrieved June 22, 2015, from http://www.huffingtonpost.com/2013/02/21/2012-national-environmental-scorecard_n_2733383.html

Adler, J. H. (2011). Heat expands all things: The proliferation of greenhouse gas regulation under the Obama administration. *Harvard Journal of Law & Public Policy, 34,* 421–452.

Ballotpedia. (2019). 116th Congress. Retrieved February 22, 2019, from https://ballotpedia.org/116th_United_States_Congress

Bump, P. (2015, January 5). The new Congress is 80 percent white, 80 percent male and 92 percent Christian. *The Washington Post.* Retrieved June 22, 2015, from http://www.washingtonpost.com/blogs/the-fix/wp/2015/01/05/the-new-congress-is-80-percent-white-80-percent-male-and-92-percent-christian/

CBS News Poll. (2018, April 11–15). Environment/CBS News Poll April 11–15, 2018. via Polling Report. Retrieved February 21, 2019, from http://www.pollingreport.com/enviro.htm

Chubb, J. E., & Peterson, P. E. (Eds.). (1989). *Can government govern?* Washington, DC: Brookings.

Cook, B. J. (1996). *Bureaucracy and self-government: Reconsidering the role of public administration in American politics.* Baltimore, MD: Johns Hopkins University Press.

Cooke, J. E. (1961). *The federalist.* Middletown, CT: Wesleyan University Press.

Croley, S. P. (2008). *Regulations and public interests: The possibility of good regulatory government.* Princeton, NJ: Princeton University Press.

Denhardt, J. V., & Denhardt, R. B. (2007). *The new public service: Serving, not steering* (Expanded ed.). Armonk, NY: M.E. Sharpe.

Denhardt, J. V., & Denhardt, R. B. (2015). *The new public service: Serving, not steering* (4th ed.). New York, NY: Routledge.

Dennis, B., Eilperin, J., & Tran, A. B. (2018, September 8). Analysis: Staff exodus hits EPA under Trump: "I could do better work to protect the environment outside." *The Washington Post.*

Dobel, J. P. (1995). Managerial leadership in divided times: William Ruckelshaus and the paradoxes of independence. *Administration & Society, 26*, 488–514.

Dresilver, D. (2018, December 18). A record number of women will be serving in the new Congress. *Pew Research Center.* Retrieved from http://www.pewresearch.org/fact-tank/2018/12/18/record-number-women-in-congress/

Gallup. (2018, March 1–8). Environment/Gallup Poll March 1–8, 2018. via Polling Report. Retrieved February 21, 2019, from http://www.pollingreport.com/enviro.htm

Goodsell, C. T. (1990). Public administration and the public interest. In G. L. Wamsley, R. N. Bacher, C. T. Goodsell, P. S. Kronenberg, J. A. Rohr, C. M. Stivers, … J. F. Wolf (Eds.), *Refounding public administration* (pp. 96–113). Thousand Oaks, CA: Sage.

Goodsell, C. T. (2004). *The case for bureaucracy: A public administration polemic.* Washington, DC: CQ Press.

Goodsell, C. T. (2006). A new vision for public administration. *Public Administration Review, 66*, 623–635.

Goodsell, C. T. (2011). *Mission mystique: Belief systems in public agencies.* Washington, DC: CQ Press.

Goodsell, C. T. (2014). *The new case for bureaucracy.* Washington, DC: Sage/CQ Press.

Green, R. T., Keller, L. F., & Wamsley, G. L. (1993). Reconstituting a profession for American public administration. *Public Administration Review, 53*, 516–524.

Intergovernmental Panel on Climate Change. (2018). *Special report: Global warming of 1.5°C.* Retrieved February 21, 2019, from http://www.ipcc.ch/

Keim, J. (2014, June 23). *Utility Air Regulatory Group v. EPA*: Separation of powers in the balance. *National Review.* Retrieved June 23, 2014, from http://www.nationalreview.com/bench-memos/380999/utility-air-regulatory-group-v-epa-separation-powers-balance-jonathan-keim

Kerwin, C. M., & Furlong, S. R. (2018). *Rulemaking: How government agencies write law and make policy.* Washington, DC: CQ Press.

Klyza, C. M., & Sousa, D. J. (2014). *American environmental policy: Beyond gridlock* (Updated & expanded ed.). Cambridge, MA: The MIT Press.

Konisky, D. M. (2008). Bureaucratic and public attitudes toward environment regulation and the economy. *State and Local Government Review, 40*, 139–149.

Kormann, C. (2018, July 11). In Andrew Wheeler, Trump gets a cannier EPA chief. *The New Yorker.*

Kraft, M. E. (2017). *Environmental policy and politics* (7th ed.). New York, NY: Routledge.

Liptak, A. (2014, June 23). Justices uphold emission limits on big industry. *The New York Times.* Retrieved June 23, 2014, from http://www.nytimes.com/2014/06/24/us/justices-with-limits-let-epa-curb-power-plant-gases.html?_r=0

Long, N. E. (1952). Bureaucracy and constitutionalism. *American Political Science Review, 46*, 808–818.

Luke, J. S. (1991). New leadership requirements for public administrators: From managerial to policy ethics. In J. S. Bowman (Ed.), *Ethical frontiers in public management: Seeking new strategies for resolving ethical dilemmas* (pp. 158–182). San Francisco, CA: Jossey-Bass Publishers.

Mann, M. E. (2012). *The hockey stick and the climate wars: Dispatches from the front lines.* New York, NY: Columbia University Press.

Martinson, E. (2014, June 23). Supreme Court Nibbles at EPA's Greenhouse Gas Powers. *Politico.* Retrieved June 23, 2014, from http://www.politico.com/story/2014/06/supreme-court-epa-early-greenhouse-gas-rules-108181.html

Mayhew, D. R. (1990). *Divided we govern: Party control, lawmaking, and investigations, 1946–1990*. New Haven, CT: Yale University Press.

McAuliff, M. (2013, February 14). Climate change: Congress warned about "High Risk" posed by global shifts. *The Huffington Post*. Retrieved June 23, 2014, from http://www.huffingtonpost.com/2013/02/14/climate-change-congress-gao_n_2687149.html

McKibben, B. (2013, December). Obama and climate change: The real story. *Rolling Stone*. Retrieved June 23, 2014, from http://www.rollingstone.com/politics/news/obama-and-climate-change-the-real-story-20131217

Meier, K. J. (1975). Representative bureaucracy: An empirical analysis. *American Political Science Review, 69*, 526–542.

Milazzo, P. C. (2006). *Unlikely environmentalists: Congress and clean water, 1945–1972*. Lawrence, KS: University Press of Kansas.

NBC News/Wall Street Journal. (2018, December 9–12). Environment/NBC News/Wall Street Journal Poll December 9–12, 2018. via Polling Report. Retrieved February 23, 2019, from http://www.pollingreport.com/enviro.htm

Pautz, M. C., & Rinfret, S. R. (2013). *The Lilliputians of environmental regulation: The perspective of state regulators*. New York, NY: Routledge.

Percival, R. V., Schroeder, C. H., Miller, A. S., & Leape, J. P. (2009). *Environmental regulation: Law, science, and policy* (6th ed.). New York, NY: Wolters Kluwer.

Quinnipiac University Poll. (2018, December 12–17). Environment/Quinnipiac University Poll December 12–17, 2018. via Polling Report. Retrieved February 23, 2019, from http://www.pollingreport.com/enviro.htm

Ramseur, J. L. (2014). *Climate change legislation in the 113th Congress*. Washington, DC: Congressional Research Service.

Rinfret, S. R., & Pautz, M. C. (2019). *US environmental policy in action* (2nd ed.). New York, NY: Palgrave.

Rohr, J. A. (1986). *To run a constitution: The legitimacy of the administrative state*. Lawrence, KS: University Press of Kansas.

Rohr, J. A. (1990). The constitutional case for public administration. In G. L. Wamsley, R. N. Bacher, C. T. Goodsell, P. S. Kronenberg, J. A. Rohr, C. M. Stivers, … J. F. Wolf (Eds.), *Refounding public administration* (pp. 52–95). Thousand Oaks, CA: Sage.

Rohr, J. A. (2002). *Civil servants and their constitutions*. Lawrence, KS: University Press of Kansas.

Statista. (2019). Resident population of the United States by sex and age. Retrieved February 21, 2019, from https://www.statista.com/statistics/241488/population-of-the-us-by-sex-and-age/

Sullivan, P. (2015, January 5). Most diverse Congress in history poised to take power. *The Hill*. Retrieved June 22, 2015, from http://thehill.com/homenews/news/228534-114th-congress-by-the-numbers

U.S. Office of Personnel Management. (2017, September). Profile of Federal Civilian Non-postal Employees. Retrieved February 22, 2019, from https://www.opm.gov/policy-data-oversight/data-analysis-documentation/federal-employment-reports/reports-publications/profile-of-federal-civilian-non-postal-employees/

Walsh, W., Erman, M. A., & Luxton, J. C. (2010). Industry cries foul to EPA's attempt to regulate GHG emissions using the clean air act. *Sustainable Development Law & Policy, 39–42*, 61–62.

2

REGIME VALUES IN DISASTER MANAGEMENT

Patrick S. Roberts

Introduction

The regime values framework identifies property and freedom as central to the small-c United States Constitution. These values have influenced the development of disaster management in the United States, but they are open to multiple meanings. The regime values framework does not assume a single meaning for these values, but it does require that bureaucrats reason through value choices and identify moral dilemmas. Disaster management, or emergency management as it is often known, presents a number of moral dilemmas that can be made visible through the lenses of various definitions of property, liberty, and equality. Promoting social capital before disaster occurs may be one way to satisfy multiple regime values in the United States context.

Regime Values

The regime values framework offers a fresh perspective on how to think about right, wrong, and the ought in disaster management. Ethics as a branch of philosophy addresses questions of doing good as well as evil. Ethics in the public service often focuses on wrongdoing, with topics such as whistleblowing or corruption (Brewer & Selden, 1998). Regime values are more elevated, and they focus attention on doing the good thing. Scholars use the term regime in the Aristotelian sense of polity rather than journalistic sense of current political leadership. As Rohr portrays it, the regime expresses the values of the political community that was brought into being by the Constitution (Rohr, 1978, pp. 2, 81–83). These values are normative for the political community, but especially for bureaucrats who have taken an oath to uphold the Constitution. Rohr advocates looking to constitutional law and United States Supreme Court decisions to derive its meaning. Other scholars include additional regime-level documents such as the Declaration of Independence or statements of presidents and civil rights leaders as offering insight into the meaning of regime values, but the Rohr method primarily looks to Supreme Court cases (Elkin & Soltan, 1993; Jaffa, 1986).

The regime values framework requires stepping back from the question philosophers are wont to ask—"Is this regime just?"—and instead asking, "How can I uphold the values of the regime?"[1] It is a form of professional ethics, and it anticipates the popular "giving voice to values" curriculum which attempts to identify relevant values in a given society and organization and develop a plan for acting in accordance with those values. The regime values framework departs from giving voice to values and some other approaches to professional ethics by warning that the study of ethics should not become "too practical" lest the principles and practice of judgment become obscured by the many particularities of individual cases (Rohr, 1978, p. 62).

Regime values are often intertwined, and Rohr finds that freedom and propriety are closely connected in the American regime (Rohr, 1978, p. 191). Property rights and human rights are considered distinct concepts today, but the Founders rarely made such a sharp distinction, usually referring to liberty and property together.[2] The constitutional meaning of freedom and property are intertwined in the 14th Amendment's due process clause, which prohibits the state from depriving a person of life, liberty, or property without the due process of law. The Fifth Amendment offers the same prohibition against the federal government.

The Constitution's use of property and liberty to imply that the government cannot deprive people of their possessions and their land is especially important in disaster management. The United States system of disaster management has evolved to give local governments control over land use and zoning. The source of much of the vulnerability in disasters is in building expensive structures and locating more people in risky locations exposed to wind, water, and fire. The federal government and the Federal Emergency Management Agency (FEMA) are often blamed for being too slow, or too stingy, to provide adequate protection after disasters, but FEMA has limited authority in a disaster (Roberts, 2013). For example, the president issues a disaster declaration, which releases new aid and FEMA capabilities after a major disaster, but only at the request of a governor. If governors think they can handle the disaster on their own, or if they are too slow, FEMA's hands are tied. FEMA's response often depends on the quality of information that the state supplies (e.g., data on severity of damages, the resources already deployed to alleviate the disaster, and a state's familiarity with cost sharing regulations).

The system of federalism and property rights provides substantial protections for local government control. These protections are not absolute, but these powers restrict the federal government's actions to reduce disaster vulnerability more than in some other more centralized systems of government.

Disaster Management in the United States

Disaster management in the United States has evolved from the responsibility of states and localities—if the government was involved at all—to a central function of the federal government. Today, if a large event occurs, the president is the responder and consoler in chief (Roberts, 2010). The growth and bureaucratization of disaster management tracks the growth and bureaucratization of the federal government. In the post-Cold War period, civil defense agencies added preparation for natural hazards such as fires, floods, hurricanes, and tornadoes to their duties. After civil defense declined, the emerging profession of emergency management began to develop to address natural hazards with a less military bent (Roberts, 2013; Rubin, 2019). The Federal Emergency Management Agency was created in 1979 as a clearinghouse bringing together pre-existing disaster aid programs. States and localities began to create their own emergency management offices, and by the 2000s, nearly every state and county and many cities employed professional emergency managers responsible for coordinating preparation and response to disasters that affect their communities. After 2001, many of these offices took on the name homeland security, but natural disasters occupy more of their time than terrorism.

The structure of the disaster state provides localities with power over zoning and land use. FEMA offers incentives and mitigation programs to encourage communities to take steps to prepare for disasters, but the participation rate in many of these programs, from the community rating system to flood insurance, is low (Dixon et al., 2013; Sadiq & Noonan, 2015). Individuals, too, retain the right to put their property at risk by, for example, not elevating homes that may be vulnerable to flooding. Individuals may also choose not to purchase flood insurance or may let it lapse and are not fined. The federal government has a wealth of programs designed to encourage preparation for disaster, including those funded by FEMA, the Department of Housing and Urban Development, and the Small Business Administration. However, local governments and individuals retain substantial discretion over what they do with their property and where they want to build—including in beautiful seaside or forested locations that may be in harm's way (Mileti, 1999).

Moral Dilemmas in Disaster Politics and Policy

Dilemma 1: Property and Liberty Regime Values Give Discretion to Build in Vulnerable Locations

The regime values of property and liberty shaped the disaster state, which leads to a recurring moral dilemma: localities and individual property owners can locate and build in risky locations, but after disaster, they rely on government aid and nonprofits—and the polity as whole—to provide assistance to help rebuild. Property owners may take the risk and bear some of the consequences, but other community members who suffer from the disaster and the government agencies and nonprofits who provide aid also bear the costs. Furthermore, property owners may develop beautiful seaside land at risk of floods and hurricanes or forested land at risk of wildfire, but once a home or school is built, others who did not end up making the choice to build may move there (or, in the case of children, *be moved*) and be in harm's way. The substantial freedom for individuals, corporations, and local groups to shape development creates risks that may harm future resident or require financial help from the rest of the nation to recover. Bureaucrats' choices are shaped by the regime values of liberty and property—and more directly their expression in law and legal interpretation. Therefore, bureaucrats following the law tend to give deference to individual and local level decisions regarding natural hazards even as they try to encourage property owners to build in less risky locations and take steps to mitigate losses from any disasters that might occur.

FEMA's new Building Resilience Infrastructure and Communities program, unveiled in summer 2019, is one example.[3] The program was conceived by FEMA public managers to provide grants for infrastructure projects meant to reduce disaster risk before a disaster occurs. The grants are funded by 6 percent set aside from estimated Disaster Relief Fund expenditures. The Building Resilience Infrastructure and Communities program is innovative because it will invest in making infrastructure more resilient before disaster occurs. The program does not affect the root causes of disaster losses, however, because it has little effect on where people locate and how they build initially. Theories of risk homeostasis predict that strengthening infrastructure and reducing disaster risk might encourage even more people to locate in a relatively vulnerable area than otherwise would have (Wilde, 1982). A community might be a good candidate for a grant precisely because it located infrastructure in a risky location, prone to hurricanes, earthquakes, or fire, and therefore need to be strengthened.

At the federal level or in nonprofit organizations, aid programs must balance how much attention to give to people who built in risky locations and need help once the inevitable fire or flood occurs, with giving help through guidance with state and federal grants or help with recovery plans to people who located in less risky locations, but were struck by a rare event. When faced with truly serious risks, bureaucrats need to decide whether to defer to individual property and liberty values or exercise power within the law to restrict individuals' exercise of these values—an area for discretion (Rohr, 1978, p. 75). For example, in some jurisdictions bureaucrats can enforce zoning or land use regulations, or choose to ignore them (WashMil, 2003, p. 113).

In some jurisdictions, bureaucrats can influence zoning restrictions to encourage less risky behavior, or they can take more of a hands off approach. Some municipalities can prohibit the subdivision of land within mapped floodplains, unless the proposed division has plans for proper drainage to prevent flooding (Nolon, 2003, p. 11).[4] The requirement for drainage and hazard mitigation is a way to protect future residents and the property owner, even though it imposes a cost on the property owner. How bureaucrats interpret what property means, and whose property, can guide how far they push for greater zoning and building code regulations.

Dilemma 2: The Regime Value of Equality Requires Bureaucrats to Confront Its Multiple Meanings

Bureaucrats looking to regime values will find law, legal interpretation, and constitutional values supporting a great deal of deference to local communities and individual property owners. But the Constitution's value of equality (e.g., the 14th amendment's "equal protection of the laws") provides a counterweight to consider how the impacts of the law are spread among all citizens.

Rohr analyzes how the contested value of equality shapes debates over race and sex (or gender) and leaves bureaucrats with a sometimes confusing and changing menu of options (Rohr, 1978, pp. 87–134). At the very least, the value of equality means equal treatment. But bureaucrats face choices about what equal treatment means in the case of disaster aid. Disasters have disproportionate effects on vulnerable communities—the poor, the marginalized, and the elderly. Studies of disaster vulnerability categorize these groups into social vulnerability scales, over and above measures of physical vulnerability. Emergency managers can choose among various notions of equality (Cutter, Boruff, & Shirley, 2003). The regime values framework requires them only to not skirt the issue or retreat to mere legalism.

To take one concrete example, local emergency managers participate in writing recovery plans for their communities. These plans guide where and when resources and attention should be devoted to repairing transportation networks, health and communication infrastructure, reopening schools, and providing and locating temporary housing. Emergency managers could treat all areas of the community equally, or they could focus more resources and attention on low incomes areas of the community, or areas with hospitals and nursing homes, and the elderly. Research shows that most county emergency managers show a preference treating all areas of a county equally rather than for plans that target low or high income areas specifically (Roberts, Wernstedt, & Velotti, 2018). How managers approach this dilemma in part depends on what they believe equal treatment requires—a focus on equal effects, which would suggest greater attention to vulnerable communities; or a focus on equal attention and effort to all, which would suggest treating all areas of a community equally.

The nature of equality in disasters is complex because disasters themselves do not affect all areas equally—an earthquake occurs in a particular place with no regard for equal treatment. However, the impacts of disasters are made better or worse by how prepared or how vulnerable a community is. The presence of a hazard does not guarantee that it will be a catastrophic disaster. For example, a magnitude 7 earthquake is a manageable event in an area with earthquake resistant building codes and building restricted to less vulnerable areas where seismic waves are less likely to be severe. A magnitude 7.1 earthquake struck Ridgecrest, CA (140 miles north of Los Angeles) on July 5, 2019, following another quake in the same location a day earlier. The earthquake seemed to cause only one death, a person found under a Jeep vehicle 100 miles from the epicenter (Fuller, Vigdor, & Taylor, 2019). The Ridgecrest quake stands in contrast to a devastating 7.0 magnitude earthquake that killed roughly 300,000 people in the less well prepared Haiti 2010 and displaced millions. Haiti lacked well enforced building codes and suffered from a greater incidence of poverty and weaker infrastructure overall.

Public managers face choices over whether to target resources and attention to all areas equally, whether to target wealthier areas worth more economically, or whether to target areas that suffered more damage and may have been more vulnerable (but worth less in economic value). In 2005, Hurricane Katrina devastated New Orleans and the Louisiana and Mississippi Gulf Coast. More than 50 percent of New Orleans residents before Karina were renters (Greater New Orleans Fair Housing Center [GNOFHC], 2011). Government programs to aid survivors favor homeowners and people with clear titles to their land (GNOFHC, 2011; Jopling, 2007). Renters, transients, and people with roots extending back generations in one home, but who lacked clear title received less aid, and were less able to get back on their feet. In many cases, these people scattered to other parts of the country.

The Louisiana state Road Home program offered the same preferential treatment to property owners. State grants for repairs to homes to help homeowners return were calculated using allocations based on the market value of homes and assessed damage (GNOFHC, 2011). Homeowners who qualified faced an easier road home than renters or transients, and homeowners with high market values received more assistance than those with relatively low market values.

At the local level, the recovery planning process after Katrina excluded some residents in an apparent quest to make quick decisions and reinvent the city (Barrios, 2017; Ford, 2010). The Unified New Orleans Plan was ostensibly a process where all New Orleanians could participate in the recovery planning process. In fact, some decisions such as the demolition of public housing had already been made before the public was involved (Barrios, 2011).

Regime Values as a Starting Point for Emergency Management Ethics

The regime values framework begins with the perspective that bureaucrats have choices about which values to emphasize and when, within constrains provided by law, their organization, and their daily tasks. Emergency management officials at all levels of government can choose to uphold the value of equality. The complication is that equality has different plausible meanings in the American regime. It could mean providing equal resources and attention to all areas affected by disaster, or it could mean devoting more attention to areas and people with more wealth—and therefore more to potentially lose and more to gain by a full recovery. It could also mean devoting more attention and resources to those who suffer more and who can least weather the shock of a disaster. These are likely the renters, the transients, the young, poor, sick, or elderly.

One area where the values of property, liberty, and equality intersect is the area of social capital. If regime values provide space for individual and community discretion over property as well as for a concern for equal treatment before the law, supporting communities in preparing for disaster and recovery could further regime values. Research shows that communities with high degrees of social capital measured by strong within group social ties and strong ties to external groups are more resilient (Aldrich, 2012; Aldrich & Meyer, 2015). In Katrina, the Vietnamese neighborhood of Village de l'Est was relatively poor, but also recovered more quickly than some wealthier neighborhoods (Rivera & Nickels, 2014; Storr & Haeffele-Balch, 2012). The community's strong social ties facilitated access to resources, mutual assistance, and rebuilding. Village de l'Est remains intact today and did not suffer the same degree of gentrification as others. Emergency managers could support social capital through community planning, small grants, education programs, and seed money for infrastructure projects—along the lines of Building Resilience Infrastructure and Communities, but with a community planning element. Strengthening social capital may be one underexploited route for disaster preparedness that supports the competing regime values of property, liberty, and equality and their multiple meanings.

Notes

1 Rohr (1978, p. 61).
2 As Rohr (1978, p. 233) notes, *Federalist* 54 makes a distinction between personal and property rights, but this is an exceptional mention.
3 For more, see: https://www.fema.gov/news-release/2019/05/22/fema-seeks-public-comment-new-pre-disaster-hazard-mitigation-grant-program
4 See Colo. Rev. Stat. secs. 30-28-133, 31-23-214.

References

Aldrich, D. P. (2012). *Building resilience: Social capital in post-disaster recovery*. Chicago, IL: University of Chicago Press.
Aldrich, D. P., & Meyer, M. A. (2015). Social capital and community resilience. *American Behavioral Scientist, 59*(2), 254–269.

Barrios, R. E. (2011). "If you did not grow up here, you cannot appreciate living here": Neoliberalism, space-time, and affect in post-Katrina recovery planning. *Human Organization, 70*, 118–127.

Barrios, R. E. (2017). *Governing affect: Neoliberalism and disaster reconstruction.* Lincoln, NE: University of Nebraska Press.

Brewer, G. A., & Selden, S. C. (1998). Whistle blowers in the federal civil service: New evidence of the public service ethic. *Journal of Public Administration Research and Theory, 8*(3), 413–440.

Cutter, S. L., Boruff, B. J., & Shirley, W. L. (2003). Social vulnerability to environmental hazards. *Social Science Quarterly, 84*(2), 242–261.

Dixon, L., Clancy, N., Bender, B., Kofner, A., Manheim, D., & Zakaras, L. (2013). *Flood insurance in New York City following Hurricane Sandy.* Santa Monica, CA: Rand Corporation.

Elkin, S. L., & Soltan, K. E. (Eds.). (1993). *A new constitutionalism: Designing political institutions for a good society.* Chicago, IL: University of Chicago Press.

Ford, K. (2010). *The trouble with city planning: What New Orleans can teach us.* New Haven, CT: Yale University Press.

Fuller, T., Vigdor, N., & Taylor, D. B. (2019, July 6). Southern California rocked by earthquake for second time in two days. *New York Times.*

Greater New Orleans Fair Housing Center. (2011). State Amends Problematic Hurricane Relief Program. Retrieved August 21, 2019, from http://www.gnofairhousing.org/2011/07/07/state-ammends-problematic-hurricane-relief-program/

Jaffa, H. V. (1986). What were the original intentions of the framers of the Constitution of the United States. *University Puget Sound Law Review, 10*, 351.

Jopling, J. (2007). Two years after the storm: The state of Katrina Housing Recovery on the Mississippi Gulf Coast. *Mississippi Law Journal, 77*, 873.

Mileti, D. (1999). *Disasters by design: A reassessment of natural hazards in the United States.* Washington, DC: Joseph Henry Press.

Nolon, J. R. (2003). *New ground: The advent of local environmental law.* Washington, DC: Environmental Law Institute.

Rivera, J. D., & Nickels, A. E. (2014). Social capital, community resilience, and faith-based organizations in disaster recovery: A case study of Mary Queen of Vietnam Catholic Church. *Risk, Hazards & Crisis in Public Policy, 5*(2), 178–211.

Roberts, P. (2010). Our responder in chief. *National Affairs, 5*, 76–90.

Roberts, P. S. (2013). *Disasters and the American state: How politicians, bureaucrats, and the public prepare for the unexpected.* New York, NY: Cambridge University Press.

Roberts, P., Wernstedt, K., & Velotti, L. (2018, November 8). How public managers make tradeoffs over lives: Evidence from a flood planning experiment. *American Public Policy Analysis and Management Conference*, Washington, DC.

Rohr, J. (1978). *Ethics for bureaucrats.* New York, NY: Marcel Dekker.

Rubin, C. B. (Ed.). (2019). *Emergency management: The American experience* (3rd ed.). New York, NY: Routledge.

Sadiq, A. A., & Noonan, D. S. (2015). Flood disaster management policy: An analysis of the United States Community Ratings System. *Journal of Natural Resources Policy Research, 7*(1), 5–22.

Storr, V. H., & Haeffele-Balch, S. (2012). Post-disaster community recovery in heterogeneous, loosely connected communities. *Review of Social Economy, 70*(3), 295–314.

WashMil. (2003, March). Keeping hazards from becoming disasters: A mitigation workbook for local jurisdictions. Washington Military Department, Emergency Management Division. Retrieved from www.metrokc.gov/prepare/docs/RHMP–LocalMitigationWkbkFinal.pdf

Wilde, G. J. (1982). Critical issues in risk homeostasis theory. *Risk Analysis, 2*(4), 249–258.

3

ADVANCING ADMINISTRATIVE ETHICS THROUGH NEEDS-BASED BUDGETING PRACTICE

Kate Preston Keeney and Michael S. Keeney

Personal values, preferences, and culture shape budgetary practice and decision-making (Douglas & Wier, 2005; Franklin & Raadschelders, 2003). An institution's budget advances strategic decisions and priorities, but it is commonly value-laden. As such, it is necessary to examine the essential organizational practice of budgeting through a public value lens, paying specific attention to outcomes related to transparent, data-informed budget practices. We argue that a new approach to budgeting is needed in order to advance freedom of reason, and to eliminate bias and related pathologies common in the public sector. In exploring this problem related to bias in budget formulation, we address the following questions:

Why is a new budgeting model necessary in the public sector?

Is it possible for a budget formulation process to be free of bias?

How can a budgeting model best support all constituents?

Is reform toward a data-informed model worth the effort, and what can it contribute?

What values or cultural shifts are necessary for institutions to embrace data-informed budgetary models?

We complete this analysis through the lens of *public value* and more specifically *regime values*. Related to this project, Piotrowski (2014) appropriately argues that the value of transparency fits Rohr's (1989) definition of *regime values*, and discusses the concept of transparency as related, but separate from *ethics*. Piotrowski (2014) defines transparency as "being able to learn about what is going on inside of an organization," and also, she connects transparency to public participation (p. 186). It is not enough, however, for organizations to be transparent in their operations and procedures. Instead, ethical practices embody transparency and *more*, a similar notion to Rohr's definition of the "high road" to administrative ethics (Piotrowski, 2014). Through an examination of budgeting in public higher education, we suggest that it is possible to demonstrate the administrative ethic, advance leadership priorities, and reduce or eliminate bias in the budget formulation process.

We examine several data-informed strategies superimposed on both centralized and decentralized budget models. This allows us to explain a data-informed budgetary model (needs-based model) in the public sector. The needs-based model offers several advantages over other types. First, the model emphasizes true costs over historical budgeting practices. Second, the needs-based model reduces budgetary slack common to the incremental approach—a process that accumulates a residue of bias over time. Third, the needs-based approach preserves elements of institutional data (or information that is of the essence of the institution) that may be lost in the most traditional of zero-based budgeting processes. Ultimately, we aim to describe the needs-based budgetary model that best reflects public value, promotes transparency, and serves contemporary, as opposed to historical, practice.

Understanding the Problem: A Residue of Bias in the Budgeting Process

We argue that the perennial problem of self-interest in the budgeting process leads to an enduring *residue of bias* in the institution's budgeting process. By residue of bias, we mean that year-over-year incremental decisions continue to build and repeat. With each increment, bias endures or residue builds. Absent a wholesale jettisoning of theories about which programs return the greatest return on investment or even the proper level of funding for mundane factor inputs (paper, pencils, and labor), budgeters repeat year-over-year support vis-à-vis standard budget formulation processes. The residue of bias, however, can be addressed when formulation activities are inclusive of better information about *how* investments leads to desired, sometimes competing, outcomes. We argue that data-informed budget formulation processes that are transparent and inclusive of ideas will lead to both the mutual adjustment of the symptom of "the way things have always been" and more effective results. To be sure, we carefully invoke "data-informed" early on to avert any tendency toward a purely positivist approach (i.e., purely data-driven).

Budget funding is the manifestation of policy preference in action (Jones & Baumgartner, 2005). One can imagine that depending on the budget environment of a college or university, budget practices will vary based on preferences. For example, a dean may prioritize a decision about deferred maintenance for the infirmary in a different way from an executive leader who oversees the operation and maintenance of the physical plant. At the exact same time, the same executive leader might not see expansion of a research program in nanotechnology as having priority over a leaking roof. This reality is at odds with the concept of all actors executing decisions with one institution in mind. Even these seemingly disparate preferences are inextricably intertwined. Although all actors may intend to serve a singular mission—such as advancing learning, promoting scholarship, and encouraging service—thus, "thinking institutionally," we are not always capable of that level of execution (Heclo, 2008). We cannot assume that decisions about budget formulation will be approximately the *same* given that actors are members of the *same* institution. Personal values, preferences, and culture can shape budgetary practice and decision-making (Douglas & Wier, 2005; Franklin & Raadschelders, 2003). Just as resources are allocated at all levels of government and in public and private organizations, economic self-interest abounds even when void of malintent. We are biased, even if we don't *mean* to be.

Other contextual realities of budgeting complicate the accumulation of residue of bias, the very first being incrementalism, where programs enjoy year-over-year success shrouded in *tradition*. Though providing a predictable basis for institutional budgeting, incrementalism (Davis et al., 1974; Fenno, 1966; Wildavsky, 1964) and its slight adjustments over time, do not demand iterative introspection about optimal allocation of resources. We also acknowledge that economic shots in the arm will have the effect of distributing new or increased resources for new programs (Wagner, 1883). Influencing factors such as increased tax base may drive increased spending in targeted areas (Choi, Bae, Kwon, & Feiock, 2009; Lewis-Beck & Rice, 1985; Thornton & Ulrich, 1999). We take this as a given. Though it is fortunate that public institutions *are* subject to the fruits of economic vitality, ethical resource allocation demands thoughtfulness.

The Higher Education Environment

Higher education institutional budget environments vary by institution. Such budget environments may be driven by administrative policies or academic areas. In the public landscape, the residue of bias exists not only within organizations, but also with state policymakers. Examining budgeting in the public higher education context is particularly illuminating as public higher education has relied on lessening state institutional support over time, experiencing deep funding cuts after the 2007 recession (SHEEO, 2018).

Colleges and universities are one step removed from the traditional democratic feedback from the polity. Although college governing boards receive critical input on one-off strategic investments and approval of overall budget operation strategies on a macro level, members likely devolve micro-level decisions to their administrators. Even though institutional funding from the state for school operations is vetted through the legislative process, gubernatorial review, and ongoing oversight for all funds and operations, administrative discretion is very much in play, thus necessitating the need for key values to be present in the formulation process. Rigorous budget formulation methods help address the equitable allocation of public resources, thereby serving as an extension of the state-level policy processes. The allocation of resources at the institutional level is as important as the allocation of resources by state and/or federal policymakers. Because citizens fund public institutions of higher education just as they do their town or county council, constituents expect results or at a minimum an explanation about how investment might lead to certain outcomes or results. Therefore, an evaluation of processes and their merit based on the key values is as critical in this context as it is in any other public context.

Administrative Ethic

This analysis began with a discussion of Rohr's regime values, specifically where we can look for—and expect—the "high road" in public budgeting practice. We argue that through data-informed, needs-based budget techniques, three values should be identifiable: transparency, participation, and accountability. These values "cut across the entire administrative process" (Rohr, 1989, p. 71), and for the sake of this research, permit us to take a step back from the minutiae of budgeting in order to refocus our attention on normative fundamentals. We position these values—transparency, participation, and accountability—within Rohr's discussion of *freedom*, arguing that freedom of reason, information, and debate should serve as a foundation to the public budgeting process. After this introduction, we analyze how well each value stacks up in light of several budgeting alternatives.

The most important value that links public budgeting to freedom is transparency. Piotrowski (2014) deftly makes the case for transparency as a regime value, highlighting the works of Rohr and Cooper (2004), among others. It is through transparency that bureaucrats can serve citizens and earn their trust in the process. Transparency begets participation—another cross-cutting public sector value. An open and participatory process allows for the freedom of information exchange that ultimately aids decision-making processes. In turn, this approach ensures that decision-makers—and in this case budget officers—are accountable to the process and to the organization. To be sure, there are operational drawbacks to permitting freedom in any administrative process. Taking the "high road" is easier said than done. However, when the forthcoming comparison of several budget techniques clarifies the elevated path, the aspirational "high road" will be shown as attainable.

Within this context, we emphasize the need for data-informed, needs-based budget allocation models. Just as institutions can be the recipient of good, they also can be subject to economic downturn, perhaps making our argument even more salient. With more information, we can respond to both stability and punctuations

(Jones & Baumgartner, 2005), and even unpredictable avalanches of change that disrupt incremental contexts (True, 2000). Posner (2009) has argued that "rules and processes can help policy makers cope by protecting their ability to make hard choices" (p. 233). Similarly, we suggest that needs-based approaches at the institutional level can have a similar effect. In this research, we argue that by including more data in budget formulation process, rather than less, we have the potential to see less bias and more objectivity bent at advancing the strategic needs of the institution; this is manifest in a rigorous approach toward allocation of scarce resources.

We do not argue that all decisions can be data-driven, but rather that they can be *data-informed*; this is a crucial distinction. Though information leads to better decisions, it is not the *sine qua non* of good policy. After all, institutions are complex and have integral human components that must be considered. Concrete examples could include decisions that would drive disinvestment in human capital, especially where in higher education, academic freedom and excellence in teaching, research, and service are built on the tradition of tenure and promotion. (We are not arguing for a disruption to that model.) Additionally, outside resources may be driven by legislative and donor intent; not all spending decisions are made in-house. This is especially the case for public institutions.

The Higher Education Budget Environment: Description and Illustration

We illustrate the budgeting process, and related complexities, within a broader discussion of centralized and decentralized higher education budget environments, as well as various budget reforms. These environments and approaches lay the foundation for the budgeting process and influence its outcomes. We do not offer a one-size-fits-all solution, but instead hope to shine light on related complexities that affect the public pursuit of transparency in the process.

The Macro View: Centralized vs. Decentralized Budget Environments

At a broad view, budget environments are characterized as centralized or decentralized. It is important to first understand this environment, before analyzing the specifics of a renewed data-informed budget model. Our analysis offers a critique of how core administrative values might be addressed by both environments. Both centralized and decentralized models tend to contribute residue, which is not necessarily positive or negative. The important takeaway is that the building of residue be data-informed. Without data-informed decisions, residue will tend to be biased toward a particular program or potentially have a self-economic bent. With data, we assuage concerns about economic self-interest.

Highly *centralized* budget environments provide for strict control over the institution's financial resources; this is seen in both the budget formulation and budget execution processes. In the centralized budget environment, most, if not all input into budget formulation comes from executive leadership. In the higher education context, executive leadership is defined as the institution's president or chancellor, the provost, the chief financial officer, and other vice-presidential level leaders. During the budget formulation process, this cadre of leadership will have the primary input on strategic policy preferences related to academe as well as to administrative operations of the institution. This may manifest in any number of decisions about budgeting and the policy preferences that come to light in that process. The pure centralized model also bears all of the burden from outside mandates imposed on the institution.

On the other end of the spectrum, imagine a budget environment that is *decentralized*. In this instance, budget prioritization relies much more on the input from leaders of academic and administrative units. Academic units may be referred to as colleges (in the case of larger universities) or as schools (in the case of smaller colleges). During the budget formulation process, the academic deans will have primary input on strategic policy preferences related to their respective schools as well as the administrative operations *within* the school. Their decisions will be closely coordinated with the chief academic officer (i.e., the provost), but their flexibility is limited. Without direct access to economic resources other than those directly driven toward their programs (i.e., through access to gift funds), their decisions are hardly decentralized, but rather dependent on resources mustered by the college writ large. Stated differently, short of the pure responsibility controlled model (Dubek, 1997; Hnat et al., 2015), where all costs and expenses are purely the responsibility of the deans, decentralized college central administration is still ultimately responsible for ensuring that unfunded mandates such as pension increases, general salary increases, and cost of living adjustments are addressed centrally.

Herein lies part of the problem: what decisions are being made? Given the complexity of the mission, allocation of resources within the institution is both complicated and imprecise. It is complicated because of the myriad of moving parts that range in the sphere of pure academic areas to administrative operations. The formulation process is imprecise because there is no single method for allocation. It may be more art than science and more political in a Lasswell (1936) sense than apolitical. Self-interest and a desire to gain economically—even if not personally (Feldman, 1982)—is at play. Much is at stake when it comes to making decisions about advancing the institution and ensuring some degree of resource availability for administrative operations. In addition to these endogenous procedural challenges, exogenous budgetary realities of stability and punctuation abound.

Examples of endogenous factors complicating the budget formulation and execution are shown in Table 3.1. Factors in the "primary mission" column represent the core mission of the educational institutions. Factors in the "supporting command" column represent administrative operations, necessary to support the primary mission. These examples are for illustrative purposes.

TABLE 3.1 Funding decision challenges: endogenous factors

Advancing the Institution's Core Mission (Primary Mission)	Purely Administrative Operations (Supporting Command)
New academic programs in which to invest	Funding and staffing for a central administrative unit, such as the controller's office
Hiring strategies for faculty (and academic areas to support mission)	Addressing deferred maintenance (i.e., operation and maintenance of the physical plant)
Competitive compensation and retention initiatives	Investing in a new major construction project such as an academic hall or dormitory
Enhancing student experience through state-of-the-art learning spaces	State-of-the-art equipment, training, and staffing for the institution's police unit
Curriculum overhauls	Efficiency initiatives

A discussion of the budgeting environment provides related challenges and justification for renewed processes. Doubtless, each example in Table 3.1 is inextricably interconnected. Therefore, a holistic approach is in order. A college focused on an enhanced student experience through state-of-the-art learning spaces cannot achieve its desire without: (1) a well equipped police force to keep its students, faculty, and staff safe and (2) maintenance of its physical infrastructure with rigorous deferred maintenance plans. Periodic evaluations of required curriculum and methods for increasing operational efficiency are needed in order to attract and retain top academic talent. However, in the absence of a rigorous needs-based budget process that is data-informed and considers key values of transparency, participation, accountability, and administrative discretion, we argue that budget preferences are susceptible to continued incrementalism, which does not address the overall needs of the college. In effect, the residue of bias will continue to build.

How to Proceed? A Brief Nod to Budget Reform

To be sure, macro-level budget reforms in the United States political context have ebbed and flowed. Budget "reforms reflect the times in which they were formulated, the public mood and needs, and the political beliefs of those who promote them. They are not simply good government proposals, appropriate for all times. If some portions of the reforms adopted do not seem to be working in the present period, they can be changed" (Rubin, 1994, p. 249). This insight is supported by years of changing budget reforms and practices in the United States (see Posner, 2009; Kettl, 2003). We saw performance budgeting (multiple times in the early twentieth century); planning-program-budgeting (1960s); management by objectives and zero-based budgeting (1970s); government performance and results and its modernization in the 1990s–2000s (see Kettl,

1992, 2003, 2018); and more recently linking performance (PART) scores to program budgets (Joyce, 2008). Each has had varied results at the federal level of government. As Gilmour and Lewis (2006a, 2006b) and Moynihan (2006) have observed, injection of objective positivist measurements into the budget process have not been fail-safe because even the data are subject to interpretation.

The lessons of budget reform are applicable as we observe tensions driven by public values. Though each practice has its merits, there may be unintended consequences or simply by-products of policymakers attempting to be objective, but unable to be so. Still, subjectivity manifests as bias. There are lessons vis-à-vis these reforms that can be considered in a data–informed model for budget formulation that are closely aligned with the zero-based budget model. In this analysis, we reimagine a flexible zero-based budget model in the context of higher education and how this model addresses key values at the institutional level.

An Illustration of the Data-Informed Processes

In this section, we present several concepts important for making data-informed decisions in the budgeting process. The first hinges on a classic approach to budgeting: the *zero-based budget model*. We then introduce *cost-effectiveness*, an analytical approach for organizing desired outcomes in policy preference. Finally, we provide an illustration that allows for either a singular or blended approach. An institution will best be able to meet its goals by using a combination of these data-informed approaches.

Zero-Based Budgeting

In the strictest sense, a zero-based budget assumes that no spending unit's budget is built upon what had been previously allocated. The base point is at zero funding. This is in stark contrast to incrementalism, where budgets approximately increase in a way that is proportional to additional resources feeding the institution (see Wildavsky, 1964). Starting at zero for each budget cycle would be impractical, or as Kettl (1992) puts it, "**simply** impossible—analytically, legally, or politically" (p. 83). We cannot jettison in whole part decisions (in the form of public programs) that had been included in a prior year's budget. Instead, budgeters begin at a certain cut point of the budget and then analyze marginal increases on top of that cut point through a rigorous analysis of programs. We argue that this stage of the analysis is where key values can be seen in practice.

Following Gordon and Heivilin (1982) and Kettl (1992), we offer a five-step sequence for analyzing programs within a zero-based budget model. In Table 3.2, we offer several potential decision units within the context of higher education, which could be subjected to each of the five steps. This analysis represents how a college may rank priorities across academic and administrative

TABLE 3.2 Analyzing decisions in a zero-based-budget higher education environment

Analysis sequence	Decision unit analysis
Step 1: Define "decision units" *VPs/Provost determine priorities*	1. Recapitalizing a campus housing unit 2. Investment in an academic program 3. Upgrade police dept. transportation

Step 2: Build "decision packages" of programs
 VP/Provost outline array of options
	1. Recapitalizing a campus housing unit
	   Option A: renovate existing footprint (est. $10 million)
	   Option B: option A and add square footage (est. $40 million)
	   Option C: raze and rebuild to meet growing needs (est. $80 million)
	 2. Investment in an academic program
	   Option A: add robotics major and lab to existing school (est. $3 million)
	   Option B: add robotics major/partner with local industry (est. $500,000)
	   Option C: add robotics concentration to mechanical engineering ($250,000)
	 3. Upgrade police dept. transportation
	   Option A: purchase new cruiser and two bicycles (est. $50,000)
	   Option B: lease three cruisers from state fleet (est. $30,000)
	   Option C: contract out traffic enforcement (est. $200,000)

Step 3: Rank decision packages *Unit chooses best option;* *$93 million investment*	1. Recapitalizing a campus housing unit: unit first choice: option B (est. $40 million) 2. Investment in an academic program: unit first choice: option A (est. $3 million) 3. Upgrade police dept. transportation: unit first choice: option A (est. $50,000)
Step 4: Consolidate rankings *VPs/Provost choose best option;* *$40.55 million investment*	1. Recapitalizing a campus housing unit: college choice: option A (est. $40 million) 2. Investment in an academic program: college choice: option B (est. $500,000) 3. Upgrade police dept. transportation: college choice: option A (est. $50,000)
Step 5: Allocate resources *Final approval by the president and* *board; $32.4 million investment*	1. Recapitalizing a campus housing unit: college funds: option A at 80% (est. $32 million) 2. Investment in an academic program: college funds: option B at 80% (est. $400,000) 3. Upgrade police dept. transportation: college funds: option A at 50% (est. $25,000)

Note: Analysis sequence adopted from Kettl (1992) and Gordon and Heivilin (1982).

functions of the institution. At a minimum, the options represent between $10.3 million and $83.2 million in discretionary spending. In the end, the college allocated $32.4 million in resources for each of the programs or initiatives.

One can imagine that the array of these budget/policy alternatives could be developed in a vacuum—that is by each area's respective leadership (void of input from other key stakeholders). Resources could then be subsequently allocated by college leadership. Such allocation could have been without information about how each marginal investment (e.g., choosing option A, B, or C) might generate a certain result. If this were the case, we would have nothing more than a *teched-up* version of incrementalism. It would be more of the same or "the way things have always been." However, we argue that the transparent and inclusive vetting processes within this framework generate rich information about intended outcomes given the availability of finite resources. This structure lends itself to thoughtful analysis and the inclusion of multivariate factors that best impact the mission of the institution. In the end, the leadership made funding decisions that positively impacted all decision units in some way. By analyzing all options, stakeholders face a win-win proposition.

Cost-Effectiveness Analysis

By coupling this framework with a cost-effectiveness analysis for each alternative, decentralized and centralized decision-makers are able to make decisions about alternative approaches and allocate scarce resources to both triage risk and make strategic enhancements to programming. Weimer and Vining (2017) suggest that cost effectiveness can follow two approaches: a fixed budget approach and a fixed effectiveness approach. Both contribute to an information-based allocation of resources, which positively addresses key institutional values of transparency, participation, and accountability. In cost-effectiveness analysis, the *fixed-budget* approach describes funding programs at some ceiling of available resources (Weimer & Vining, 2017). In the *fixed-effectiveness* approach, decision-makers can allocate resources to the alternative that meets a desired outcome at the lowest cost (Weimer & Wining, 2017).

In order to illustrate the need for multiple data-informed budget approaches, we imagine three options related to expanding an academic program and their related effects on three institutional goals. Such alternatives matrices should support all new program requests as part of the budget formulation process. Further, decisions about what new programs should be analyzed are made at the decentralized level. For example, in the case of the robotics illustration, we suggest that the dean of the college involve her faculty and staff on such initiatives on an ongoing basis. The result of this exercise has the potential to put forward the best array of options for budgeters to consider when making holistic decisions for the college. More importantly for the purposes of this analysis, it offers a data-informed approach to budgeting. Rather than allocating the maximum amount of resources possible to a particular policy or program, the data inform decision-makers so that they may achieve the same or better results in a transparent, participatory, and accountable manner. Absent such analysis, the allocation of resources is unable to resist the perennial addition of bias over time.

The alternatives matrix in Table 3.3 does not explicitly reveal that the college leadership heavily weights a relationship with a local firm that is eager to support experiential learning at the college (and needed a ready professional workforce).

TABLE 3.3 Alternatives matrix: comparing options and goals for academic program expansion

	Option A *Add robotics major and lab to existing engineering school ($3 million)*	*Option B* *Add robotics major/partner with local industry ($500,000)*	*Option C* *Add robotics concentration to mechanical engineering ($250,000)*
Goal A *Contribute to a prepared workforce*	Provides an avenue to expand offerings to existing and new students.	Provides an avenue to expand offerings to existing and new students.	Provides avenue to expand offerings to existing and new students. However, only providing a concentration may divert potential students to other institutions.
Goal B *Cost effectiveness*	Least cost-effective option considering the start-up and recurring/replacement costs of equipment.	Medium cost effectiveness as it does not require the purchase of equipment, but does require increased faculty and staff support.	Although costs will be low with few new faculty and staff requirements, new enrollment is unclear.
Goal C *Missed opportunity*	Provides the greatest opportunity to be a national leader in areas of teaching and research.	Provides substantial advantage to students through new experiential learning opportunities in cooperation with industry and high likelihood of employment with the firm upon graduation.	Low opportunity for institution to hinge national prominence on minimal investment.

Note: See Weimer and Vining (2017) for comprehensive treatment on solution analysis.

Therefore, the presented analysis might quickly point to option B. Not only would it realize an immediate first-year cost savings of $2.5 million, but it also provides a strong linkage to industry, which is mutually beneficial to students and the local economy. Option A is costlier and lacks the experiential learning component; option C touches only the surface.

Evaluating the Administrative Ethic in the Budgeting Process

Through an illustrative budget analysis, we present complexities in the budgeting process and offer a lens through which to make difficult financial decisions. How do these approaches measure up when mapped onto the core public values of transparency, participation, and accountability? We evaluate each in the centralized and decentralized budget environments and through the incremental and needs-based budget approaches (Table 3.4).

When one compares environments and budgeting approaches side-by-side, it is clear that while some better advance public values, institutions will certainly experience a combination of approaches in their day-to-day budget operations. Overall, the centralized environment may confound the principles of participation and accountability through both the incremental and data-informed budget approaches. Yet, there may be instances when the centralized environment is necessary in order to advance an institution's strategic goals. For example, there are certain costs to the institution such as mandated cost-of-living adjustments and pension cost increases that, in reality, can only be addressed through "pulling levers" by the central administration. The decentralized environment, on the other hand, prioritizes participation, yet may hinder an institution's strategic advancement through the objectives of multiple stakeholders. To use the mandated cost-of-living adjustments and pension cost increase example, a pure decentralized model (short of a responsibility controlled model) is unlikely to be able to foot such a bill. Fortunately, institutions have the ability to consider multiple data-informed approaches no matter the broader environmental contexts. Rohr underscores this sentiment by stating, "The purpose of regime values is not to make all bureaucrats march in lock-step. There is no one 'authoritative' interpretation of the American experience that all bureaucrats must adopt" (Rohr, 1989, p. 84). Data-driven budgeting approaches provide a veritable rainbow of options from which the bureaucrat can choose. This works to eliminate or at least start to mitigate the residue of bias that undermines administrative ethics. Higher education institutions face uncertain financial futures, yet these institutions can be sure that true needs are being met through data-informed financial decision making.

TABLE 3.4 Analysis of budget environment contexts

| | Centralized budget environment | | Decentralized budget environment | |
	Incremental approach	*Needs-based approach*	*Incremental approach*	*Needs-based approach*
Transparency	The status quo is preserved. Residue tends to build over time which obscures true needs.	Central administrators present the necessity of funding with full transparency by.	College units will request the status quo, which may be void of data and consideration of constraints.	College units will put forth multiple options for funding based on both fixed-cost and fixed effects considerations and have "buy-in" on alternatives.
Participation	There is less participation across the college; resources are allocated as they have always been allocated.	Cost-effectiveness, fixed-based, and goals-alternatives techniques help central decision-makers to optimize resource allocation. Participation is limited to central administrators.	Though participation is encouraged, true decentralized models may place inequitable demands on college units, especially in light of outside mandates.	College units will be fully engaged with policy alternatives put forward for consideration.
Accountability	College units may have carte blanche in expenditures and not consider exogenous impacts from outside the college.	College units are held to intended outcome measures as selected by central administrators rather than all stakeholders.	Though accountable for outcomes, college units will not be able to guarantee results with incremental approaches, especially when considering scarce resources.	College units will have considered effects of alternative approaches and be able to address various outcomes based on selected levels of policy choices.

References

Douglas, P. C., & Wier, B. (2005). Cultural and ethical effects in budgeting systems: A comparison of U.S. and Chinese managers. *Journal of Business Ethics, 60*(2), 159–174. https://doi.org/10.1007/s10551-004-6711-z

Dubeck, L. W. (1997). Beware higher ed's newest budget twist. *Thought and Action, 13*(1), 81–91.

Feldman, S. (1982). Economic self-interest and political behavior. *American Journal of Political Science, 26*(3), 446–466.

Franklin, A., & Raadschelders, J. (2003). Ethics in local government budgeting: Is there a gap between theory and practice? *Public Administration Quarterly, 27*(3/4), 456–490.

Fenno, R. F. (1966). *The power of the purse: Appropriations politics in Congress.* Boston, MA: Little, Brown.

Heclo, H. (2008). *On thinking institutionally.* Boulder, CO: Paradigm Publishers.

Gilmour, J. B., & Lewis, D. E. (2006a). Does performance budgeting work? An examination of the office of management and budget's PART scores. *Public Administration Review, 66*(5), 742–752.

Gilmour, J. B., & Lewis, D. E. (2006b). Assessing performance budgeting at OMB: The influence of politics, performance, and program size. *Journal of Public Administration Research and Theory, 16*(2), 169–186.

Gordan, L. A., & Heivlilin, K. M. (1982). Zero base budgeting in the federal government: An historical perspective. In V. R. Kavassari & P. H. Larry (Eds.), *Management control in non-profit organizations* (p. 319). New York, NY: John Wiley & Sons.

Hnat, H. B., Mahony, D., Fitzgerald, S., & Crawford, F. (2015). Distributive justice and higher education resource allocation: Perceptions of fairness. *Innovative Higher Education, 40*(1), 79–93.

Kettl, D. F. (1992). *Deficit politics: The search for balance in American politics.* New York, NY: Macmillan.

Kettl, D. F. (2003). *Deficit politics: The search for balance in American politics* (2nd ed.). New York, NY: Longman.

Kettl, D. F. (2018). *Politics of the administrative state* (7th ed.). Thousand Oaks, CA: CQ Press.

Lasswell, H. D. (1936). *Politics: Who gets what, when, and how.* New York, NY: McGraw Hill.

Lewis-Beck, M. S., & Rice, T. W. (1985). Government growth in the United States. *The Journal of Politics, 47*(1), 2–30.

Moynihan, D. P. (2006). What do we talk about when we talk about performance? Dialogue theory and performance budgeting. *Journal of Public Administration Research and Theory, 16*(2), 151–168.

Piotrowski, S. J. (2014). Transparency: A regime value linked with ethics. *Administration & Society, 46*(2), 181–189. https://doi.org/10.1177/0095399713519098

Posner, P. L. (2009). Budget process reform: Waiting for Godot. *Public Administration Review, 69*(2), 233–244. https://doi.org/10.1111/j.1540-6210.2008.01969.x

Rohr, J. (1989). *Ethics for bureaucrats: An essay on law and values* (2nd ed.). New York, NY: Marcel Dekker.

Rohr, J. (2004). On Cooper's "big questions." *Public Administration Review, 64*(4), 408–409. https://doi.org/10.1111/j.1540-6210.2004.00387.x

Rubin, I. (1994). Early budget reformers: Democracy, efficiency, and budget reforms. *American Review of Public Administration, 24*(3), 229–252.

State Higher Education Executive Officers Association. (2018). *SHEF: 2017: State Higher Education Finance.* Retrieved January 28, 2019, from http://www.sheeo.org/sites/default/files/project-files/SHEEO_SHEF_FY2017_FINAL.pdf

Thornton, M., & Ulrich, M. (1999). Constituency size and government spending. *Public Finance Review, 27*(6), 588–598.

True, J. L. (2000). Avalanches and incrementalism – Making policy and budgets in the United States. *American Review of Public Administration, 30*(1), 3–18.

Weimer, D., & Vining, A. R. (2017). *Policy analysis: Concepts and practice* (6th ed.). New York, NY: Routledge.

Wildavsky, A. (1964). *The politics of the budgetary process.* Boston, MA: Little, Brown.

4

FREEDOM v. FAIRNESS

How Unresolved Normative Tension Contributed to the Collapse of the U.S. Housing Market in 2008—and Policymaker Inability to Reform It a Decade On

Susan W. Gates

Introduction

The second edition of John Rohr's seminal *Ethics for Bureaucrats* made a compelling case for the use of regime values, the values that define a people, to guide public administrators through the gray space of administrative discretion. Although the law gives broad policy contour, and detailed regulations follow with the specifications, there remains a time and place for ethical reasoning on the part of unelected bureaucrats. *What is the right thing to do?*

For the purpose of ethical training, Rohr distinguished the use of regime values from the "low road" of conflict-of-interest style rule adherence with its "emphasis on meticulous attention to trivial questions." Using United States Department of Agriculture (USDA) "check the box" ethics training as the bête noir, Rohr said rules-based ethics training "runs the risk of developing a dangerous attitude of pharisaism" where bureaucrats strain gnats while swallowing camels (Rohr, 1989, p. 63).

Rohr also took issue with basing ethical training on the "high road" of social equity, which would add egalitarian concerns to traditional administrative norms of "efficient, economical and coordinated management" (Rohr, 1989, p. 64). Perhaps dating himself here, Rohr argued that basing the ethical education of "professional bureaucrats" on the equalitarian aspects of Rawlsian-style political theory would be "questionable" (Rohr, 1989, p. 65).

A more promising and operational approach, he argues, is to use regime values that "can be discovered in the public law of the regime" (Rohr, 1989, p. 68). By considering the nuanced arguments of United States Supreme Court cases, public administrators not only gain insights into "the values of the American people" (Rohr, 1989, p. 74), but also are exposed to a disciplined methodology for thinking through ethical quandaries. Because of the bureaucrat's oath to the Constitution, regime values could thus be viewed as normative flashlights they could use when implementing regulations, disbursing funds, meting out enforcement, etc.

Sounds straightforward, but what to do when treasured constitutional norms conflict? Acknowledging the imperfect science of balancing norms and the not-unheard-of occurrence of "dirty hands," Rohr relieves the conscience of the conscientious bureaucrat by saying that "not every moral principle is an absolute principle, that is, a principle that must be followed regardless of cir-cumstances." Like De Tocqueville, Rohr hints that there are normative trade offs to be made, particularly between cherished American norms of freedom and equality and that governing does, indeed, involve horse trading at times. At its best, it's called compromise, which Rohr calls "one of the most important values of any organization [because] it is the catalyst that makes possible the realization of other values" (Rohr, 1989, p. 10). A timely reminder.

Helping bureaucrats develop a deeper ethical awareness of the regime value of property (in its "redeemed" form) is instructive for regulatory agencies over-seeing their shareholder-owned charges. Rather than seek to squelch "corpo-rate greed," Rohr posits that government overseers might do better to "regard the acquisitive spirit" as a "great national resource and to point this mighty engine in directions that are socially useful" (Rohr, 1989, p. 244). Of course, regulators also need to take an aggressive stance toward the industries they regulate; this kind of muscle does not come from mere rule adherence. Rather, deeper ethical reflection about competing norms is necessary to operate well in the discretionary administrative space, particularly where money and power cast a long shadow.

Analysis of the normative tension that contributed to the collapse of the United States (U.S.) housing market in 2008 indicates that John Rohr was on to something. As will be explored below, large financial institutions, nota-bly government-sponsored enterprises (G.S.E.s) Fannie Mae and Freddie Mac, responded competitively to free market incentives by lowering mortgage underwriting standards, thereby pushing house prices to unsustainable highs. At the same time, regulatory and societal expectations that the firms expand homeownership among traditionally underrepresented groups—requirements which heretofore had tempered G.S.E.s animal spirits—became an unwitting partner to the firms' outsized purchases of higher-risk mortgages in the name of affordable housing. Unnoticed and unchecked, the lethal normative combina-tion crippled the nation's housing markets.

In hindsight, federal regulators should have recognized and sought to assuage the dangerous interplay between the regime values of freedom and equality masquerading, in this instance, as private profiteering and efforts to equal-ize homeownership rates across groups. Instead, as Rohr predicted, regulators were traveling the low road of rule adherence: straining remedial accounting reports while the G.S.E.s loaded their balance sheets with high-risk mortgage assets in the name of affordable housing. In the fall of 2008, Fannie Mae and Freddie Mac were essentially bankrupted and placed under government control, where they remain at this writing in 2019. Tragically, the homeowners who had been the focus of well intended social policy were the most hurt by the 30 percent collapse in house prices—and have taken the longest to recover.

Drawing on Rohr's insights into regime values, this chapter seeks to elucidate the normative tension between freedom and equality in U.S. housing markets. It is not a mere philosophical exercise. The central institutions at the heart of the crisis have remained in a 2008 freeze frame for over a decade and, as of this writing, have yet to be structurally reformed. Difficulty triangulating the age-old tension between freedom and equality is at the heart of the policy gridlock then—and now.

The 2008 Financial Crisis

The financial crisis of 2007–2008 stands as a dismally remembered and hotly debated U.S. economic debacle with painful global repercussions. To recap the arc of the disaster: On the heels of a decade that saw a 30 percent rise in national house prices, beginning in 2007, there was a sudden and concomitant house price collapse that set off a tsunami of mortgage defaults. The problems began in the so-called subprime mortgage market, which was characterized by high-risk mortgages made to high-risk borrowers, such as those who had weak credit scores or other financial anomalies. Many subprime loans were adjustable-rate mortgages with very low introductory mortgage rates that increased dramatically after the first two years, otherwise known as exploding adjustable-rate mortgages. When the United States Federal Reserve began increasing interest rates from their post 9/11 lows, the staircase of rate increases made the payments on subprime mortgages too expensive for many borrowers—and they defaulted. As these defaults spread through the broader housing market, house prices began to weaken, which caused more borrowers to go "underwater" when homes values fell below the level of debt they owed to the bank or other creditor. With zero or negative equity in their homes, many borrowers simply abandoned their properties. Still other defaults were driven by predatory lenders talking unsuspecting borrowers into mortgages they could neither understand nor afford. Taken together, upwards of 10 million Americans lost their homes to foreclosure as a result of the housing bubble and subsequent crash.

The losses were as staggering as they were widespread. The financial pain extended from Main Street to Wall Street and eventually around the world. In 2013, the U.S. Government Accountability Office estimated that the housing market collapse had cost Americans $9.1 trillion in home equity and a year's worth of Gross domestic product (GDP) (U.S. Government Accountability Office [GAO], 2013, p. 21). As losses mounted, businesses shuttered, jobs were lost, and unemployment skyrocketed. Local governments, which had relied on property taxes, were suddenly strapped, if not bankrupted. The federal government responded with billions in bailouts, unemployment insurance, and stimulus packages, but most of the funds went to maintain systemically important institutions, not to individual homeowners. To maintain mortgage market liquidity, the Federal Reserve bought up billions in mortgage assets that remain on its balance sheet a decade on.

As widespread as the economic calamity was, lower-income and minority communities bore the heaviest brunt of foreclosures, and negative secondary effects. These neighborhoods have been the slowest to recover, if they ever will.

Whodunnit?

After a decade of analysis, reflection, and debate, and a trove of academic papers on a broad array of variables, there continues to be a clear lack of consensus about the root cause of the crisis. The dominant explanations fall into two opposing camps: unwitting government housing policy caused the dangerous house-price bubble or unregulated and rapacious Wall Street banks did it.

The official government account—the 2011 Report of the Financial Crisis Inquiry Commission—takes the latter view. The F.C.I.C. laid the lion's share of the blame at the feet of the "shadow" banking system driven by Wall Street firms which had turned traditional mortgage finance upside down. Instead of *borrower* demand for mortgages driving the market, Wall Street firms fed *investor* demand for high-risk mortgages. These loans, which at first flunked G.S.E.s quality standards, were needed to fill complex financially engineered asset-backed securities that investment firms (think Lehman Brothers, Goldman Sachs, and others) pedaled around the world as safe and sound, and profitable due to their higher yields. Aside from castigating individual firms for shameless greed, along with co-opted credit rating firms, and moribund regulators, the broader indictment here is that financial de-regulation started under the Reagan administration had opened the door for the abuses that occurred (Financial Crisis Inquiry Commission [FCIC], 2011, p. xviii).

Not everyone agreed with this diagnosis. In the back of the F.C.I.C. report are the dissenting voices from the 10-person commission. Chief among them is Peter Wallison, an economist with the conservative American Enterprise Institute. Wallison disagreed strongly with the official narrative and turned the blame on the government itself, particularly Fannie Mae and Freddie Mac, gigantic firms with murky government ties that were undergirding the U.S. housing market. Fannie and Freddie were creatures of Congress, created in 1938 and 1970, respectively, with the job of ensuring wide availability of mortgage money by purchasing mortgages from lending institutions, thereby replenishing funds for homeownership. The G.S.E.s accomplished this by packaging loans into mortgage-backed securities for sale to investors. With the G.S.E.s guaranteeing the securities against borrower default, investors viewed the securities as safe and desirable investment instruments. This system of transactional relationships comprises the secondary mortgage market.

Wallison—and other conservatives—argue that the G.S.E.s were goaded into expanding their purchases of higher-risk mortgages by government regulation and the politics of expanding homeownership. Specifically, the G.S.E.s were required to purchase a growing share of mortgages that financed homes for families in lower-income and minority communities. Over two decades, the G.S.E.s affordable housing goals had risen from around 32 percent of business to above 50 percent. To meet those increasingly tough regulatory requirements, the firms competed furiously for "goal-rich" mortgages by any means possible: They adversely selected against—or raided—FHA, the government's mortgage insurance program; crafted dubious mortgage rental arrangements with banks; and "paid up" for the desired loans when market conditions did not produce the mortgages needed to fill the regulatory buckets. The low-road rationale was that even if their purchases were unethical and market-distorting, it was preferable than the political fall out of "missing" a regulatory goal.

More broadly, Wallison and others argue that the existence of two systemically important, lightly regulated, and minimally capitalized institutions was a recipe for disaster. Not only did G.S.E.s special privileges lead to complaints of an "unfair playing field" that stifled competition, there were also graver concerns that the fast-growing balance sheets of the firms could someday cause systemic threats to the economy. Decades of reports by the Office of management and budget (OMB), U.S. Treasury, and others fretted that due to their unusual structure and privileges—which gave rise to the notion that the entities were "implicitly" backed by the U.S. government—the G.S.E.s would eventually "privatize the profits and socialize the losses" of their activities. Which is essentially what happened.

The housing lobby and progressives have generally sided with the findings of the F.C.I.C. report and defended the G.S.E.s structure and their affordable housing goals against conservative claims that they were a root cause of the crisis. With increasing perspective on the events of 2008, researchers have ascertained that the high-risk mortgages swept into Wall Street securities defaulted at significantly higher rates than those securitized by the G.S.E.s, indicating that the worst offending loans were not those that counted for G.S.E.s housing goals that targeted low- and moderate-income households.

The F.C.I.C. report noted that the G.S.E.s had a "deeply flawed business model," and they did. They were publicly traded corporations that enjoyed implicit backing from the U.S. government. Even so, the F.C.I.C. did not finger the companies as the primary cause of the crisis. While the two firms did participate in the expansion of subprime and other risky mortgages, they were followers, not leaders in this regard; company documents indicate the G.S.E.s entered those markets largely to maintain market share against growing competition from Wall Street firms. As recounted by the Commission:

> [The GSEs] relaxed their underwriting standards to purchase or guarantee riskier loans and related securities in order to meet stock market analysts' and investors' expectations for growth, to regain market share, and to ensure generous compensation for their executives and employees—justifying their activities on the broad and sustained public policy support for homeownership (FCIC, 2011, p. xxiv).

The continuing debate about the role the G.S.E.s played in the crisis goes to the heart of the normative tension between freedom and fairness. If they were merely shareholder-owned companies, then pursuing profits and perks should hardly have been surprising. Yet because they were chartered by Congress and given certain statutory purposes, they also had a public mission to make mortgage money widely available so that more people could become homeowners— and not just for a day. The G.S.E.s were also expected to provide stability, which meant that the mortgages those homeowners received could stand the test of time. Unfortunately, way too many did not.

Were the seeds of the financial crisis sown into the founding documents of these two systemically important firms?

Creation Story

In the ashes of the Great Depression, the U.S. government created institutions to restore confidence to the nation's battered mortgage delivery system. Fannie Mae was one of them. Chartered by Congress in 1938, its job was to purchase mortgages originated by private lenders and insured by another government agency—the Federal Housing Administration (F.H.A.), which had been established a few years earlier in 1934. In purchasing F.H.A.-insured mortgages, Fannie Mae replenished lender funds for housing and increased investor confidence; the purchases were financed by bonds issued by the F.H.A. Over the years, Fannie Mae's job grew to include purchasing mortgages guaranteed by the Veterans Administration.

In 1968, legislation converted Fannie Mae to a publicly held company; its growing debt obligations were conveniently moved off-budget, but it retained its federal charter and the accompanying privileges. It was also given a green light to purchase mortgages originated by mortgage bankers; unlike the nation's savings and loan institutions, mortgage bankers lacked a depository base for originating mortgages and so needed a different source of liquidity.

In 1970, Congress chartered another entity—Freddie Mac—to purchase mortgages originated by the savings and loan institutions. Initially capitalized by the 12 Federal Home Loan Banks, Freddie Mac purchased mortgages alongside Fannie Mae, packaging them all into securities and selling them to investors. Rising interest rates in the late 1970s and early 1980s exerted pressure on the savings and loan institutions, which were squeezed between the low interest rates they were receiving on the long-term fixed-rate mortgages they held on their balance sheets and the high interest rates they had to offer savers to attract deposits. Caught in the same squeeze, Fannie Mae was essentially insolvent for several years until interest rates eased.

The response of the Reagan administration was to deregulate the mortgage market to attract private capital and create competition. In 1982, the President's Commission on Housing called for as much, with the assumption that old-school players Fannie Mae and Freddie Mac would lose out to more innovative competitors. It didn't turn out that way, however. The special quasi-governmental status of the firms resulted in an uneven playing field where new entrants could not compete with the firms that "paid less taxes, could borrow at cheaper rates and were lightly regulated in that they faced low capital requirements for holding similar risks compared to private-sector counterparts" (Acharya, Richardson, Nieuwerburgh, & White, 2011, p. 22). Instead of being sidelined under deregulation, the G.S.E.s thrived. In 1989, Freddie Mac paid off the Federal Home Loan Banks and became a shareholder-owned corporation traded like Fannie Mae. Both firms retained their original congressional "charters," which resulted in strong growth and profits. The unique charters barred other firms from market entry; they also gave the impression that the G.S.E.s were safer than they really were.

Operating as a protected duopoly with widespread political support, the combined G.S.E.s share of the mortgage market grew from 7.1 percent in 1981 to 28.4 percent in 1991 and nearly 45 percent by 2002 (Acharya et al., p. 20). Along with their charters, G.S.E.s activities and innovations, such as standard mortgage documentation and development of new securities, attracted new funds to housing and expanded the investor base for mortgages.

But complaints and worries abounded. Lenders balked at the dominance of the two firms, which were flexing their market muscle and pushing the boundaries of the secondary market. Progressives pounced on their outsized profits and prodded the firms to expand homeownership to so-called "underserved" households and neighborhoods. Regulations expanded to require the firms to meet tougher affordable housing goals, meet "duty to serve" requirements, and contribute funds to magnet funds commensurate with their profits.

Conservatives were increasingly concerned about the growth of the entities. By 2007, the firms were two of the largest and most profitable firms in the country, together supporting a $5.5 trillion mortgage market. Many railed against the increasing political power of the G.S.E.s and the daunting system risk they posed should anything go wrong.

Despite their differences, both conservatives and progressives gave continued allegiance to the American dream of homeownership.

The Collapse

In early September 2008, amid rising mortgage foreclosures and losses on sub-prime bonds, Fannie Mae and Freddie Mac teetered on the edge of insolvency. Investor confidence had collapsed, and short sellers were dragging company stocks to single digits. To stave off a broader collapse, then—Treasury Secretary Paulson acted expeditiously and placed the pair in government conservatorship. The disgraced outgoing executives signed over control of the firms to their regulator, cum conservator, and acquiesced to a stringent bailout agreement that gave the Treasury an 80 percent stake in the companies, thereby wiping out common shareholders.

Over the next few years, as mortgage losses ran through their balance sheets, the firms required close to $200 billion in bailout funds, which came with a hefty 10 percent dividend. In 2012, as the tide of red ink seemed to be ending—and hedge funds eagerly piled into the penny stocks—the government increased the dividend to almost 100 percent of profits. This bold move immediately drew legal action on the part of shareholders who expected the newly profitable firms to be soon released from conservatorship, with bountiful profits to be made. At this writing, the total bailout of $191 billion has been more than repaid; Fannie and Freddie have paid $267 billion in dividends to the general fund of the Treasury where they are applied to deficit reduction.

Reform Attempts Fail

In the 11 years since the government take over, Congress has attempted, on numerous occasions to pass G.S.E.s reform legislation that would end the conservatorship, but to no avail. Without agreement on the fundamental cause of the crisis, particularly the contributory role of Fannie and Freddie, and with so much money riding on the outcomes and so much at stake if zealous reformers get it wrong, congressional hearings invariably devolve into arguments and make little progress. In the meantime, the Federal Housing Finance Agency, the regulator and conservator of Fannie and Freddie, has made a number of administrative reforms that likely would be included in any broader legislative solution.

Notwithstanding the political inertia, the G.S.E.s once again are the dominant players in the nation's mortgage markets. In 2019, the firms financed nearly one-half of all mortgages. Their dominance is a direct result of being fully backed by the government, which makes it impossible for private firms to compete. Housing and real estate trade groups, builders, and bankers are comfortable with the status quo (primarily because of the homeownership subsidy government control affords), but taxpayers should not be. Unlike before the crisis when the firms had retained earnings and a capital cushion, today they have none. Fully 100 percent of G.S.E.s risk rides on taxpayer shoulders.

In 2019, the newly confirmed director of the F.H.F.A. has signaled fresh determination to work with Congress to find a market-based solution that does not eviscerate the G.S.E.'s traditional public mission to expand homeownership. Can it be done? How will this bureaucratic agency thread the needle between freedom and equality?

Normative Tension

Very little of the past decade of research into the financial crisis has looked at its normative roots. There is no shortage of books decrying Wall Street excesses in the wake of deregulation (Lewis, 2010), the political power of firms, and their weak regulators (McLean & Nocera, 2010; Morgenson & Rosner, 2011). A few have looked at the unintended consequences of government intrusion in the housing market (Wallison, 2016). Housing economists have plumbed mortgage default data for clues into underlying causes, while others have considered the weaknesses of predictive models and underestimation of risk.

A former Freddie Mac employee, Gates (2017) wrote an insider account of the G.S.E.s role in the crisis with an eye to the normative conflict between freedom and equality and the critical importance of "high-road" ethical reflection. Gates likens the housing's normative conflict to "fault-lines under major cities," which, because they are hidden, "make true recovery elusive and unsustainable." Invariably, the "competing philosophies and ideologies" running beneath the debate on housing finance reform pit freedom against fairness, tracking political divides (Gates, 2017, p. 10).

Normative preference for freedom shows up in debates about the government's role in the provision of private goods, like homeownership. The conservative rap on the G.S.E.s was that by allowing them to retain their congressional charters, which gave the firms preferential treatment in the capital markets, the government was enabling private individuals to borrow funds as cheaply as top-rated corporations, which led to an "overinvestment" in housing. To many conservatives, the economic returns to homeownership were not worth it. Former Federal Reserve Chairman Greenspan was particularly emphatic that the nation would be better served if it eliminated subsidies to Fannie Mae and Freddie Mac and invested instead in factories, jobs, and other more productive sectors of the economy. Freedom also shows up in the debate about mortgage products. Proponents for consumer choice regularly opposed policies that would restrict access to certain mortgage types that others deemed higher-risk or even dangerous.

On the other hand, preference for fairness and equality were seen in the growing reliance on the G.S.E.s as an off-budget tool to expand housing opportunities, combat discrimination, bring liquidity to central cities, Native American communities, and rural housing, particularly in the form of manufactured housing. Homeownership is a significant emblem of having made it to the middle class, and, for most middle-income families, home equity represents a greater component of retirement savings that stock market investments. Homeownership rates for African Americans and Hispanics significantly trailed rates for whites and Asians. Greater equality in homeownership rates therefore became a rallying point, and tight G.S.E.s underwriting was often viewed as a barrier to accession to the rolls.

Not surprisingly, these external normative tensions led the G.S.E.s to play their political masters off one another. Maximizing either norm could spell disaster for the delicate political balance the firms had carefully cultivated over the years. In the early 1990s, Fannie Mae lobbied hard for the affordable housing goals to be added to the G.S.E.s charters; it was more a shrewd move than an altruistic one. By appeasing progressives, G.S.E.s housing goals had the perverse effect of strengthening the government ties with the two firms, further "hardening" the lucrative implicit government guarantee.

For its part, in 2002, Freddie Mac talked the Bush administration into making a commitment to boost homeownership rates among minority homeowners. The policy plank focused on assuaging wealth inequality through increased access to low-cost mortgages, but it was also a Trojan horse. It was a political win to be positively associated with a president whose party sought to privatize the G.S.E.s to reduce systemic risk. Aligning with President Bush to expand minority homeownership thus neutralized privatization (for a time), and G.S.E.s stock prices rose in response.

First-Hand Account

Having worked at Freddie Mac during the two decades prior to the government take-over, Gates experienced firsthand the ideological rifts that were embedded in the firm's valuable—but schizophrenic—congressional charter and which would turn business decisions into political standoffs.

> The G.S.E.s and the broader housing market comprise a highly complex and interrelated system crisscrossed by very serious political and ideological fault lines. The refusal to acknowledge, at a minimum, or better, to seek to reconcile these fault lines spelled the doom of the entire system (Gates, 2017, p. 23).

What were these lines? Hewing to free market economics, conservative Republicans regularly called out the firms for trading on their government ties, wrung hands over their thin capital cushions, and called them "spongy conduits" for soaking up profits and passing along relatively little to homeowners. Democrats, on the other hand, railed against the firms' eye-popping profits and exceedingly low losses, which suggested to them that the firms were discriminatory by cream-skimming the market and not adequately serving more challenging borrowers. "How to please a powerful Representative who wanted the firm to invest in higher-risk apartment buildings? Or a Senator who wanted Freddie Mac to hold more capital?" To choose a path forward, the companies struggled to reconcile competing regime values, which were embedded in sharp political realities, with the temptation of alluring profits to be made in the subprime market.

> These rifts were keenly felt at Freddie Mac. Nearly every major business decision required managing competing politics and players, reconciling jarring differences in public policies, and bridging deep ideological divides between supporter and naysayer, friend and foe. In the years leading up to the crisis, managing the company was a constant game of three-dimensional chess (Gates, 2017, p. 23).

Gates recalled tensions within the employee base between the "housers," those deeply committed to the company's housing mission, and the "Wall Street types," whose entire job was to buy and sell securities for the sole purpose of making money—on which their handsome commissions depended. Concerns about fairness, predatory lending, and the dangers of portfolio growth were not easily raised on the trading room floor. Gates recalled bringing "peer mediators" to meetings to help manage the tension.

> The fact that our friendly discussions became heated debates is revealing. Almost parallel to the political debates exploding around us, some employees thought Freddie's primary job was about expanding homeownership, while others thought it was to make the secondary mortgage market more efficient. Yet others said our fundamental purpose was to "maximize shareholder value (subject to not losing the charter).
>
> That rankled some of us, but here was their point: By maximizing profits, they claimed, we would be the most efficient by definition, and that would be the best way to support homeownership. It was classic business theory for a shareholder-owned company. But we had a problem: Freddie was a G.S.E. Maximizing profits might have been what the traders thought about every day, but it was not the mission politicians expected us to fulfill (Gates, 2017, p. 165).

Freddie Mac's 2003 accounting scandal, in which the firm understated earnings by $5 billion, resulted in "one of the largest restatements in corporate history." In addition to imposing a fine of $125 million, the regulator required the company to develop a plan to change its corporate culture from being so focused on earnings, profits…and employee bonuses…and to be more focused on mission. It was a hard assignment. How could a shareholder-owned company not think or behave like one?

G.S.E.s leaders operated at the fateful intersection of freedom and equality. "Their inability to manage this great schism, to bridge this enormous ideological fault line, contributed to the undoing of both firms. Politicians also could have played their cards differently; certain political appeasements would have helped the companies steer clear of the more dangerous shoals. The GSEs needed Congress to provide bipartisan support for the GSE housing mission, while upholding traditional strong underwriting standards. Instead of taking a balanced approach, the political parties moved to the edges like two boats widening. The GSEs tried unsuccessfully to straddle both norms. The divided Congress became the GSE divide, and management struggled to balance these two important (and sometimes competing) objectives" (Gates, 2017, p. 27).

Threading the Needle

To deal with the tension, G.S.E.s managers became good at satisfying norms by "threading the needle." The decision to enter the subprime market in the years before the crisis was a way to gain back market share while meeting the company's understood mission to expand homeownership to underserved households. At the time, company leaders rationalized that by participating in the subprime mortgage market, Freddie Mac could bring its efficiencies and high standards to "the wild west" of the mortgage market, which was serving (or taking advantage of), borrowers in low-income communities. A classic case of "doing well while doing good." Except that it didn't turn out that way.

The tension over subprime pitted David Andrukonis, the company's chief credit officer, responsible for ensuring the firm invested in quality instruments, and new chief executive officer, Dick Syron. In a damning internal memo that appeared later on congressional oversight websites, Andrukonis urged Syron to exit the high-risk market, saying, "What better way to highlight our sense of mission than to walk away from profitable business because it hurts the borrowers we are trying to serve" (Gates, 2017, p. 181).

Where were the regulators while all this gamesmanship was going on? They too seemed oblivious to the normative tension that the firms were able to exploit. Believing in the power of market discipline and that firms would act in their own self-interest, former Federal Reserve chair, Alan Greenspan, spurned calls to use federal regulatory authority dating from 1994 to govern subprime mortgages and protect consumers.

G.S.E.s regulatory oversight was similarly bifurcated along normative lines. The housing goals were under the purview of housing and urban development (HUD), while the safety and soundness of the firm was managed separately by independent regulator, the Office of Federal Housing Oversight (O.F.H.E.O.). This unfortunate structure aggravated the normative tension. When the G.S.E.s protested against unrealistically high (and risky) affordable housing goals, they could not appeal to the prudence of the safety and soundness regulator.

As the G.S.E.s proved to be difficult and wily charges, O.F.H.E.O. sought additional legislative authority while failing to use the authority it already had to oversee and limit the types of mortgages the companies were purchasing. Reproving the company after its 2003 accounting scandal became so central to O.F.H.E.O.'s oversight that it blinded the regulator from grosser sins. From the perspective of Freddie Mac employees, O.F.H.E.O. was still checking compliance reports dating back to the 2003 scandal when the company gorged itself on high-risk mortgages without the ability—or capital—to manage the added risks.

In the summer of 2008, Congress enacted comprehensive reform legislation that finally unified the G.S.E.s regulator (thereby dismantling O.F.H.E.O. and replacing it with the Federal Housing Finance Administration), enabling a unified approach to balancing mission and risk. Unfortunately, the reforms came too late. The G.S.E.s were placed into conservatorship just two months after passage of that landmark legislation. For over a decade, both firms had funded lobbying efforts to block enactment of legislation that would unduly curb their business interests.

Challenges Going Forward

Important policy ramifications flow from the different explanations of what/who/why caused the financial crisis. Democrats, for their part, tend to draw a direct line from the deregulation that began under President Reagan to the Wall Street firms that pushed bad mortgages to unsuspecting borrowers and sold complex mortgage related instruments to unsuspecting global investors. Their policy prescription, it follows, is a clamp down on banks in terms of greater oversight and accountability, enhanced investment disclosures, and the institution of consumer protections, including greater legal recourse. In short, more regulation.

Many of these changes are well underway. In 2010, Congress passed the Dodd-Frank Wall Street and Consumer Protection Act, the most mammoth reconstruction of the U.S. financial services system since the Great Depression. The hundreds of regulations spawned by the watershed legislation took years to develop, promulgate, and implement. Some have not yet gone into effect. At this juncture, the full impact on mortgage lending of these complex and interactive regulations is still unknown.

On the other side of the aisle, Republicans generally despise the Dodd-Frank Wall Street Consumer Protection Act as overreach and have taken initial steps to rescind part of it. They tend to agree with Wallison that government intrusion into the housing market distorted market incentives, creating a government-sanctioned erosion of underwriting standards, and subsequent house-price bubble and collapse.

Given these largely irreconcilable viewpoints, it is no wonder that congressional hearings designed to sift through difficult and complex restructuring choices invariably end up in a shouting match, where Republicans blame Democrats and Democrats blame Republicans for their role in the crisis. It has become a national sport to blame the G.S.E.s.

For Gates, truth is somewhere in between these two views.

> Government indicia and intervention (at times well intended and at times not) did complicate, incent and reward some of the worst behavior on the part of the GSEs. But it is equally true that had fly-by-night brokers been regulated and Wall Street firms been prevented from jumping headlong into the riskiest mortgages, Freddie Mac, at least, would have been far less inclined to abandon tried and true mortgage underwriting standards in the name of market share. Hence, both sides of the aisle have something important to contribute to our understanding of how things got so badly out of control—and how to see our way forward (Gates, 2017, p. 22).

Normative Separation—or Compromise?

A first pass at the question of reform might suggest that freedom and equality need to be separately pursued—given that their interplay, according to this thesis, wreaked havoc on U.S. housing markets and homeowners. Under this view, the G.S.E.s should be completely privatized; their government ties would be severed such that if they failed to manage their businesses profitably in the future, their shareholders—and not taxpayers—would be the ones to suffer. The corollary to this bifurcated approach would be that government agencies—not shareholder-owned companies—should be the ones to implement pro-social housing policies that could entail social costs. By keeping freedom and equality at arms' length, the argument goes, mortgage markets would be safer and more transparent, with targeted benefits placed on-budget for all to see. However, the separation would come at a price: mortgage rates would be noticeably higher and there could be shortages of mortgage capital as investors adjust to a world without government backing.

Conservatives tend to support this clear-cut distinction. But is it realistic? Now that the government has shown its willingness to "save" housing, will it not do it again? Representing a large share of GDP, housing itself is "too big to fail," not just the entities that make the mortgages available. Under this view, policymakers should not be so naïve as to think that investors won't be fooled by a governmental statement that the privatized firms will not be bailed out again. "Merely stating that the companies are private and will not be rescued again is not credible if there are only two of them, because the government will not allow the resulting disruption to the housing market if they fail," (Gates, Schnare, & Swagel, 2017).

By the same token, progressives tend to look askance at the moral hazard raised by two firms operating with a government guarantee without the discipline of market competition. Amnesia also has set in. The recovery of the housing market and today's seemingly "safe" mortgage delivery system is turning policy attention away from free markets back to equality. Once again, presidential hopefuls are focused on policies to address the inequality of home-ownership rates (Riley, 2019). Equality-focused reform seeks to create opportunity by providing subsidies and liberalizing underwriting standards. However, to become a homeowner only to lose one's equity or home when house prices collapse hits vulnerable borrowers the hardest, as we have sadly seen.

Maxing out on either freedom or equality is politically unstable, if not dangerous. Something less ideologically pure is needed to resolve the normative puzzle that has engulfed housing for over a decade. Rohr's wizened insight that "not every moral principle is an absolute principle" suggests that freedom and equality must find a way to co-exist, that some sort of pragmatic approach is urgently needed.

Conclusion: Normative Accommodation

By considering examples of normative tension running beneath the nation's mortgage market prior to 2008, it is possible to discern the dangers of ideological gridlock. Both freedom and fairness are deeply held American values. Rather than play one against the other, it ought to be possible to construct a housing finance system that incorporates both. There is a place, even within the hyper-charged politics of housing finance, for compromise. In fact, Rohr goes so far as to say that when practiced earnestly, compromise becomes its own regime value. It also has a catalytic quality, breaking the logjam and making "possible the realization of other values." In this case, compromise would pave the way for a stronger housing finance system.

What might a compromise look like for G.S.E.s reform that honors both regime values of freedom and equality? Is there a "golden mean?"

Despite a decade of standoff in Congress, there are hints that policymakers are finding a bipartisan way forward. First, there is growing realization, albeit reluctantly among progressives, that the quasi-government structure of the G.S.E.s led to market misperceptions about the risks they posed. This has led to greater openness to allowing more market competition; the unique nature of the two firms created a privileged space where other firms could not enter or compete. Allowing more players to compete also spreads the risk that any one of them might fail, reducing taxpayer exposure.

Second, there appears to be grudging acceptance among conservatives that because of the size and importance of housing to the U.S. economy, privatization is unrealistic; given the G.S.E.s bailout in 2008, investors will not believe that the U.S. government would let housing fail in the future. A second-best solution would be to provide a limited government guarantee on mortgage securities—not on the firms issuing them—to keep mortgage money flowing and to ensure the continued availability of the popular 30-year fixed-rate mortgage. Fannie Mae, Freddie Mac, and other securitizing firms would pay a fee for having a government guarantee on their bonds, which would be passed along to homeowners. Although higher costs could dampen enthusiasm for homeownership, the system would provide a truer reflection of the costs and risks of a homeownership society.

These are simply broad contours of how a new housing finance system might evolve. The key point is that whatever reform scheme is ultimately adopted, it will not be normatively pure. Housing will always be messy and involve normative compromise. Hopefully we're wiser to the mischievous bedfellows freedom and equality can become—especially when lots of money and political power are at stake. Going forward, mindful oversight and strong enforcement is needed to prevent the dangerous entanglement of these norms, despite the tempting political elixir they represent. If policymakers can keep their eye on the normative concessions that need to be made, progress is possible. A housing finance system that is both resilient and broadly accessible is solidly in the national interest. As such, it deserves strong bipartisan support.

References

Acharya, V., Richardson, M., Van Nieuwerburgh, S., & White, L. J. (2011). *Guaranteed to fail, Fannie Mae, Freddie Mac and the debacle of mortgage finance*. Princeton, NJ: Princeton University Press.

Financial Crisis Inquiry Commission. (2011). *The financial crisis inquiry report*. New York: Public Affairs.

Gates, S., Schnare, A., & Swagel, P. (2017). Privatize Fannie and Freddie, Yes. But be pragmatic. Retrieved from https://www.rhsmith.umd.edu/files/Documents/Centers/CFP/research/swagel_march_2017.pdf

Gates, S. W. (2017). *Days of slaughter: Inside the fall of Freddie Mac and why it could happen again*. Baltimore, MD: Johns Hopkins University Press.

Lewis, M. (2010). The Big Short. New York: W.W. Norton & Company, Inc.

McLean, B., & Nocera, J. (2010). *All the devils are here, the hidden history of the financial crisis*. New York, NY: Penguin Group.

Morgenson, G., & Rosner, J. (2011). *Reckless endangerment: How outsized ambition, greed and corruption led to economic Armageddon*. New York, NY: Times Books.

Riley, J. L. (2019, July 9). Democrats may inflate another housing bubble. *Wall Street Journal*. Retrieved from https://www.wsj.com/articles/democrats-may-inflate-another-housing-bubble-11562713530l

Rohr, J. (1989). *Ethics for bureaucrats: An essay on law and values* (2nd ed.). New York: Marcel Dekker.

U.S. Government Accountability Office. (2013). Report to Congress: Financial crisis losses and potential impacts of the Dodd Frank Act. GOA-13-180. Washington, DC. Retrieved from http://www.gao.gov/assets/660/651322.pdf

Wallison, P. (2016). *Hidden in plain sight: What really caused the world's worst financial crisis and why it could happen again*. New York, NY: Encounter Books.

PART II
Property: New Forms of Property Reinvigorating Long-standing Debates

5

DUE PROCESS AND PROPERTY

What Process Is Due?

Amanda M. Olejarski and Sue M. Neal

Introduction

Rohr was a student of Straussian theory which, in part, rests in the ancient Aristotelian tradition, striving to "preserve regimes by moderating their tendencies toward conflict, decline, and transformation" (O'Neill, 2009, p. 467). Strauss, and Rohr by extension, value the constancy provided by the Constitution as a mechanism for providing an ethical bellwether for the public administrator. How then do the transformational interpretations of the Constitution, as manifested by United States Supreme Court decisions, inform the normative nature of property and the role of property as a regime value in the modern administrative context?

Dating back 200 years, the Supreme Court has viewed property rights as a mechanism to achieve national and political goals of economic development. In *Gibbons v. Ogden* (1819), the Court ended a monopoly to promote a competitive environment and prosperity. Fast forward to 2005 and the Court again rules in favor of using property to grow the economy by facilitating some degree of private gain (*Kelo v. New London*). These cases present strong evidence that there is a fundamental regime value of property as a legitimized tool to grow private development and thereby support the public interest via economic growth. Property as the concept then includes dimensions of private rights, public economic benefits, and private economic gain against a shifting backdrop of due process and public interest protections. How broadly the public interest is defined and what constitutes due process puts public administrators in the center of the debate.

Property is dynamic, as to what constitutes economic development evolves over time; consider traditional notions of the nineteenth and twentieth centuries meaning of lines of travel (*Charles River Bridge v. Warren Bridge*, 1837), mortgage moratoriums (*East New York Savings Bank v. Hahn*, 1944), welfare benefits (*Goldberg v. Kelly*, 1970), and blighting communities for gentrification (*Berman v. Parker*, 1954). These could have been cases from the twenty-first century because the policy issues persist. Property rights, however, remain held in the Takings Clause of the Fifth Amendment of the U.S. Constitution: "nor shall private property be taken for public use, without just compensation." Though this language has been chipped away by the courts and legislatures (Olejarski, 2018; Olejarski & Webb Farley, 2015), two due process provisions of public use and just compensation remain as protections. Due process in the Fifth and Fourteenth Amendments requires "nor shall any person be deprived of life, liberty, or property, without due process of law." What remains is the need to discern what constitutes property and how property may be used to support the public interest.

The purpose of this chapter is to use property rights as an example of a normative policy argument: the regime value of property remains a central tenant of our nation that should be protected. While property endures as a regime value, what shifts over time and must be under constant scrutiny by public administrators is the process of governmental takings, the due process, and public interest value judgments involved. Property can continue building the public interest through economic development, just as it has for centuries, while remaining constrained by the promises of protection provided within the Constitution.

Property as a regime value is inherently normative because it involves prescriptions for the ways governmental actors should make ethical decisions. Understanding the role of due process adds to the analysis and is of practical import when considering the policy implications of economic and private development and the competing interests that policymakers confront. Those studying and practicing in the field carry the heavy burden to ensure balance between protecting individual property rights and advancing the goal of economic development. This dilemma is not limited to the legal and philosophical canon surrounding the issue. Instead, it also calls on the administrator to practice administrative discretion and to do so within an ethical context at the intersection of public interest, economic goals, and private property rights. The public administrator, as frontline decision-maker, may draw on normative roots in order to guide ethical decisions in their functions of administrative discretion that position them as de facto policymakers.

Property as a Regime Value

In Rohr's *Ethics for Bureaucrats* (1989), he argues that property is a regime value because "the connections between property, independence, individualism, and freedom …are seen as contributing to the common good" (p. 245).

Administrators then exercise their discretionary authority in how they interpret legislation, regulations, rules, and case law. In this way, bureaucrats are making public policy. Eminent domain is the best suited policy area to study property as a regime value for three reasons. First, the Court has consistently ruled on eminent domain for well over 100 years, so the precedent is strong and stable. Second, property rights are inherently governmental, meaning that the right to private property predates the Constitution. In other words, individuals had the right to be secure in their own property in the state of nature, before the social contract. Eminent domain applies to personal property, such as homes, land, and commercial property like businesses and farms. Third, as Rohr maintains, due process protections found in the Fifth and Fourteenth Amendments of the Constitution "do not confer property on anyone; rather it protects property as the security of interests that a person has already acquired in specific benefits" (1989, p. 265).

As administrators make policy and implement eminent domain, ensuring due process requires two steps, as Rohr explains. The first, and rather obvious, step is to confirm that due process is relevant, or whether an individual has been deprived of life, liberty, or property. Confirming this leads to the second step, determining what process is due. Agency responses to this line of inquiry vary substantially based on the degree of deprivation. This is where the public administrator is left to consider how past cases and normative practice inform ethical exercise of their authority under the law. A review of the history of landmark cases in the Supreme Court can provide a foundation for public administrators confronted with these competing values.

Eminent Domain and Due Process in the Courts

The first time the Court ruled about eminent domain, economic development, and the public interest was in *Fallbrook Irrigation District v. Bradley* in 1896. California passed a statute to create artificial irrigation districts, private organizations, that would be funded from taxes paid by area property owners. All of the property owners would not benefit from these irrigation districts, but the Court held that was unnecessary, arguing "It is not essential that the entire community or even any considerable portion thereof should directly enjoy or participate in an improvement to constitute a public use... The water is intended for the use of those who will have occasion to use it on their lands" (pp. 161–162).

In *Fallbrook*, the broader economic development goals of the state of California were at issue, as the growth of the region depended on building these new irrigation districts. The Court's rationale was that all property owners would pay the new tax because they would all benefit from a general economic improvement. Stating explicitly that all property owners did not have to use or even have access to use the irrigation systems was a powerful statement.

Due process protections were managed in that the balancing test was between the property owners paying the increased tax and an overall boost to the economic growth of the region. That only a portion of the public had access to the system was irrelevant insofar as the public use requirement of the Fifth Amendment was concerned, as the Constitution does not require that all the public have occasion to use or access.

Due process protections in eminent domain saw higher stakes in the next landmark case, 1954's *Berman v. Parker*. At issue was blighting a community in Washington, D.C., or gentrification as it would be called today. This case occurs in the midst of the civil rights movement, and Congress was the legislature in control of taking the private property. Evidence of poor living conditions were evident in that 60 percent of the properties in the community lacked bathrooms, 58 percent had outside toilets, and 84 percent lacked central heating (*Berman v. Parker*, 1954). Congress was balancing urban renewal of the community against claims of public health and safety, invoking the police powers argument.

Legislatures have the power to regulate "public safety, public health, morality, peace and quiet, and law and order" and that "the power of eminent domain is merely the means to the end" (p. 32). Here, the economic development associated with blighting the community to rebuild newer, more robust structures producing higher taxes, solidifies the evolution of property as a regime value. Bolstering the precedent set forth in *Fallbrook*, *Berman* maneuvered eminent domain as a tool to support the public interest, albeit in a politically challenging way. From a normative perspective, the legislature in this case made decisions in a top-down style indicative of the time.

The tides of reform began to shift by the next time the Court ruled on an eminent domain case, *Hawaii Housing Authority v. Midkiff* (1984). Across the state of Hawaii, property ownership was highly concentrated, with just over 70 individuals owning about half the land (47 percent) and the other half owned by the government (49 percent) (*Hawaii v. Midkiff*, 1984). To diversify land ownership, the legislature passed a statute to enable renters to purchase their rental property from the property owner, all with the help of loans from the state housing authority. In more of a bottom-up approach, the state feared market failure and sought action to intervene. The Court notes, "it is only the taking's purpose, and not its mechanics, that must pass scrutiny under the Public Use Clause" (p. 244).

Midkiff differs from *Fallbrook* and *Berman* in that while both precedents failed to incorporate a substantial portion of the population as having access or use, Hawaii's legislature assured the Court that the Land Reform Act of 1967 was a public good. The act provided for grants by the state to renters to enable them to purchase their rental property. Moreover, the program was driven by the renters calling the state and requesting to have the property condemned, thus allowing the renters to purchase the property directly from the state. Property owners in this case were to be paid the fair market value of their property, per the just compensation requirement. According to the Court, "what in its immediate aspect is only a private transaction may be raised by its class or character to a public affair" (p. 244). Due process protections in *Midkiff* balanced a much broader public purpose of diversifying land ownership against preserving private property monopolies.

The Case of the Little Blue Pill

Thus far, the Supreme Court landmark cases have focused on the process of eminent domain, or the due process protections in place to guard over individual property rights, via the just compensation and public use requirements as well as the community's need for economic development. This balancing act came to a tipping point in *Kelo v. New London* (2005). In the much publicized *Kelo* case, the central issue surrounds a redevelopment agency, funded heavily by the state of Connecticut, using eminent domain to take private homes and businesses to support new construction of a research and development site for Pfizer, Inc., a large pharmaceutical company.

The city in *Kelo* is New London, and it was declared as distressed by Connecticut in 1990 due mostly to rising unemployment. Growth in the city was stunted. Following the shuttering of a federal naval center in 1996, population levels were so low they reached 1920s numbers. What began as a public-private partnership hybrid collaboration to redevelop New London turned quickly into the state taking a stronghold over the city.

Pfizer had just released Viagra, leading to exponential growth in the company and rapid expansion of its research and development facilities. In 1998, Connecticut approved a $5 million bond to reactivate and support the New London Development Council to create a redevelopment plan for the community. Moreover, the state provided a $10 million bond to build a park in the neighborhood. The work of Pfizer officials and the New London Development Council resulted in a plan to stimulate job growth and increase tax revenues.

Connecticut approved this plan, which called for the following components: the new Pfizer facility, the aforementioned park, a marina, 80 new residences, a museum, retail stores, and parking. Pfizer was the lynchpin to the project and the surrounding niceties were designed to attract high-income workers to the community, employees who would work for Pfizer. It is important to note that in its *Kelo* decision, the Court listed Pfizer's benefits first, with the public interest benefits to follow. This is a clear statement that economic development can and does serve the public interest, whether or not the public has access or opportunity to the development, keeping with precedent.

Due process balance continued to persist in *Kelo*. On one hand, the economic development and growth of the community, and on the other, protecting private property rights via a stronghold on defining public use. The latter has been eroded by the Supreme Court to the point of lacking substantive protections (Olejarski, 2018). Key actors involved, including the state, the New London Development Council, and puppet actors in the city relied on a broad definition of public use, which aligns with the Court's precedent cases. The public does not have to have direct access to the redevelopment property. In *Kelo*, the Court held: "Without exception, our cases have defined that concept broadly" (p. 480). The majority opinion added a third dimension to the due process balancing act: administrative efficiency. In other words, the Court balanced the individual private property rights against the community's right for economic development now also inclusive of the procedural requirements of opening the entire property to the public or determining how much of the public should or could have access to the property. Also at issue were the administrative responsibilities associated with slowing down the redevelopment plans to make such determinations, as well as limiting flexibility in implementing the plan.

Kelo strikes a three-way due process balance that combines individual property protections with administrative efficiency and economic development. In its decision, the Court relied on a state statute that specially includes economic development as a type of public use. Building on the two prior cases in *Berman* and *Midkiff*, the Court determined that economic development, even with some degree of private gain to Pfizer, serves the public interest. Focusing on the purpose of the eminent domain, rather than its "mechanics" (p. 499), solidified the ruling.

What is especially interesting from a due process perspective is that the Court explicitly invites states to enact stricter legislation, as many states have done to some degree (Olejarski, 2018). The Court states: "We emphasize that nothing in our opinion precludes any state from placing further restrictions on its exercise of the takings power [eminent domain]" (p. 489). While the Supreme Court was unwilling to depart from historical tradition in its ruling, it opened the door for state legislatures to do so. This squares with their practice of deference to the legislatures in Connecticut, Hawaii, and Washington, D.C., in the previous decisions.

These landmark precedent cases were all unanimous rulings; however, *Kelo* was 5-4. At the time, scholars often thought that meant the Court was likely to hear another eminent domain case in the near future, but alas, *Kelo* remains the prevailing law of the land. The dissenting opinion calls the Court's legislative deference an "abdication of our responsibility" (p. 504). The dissent continues: "States play many important functions in our system of dual sovereignty, but compensating for our refusal to enforce properly the Federal Constitution (and a provision meant to curtail state action, no less) is not among them" (p. 504).

Administrative Discretion

A major premise of this chapter is that public administrators make public policy through their power of administrative discretion. Through their decision-making process, informal discretion and soft policy choices are made that impact the daily lives of Americans. This argument is reinforced by the work of Friedrich (1972) as he establishes that the public administrator is an essential link between public interest and governmental action in the increasingly complicated modern environment. As we continue studying and practicing public administration in the middle of this constitutional crisis, we should go back to our normative roots and rediscover how it is we make decisions.

Due process protections and establishment of the public interest warrants discussion of how the contemporary bureaucrat can make ethical decisions in these complex cases. Rohr's definition of administrative discretion is a good starting point. He maintains that discretion is a process surrounding administrators' responsibilities to "advise, report, respond, initiate, inform, question, caution, complain, applaud, encourage, rebuke, promote, retard, and mediate" (1989, pp. 36–37). Understanding ethical decision-making processes should also involve consideration of some classical works in the field. Behn (1998) focuses on how administrators can cultivate their discretion toward leadership and providing goal clarity. For Simon (1997), he makes a distinction between how practitioners and legislators go about the process of decision-making, explaining that legislators make their decisions based on facts, yet practitioners do so based on values or what they consider to be ethical. Likewise, Foster (1981) looks at moral and legal decisions and explores connections between value-based ethical decisions and how they emphasize the context of a situation. While Denhardt puts it quite simply by calling on the public administrator to ensure that their decisions "are consistent with the wishes of the citizenry" (Denhardt, 2013, p. 260). In the previous cases, however, the wishes of the public may at times conflict with, or be a subjective examination of, public opinion versus public interest.

The Public Interest Question

Property as a regime value, and eminent domain as an example of a normative policy problem, benefits from an understanding of the evolution of the public interest as some tangible requirement (Olejarski, 2011). While the U.S. Constitution requires that eminent domain be used for a narrow public purpose, the case analyses above show that this has been gradually expanded to a broader purpose or public interest. Goodsell (1990) and Douglass (1980) argue that the public interest is inclusive of the public use/public good because it encompasses all likely stakeholders in the process. Goodsell identifies a subjective-objective type of argument in that the public interest includes objective benefits and also the more subjective policy outcomes and determinants of success and should act on behalf of citizens.

Scholars in the Constitutional School of American Public Administration often rely on the framers of the Constitution and their interpretations as a starting point. During the 1990s and 2000s, at the birth of the Constitutional

School, the field saw an influx of attention paid to *The Federalist Papers* and the ratification debate. Most relevant to the current literature is Morgan's (2001) perspective that the public interest pulls together diverse private interests to ward against Madison's factions. Much like in the Supreme Court's eminent domain decisions, the public interest includes some degree of private benefits, whether it is health, safety, and morality; diversifying property ownership, or increasing jobs and tax revenues.

Lewis's (2006) approach is also particularly useful because of her process-centric focus to learning about the public interest. She characterizes the public interest as an ongoing and flexible pursuit, rather than an ending point. This fits especially well with studying property as a regime value, given the need for adapting over time to maintain salience. Closely related is Herring (1997, p. 78) who calls the public interest the "verbal symbol designed to introduce unity, order, and objectivity into administration." His call for objectivity pulls together Goodsell's approach for objective benefits with Lewis's designs on the process.

Finally, Long's work (1988, p. 341, 1991) rounds out the classical studies of the public interest. He calls it the search for the Holy Grail, much like Lewis and Herring. But he also draws on Rohr's regime values, calling for attention to "principle dimensions" of determining if a policy serves the public interest. This stance does not provide clear guidance for decision-makers and instead is a value judgment. The question of whether a policy meets the bar of serving the public interest in an eminent domain case requires careful consideration by the public administrator entrusted with policy development and implementation.

Aligning Discretion and Public Interest

In what has come to be known as the Blacksburg Manifesto, the faculty at Virginia Tech's Center for Public Administration and Policy, led by Wamsley as editor, offer some musings as to how administrators can align their decisions with the public interest. The Manifesto wrestled with the big questions of public administration, such as how bureaucrats could exercise discretion while still upholding the rule of law. The authors (1990, p. 41) explain: "Surely The Public Administration does not 'know' the content of the public interest; but it is in a relatively good position to nurture the kind of process essential for its ongoing pursuit, partially when it takes the enlarged view of the process that encompasses efforts to render faithful interpretations of the interests of all relevant stakeholders, including citizens at large."

From this perspective, practitioners are charged with the responsibility to make normative decisions about regime values, such as property, as they make public policy. Implementing policy decisions based on case law or Supreme

Court decisions requires a fair amount of creative problem solving to bridge the gap between vague mandates from the judiciary and statutes and regulatory actions. As Newswander (2015, p. 868) notes, "governing is ugly." And yet, administrators govern with robust, active responsiveness to the public interest and the citizens (Gooden, 2004; Meier & Bohte, 2007). Bamberger (2008) maintains that such decisions should be made as mindful of both the policy goals and also constitutional norms, echoing earlier sentiments about the meaning of the public interest. Most importantly, Newbold (2010) calls for bringing forth the practical value of constitutional approaches or what Rosenbloom (2013) describes as the administrative state as a mix of implementing and policymaking.

Relevant literature on constitutional dimensions surrounding eminent domain remains sharply divided. The traditional view argues that the public use expansions of the U.S. Supreme Court weaken individual rights and property protections (Coyne, 1985; Fawcett, 1986; Mushkatel & Nakhleh, 1978). Once it became clear that economic development would continue meeting the Fifth Amendment's public use requirements, scholars began calling for restrictions on private development (Boudreaux, 2005; Cohen, 2006; Han, 2008). Alternatives favor economic development involving private gain because of the value in public-private partnerships (Melton, 1996; Salkin & Lucero, 2005).

This dynamic interplay of making ethical decisions vis-a-vis implementing policy holds especially true for eminent domain as an example of a normative policy problem. Property is a regime value of the republic because it is a value of the people (Rohr, 1989) to own homes, businesses, land, farms, etc. In a post-*Kelo* environment, due process protections have been put into place by most of the states to guard against governmental abuse. Olejarski's (2018) study of all state responses to the case finds that the public use requirement has been eroded to the point of insignificance and that most states reproduce the term to harken back to the U.S. Constitution. Hudson (2010) examines the specific due process protections of the legislative responses to *Kelo*, focusing on whether hearings and official notifications are required. His study reveals that a dozen have surface-level protections, over 20 lack protections, and over 15 include deficient protections. Mihaly and Smith (2011) take a different direction, instead focusing on the economic growth and development angle of eminent domain proceedings, noting that states with stronger economies passed the most substantial reforms, which they attribute to those state's ability able to shoulder the cost of pricey reforms. Olejarski's (2011, p. 336) study advocates for a "principle of tangibility" that would mandate direct use by the public in eminent domain cases. Finally, Somin (2009) maintains that much of the *Kelo* legislative responses that lacked substance resulted from what he calls political "ignorance" (p. 2170).

Conclusions

This chapter argues that property continues to be a regime value, and that this status guides how administrators make ethical decisions. As Rohr (1989, p. 5) urges: "The values in question are not popular whims of the moment, but rather constitutional or regime values. This is because the bureaucrat has taken an oath to uphold the Constitution…. The best educational means for preparing bureaucrats to fulfill this obligation is to use Supreme Court opinions on salient regime values to encourage them to reflect on how those values might best influence their decision making as persons who govern." The preceding discussion and analysis of landmark cases show how eminent domain endures as an example of a normative policy problem and highlights the role of property as a regime value. It also provides a framework for the public administrator to consider ethical implications of administrative discretion decisions that are, in effect, policy-making actions.

Assaults on the constitutional protections for private property have been working their way through the courts for decades as outlined in this chapter. Continually changing parameters surrounding due process protections add to the uncertainty, as do questions surrounding whether the public should have access to the process and the evaluation of how much private gain should be permissible. These shifting sands leave administrators in a challenging position as they look to uphold their responsibilities to the Constitution, while also serving the public interest of economic development. The degree of gain in economic activity associated with takings under eminent domain, the timeliness of the procedural implications, and the level of distress of their communities remain as compounding factors worthy of examination and reflection for both practitioners and researchers. Administrative discretion in these cases thrust the public administrator (PA) into the role of policymaking. What endures is the normative nature of property policy and the position of property as a regime value. Grounding property as a regime value can provide continuity for these decisions, and understanding these ethical dimensions should be central to bureaucrats' decision-making process.

References

Bamberger, K. A. (2008). Normative cannons in the review of administrative policy-making. *The Yale Law Journal, 118*, 64–125.

Behn, R. D. (1998). What right do public managers have to lead? *Public Administration Review, 58*, 209–224.

Berman v. Parker (1954).

Boudreaux, P. (2005). Eminent domain, property rights, and the solution of representative reinforcement. *Denver University Law Review, 83*, 1–55.

Charles River Bridge v. Warren Bridge (1837).

Cohen, C. E. (2006). Eminent domain after Kelo v. City of New London: An argument for banning economic development takings. *Harvard Journal of Law & Public Policy, 29*, 491–568.

Coyne, T. J. (1985). Hawaii Housing Authority v. Midkiff: A final requiem for the public use limitation on eminent domain? *Notre Dame Law Review, 60*, 388–404.

Denhardt, R. B. (2013). *Public administration: An action orientation* (7th ed.). Boston, MA: Cengage Learning.

Douglass, B. (1980). The common good and the public interest. *Political Theory, 8*, 103–117.

East New York Savings Bank v. Hahn (1944).

Fallbrook Irrigation District v. Bradley (1896).

Fawcett, D. B., III. (1986). Eminent domain, the police power, and the Fifth Amendment: Defining the domain of the takings analysis. *University of Pittsburgh Law Review, 47*, 491–515.

Foster, G. D. (1981). Law, morality, and the public servant. *Public Administration Review, 41*, 29–34.

Friedrich, C. (1972). Public policy and the nature of democratic responsibility. In F. Rourke (Ed.), *Public policy and the nature of democratic responsibility* (pp. 176–186). Boston, MA: Little, Brown.

Gibbons v. Ogden (1819).

Goldberg v. Kelly (1970).

Gooden, M. A. (2004). A history of black achievement as impacted by federal court decisions in the last century. *The Journal of Negro Education, 73*, 230–238.

Goodsell, C. T. (1990). Public administration and the public interest. In G. L. Wamsley et al. (Eds.), *Refounding public administration* (pp. 96–113). Newbury Park, CA: Sage.

Han, A. S. (2008). From New London to Norwood: A year in the life of eminent domain. *Duke Law Journal, 57*, 1449–1483.

Hawaii Housing Authority v. Midkiff (1984).

Herring, E. P. (1997). Public administration and the public interest. In J. M. Shafritz & A. C. Hyde (Eds.), *Classics of public administration* (4th ed., pp. 76–80). Fort Worth, TX: Harcourt Brace.

Hudson, Z. D. (2010). Eminent domain due process. *The Yale Law Journal, 119*, 1280–1327.

Kelo v. New London (2005).

Lewis, C. W. (2006). In pursuit of the public interest. *Public Administration Review, 66*, 694–701.

Long, N. E. (1988). Public administration, cognitive competence, and the public interest. *Administration & Society, 20*, 334–343.

Long, N. E. (1991). Politics, political science and the public interest. *PS: Political Science & Politics, 24*, 670–675.

Meier, K. J., & Bohte, J. (2007). *Politics and the bureaucracy: Policymaking in the fourth branch of government* (5th ed.). Belmont, CA: Wadsworth.

Melton, B. F., Jr. (1996). Eminent domain, "public use," and the conundrum of original intent. *Natural Resources Journal, 36*, 59–85.

Mihaly, M., & Smith, T. (2011). Kelo's trail: A survey of state and federal legislative and judicial activity five years later. *Ecology Law Quarterly, 38*, 703–730.

Morgan, D. F. (2001). The public interest. In T. L. Cooper (Ed.), *Handbook of administrative ethics* (2nd ed., pp. 151–178). New York, NY: Marcel Dekker.

Mushkatel, A., & Khalil, N. (1978). Eminent domain: Land-use planning and the powerless in the United States and Israel. *Social Problems, 26*, 147–159.

Newbold, S. P. (2010). Toward a constitutional school for American public administration. *Public Administration Review, 70*, 538–546.

Newswander, C. B. (2015). Guerilla statesmanship: Constitutionalizing an ethic of dissent. *Public Administration Review, 75*, 126–134.

O'Neill, J. (2009). Straussian constitutional history and the Straussian political project. *Rethinking History, 13*(4), 459–478. https://doi.org/10.1080/13642520903292898

Olejarski, A. M. (2011). Public good as public interest? The principle of tangibility in eminent domain legislation. *Public Integrity, 13*, 333–351.

Olejarski, A. M. (2018). Irrelevance of "public use" in state eminent domain reforms. *American Review of Public Administration, 48*, 631–643.

Olejarski, A. M., & Farley, K. W. (2015). The little blue pill that killed the little pink house: A narrative of eminent domain. *Administration & Society, 47*, 369–392.

Rohr, J. A. (1989). *Ethics for bureaucrats: An essay on law and values* (2nd ed.). New York, NY: Marcel Dekker.

Rosenbloom, D. R. (2013). Reflections on "Public Administrative Theory and the Separation of Powers." *The American Review of Public Administration, 43*, 381–396.

Salkin, P. E., & Lora, A. L. (2005). Community redevelopment, public use, and eminent domain. *Urban Lawyer, 37*, 201–242.

Simon, H. A. (1997). *Administrative behavior: A study of decision-making processes in administrative organizations* (4th ed.). New York, NY: Free Press.

Somin, I. (2009). The limits of backlash: Assessing the political response to Kelo. *Minnesota Law Review, 93*, 2100–2178.

Wamsley, G. L., Goodsell, C. T., Rohr, J. A., Stivers, C. M., White, O. F., & Wolf, J. F. (1990). Public administration and the governance process: Shifting the political dialogue. In G. L. Wamsley, R. N. Bacher, C. T. Goodsell, P. S. Kronenberg, J. A. Rohr, C. M. Stivers, ... J. F. Wolf (Eds.), *Refounding public administration* (pp. 31–51). Newbury Park, CA: Sage.

6

PROPERTY, INTELLECTUAL PROPERTY, AND ETHICS IN PUBLIC ADMINISTRATION

Sara R. Jordan

What guidance does the Constitutional School of Public Administration offer for public officials grappling with issues of intellectual property protection? Whether through sponsorship of basic and applied research, through production of program evaluations, or through production of the troves of data essential to the conduct of agency tasks, modern states are pre-eminent intellectual property generators. Likewise, the state is the primary organ through which the intellectual property of others is protected.

Considerations of property and intellectual property occupy considerable numbers of scholars of law and legal studies. These same considerations, somewhat curiously, do not occupy scholars of public policy and public administration. The authors of the Blacksburg Manifesto, *Refounding Public Administration*, and *Refounding Democratic Public Administration* (hereafter, the Blacksburg School), are among the set of scholars strangely quiet on issues of property and intellectual property (Wamsley, 1990; Wamsley & Wolf, 1996). At least vis-a-vis the Blacksburg School of Public Administration, the silence is strange. Given the overwhelming concern of the founders with protection of property, including the protection of an individual's letters, home, and other effects that might live in a desk, it is a significant gap that the constitutional school does not take on the *overall* topic of property as such with any notable ardor, much less address the question of intellectual property.

This essay does not offer a lengthy speculative exegesis as to why property does not loom large in the *Refounding* texts or in the separate texts of scholars of the Blacksburg perspective, such as those by John Rohr (1989) and Charles Goodsell (1985). Instead, I start from the position that the oversight is an unintentional opportunity for later scholars, left open by the Blacksburg School founders for reasons of expediency and methods. As a historical matter, from the late 1980s to early 2000s, there were few major political debates on the nature of property ownership, over the states' rightful claims as a property owner, or debating the merits of the state as a claimant upon citizens' property. The Federal Land Policy and Management Act having been largely settled in 1976 and the associated "Sagebrush Rebellion" largely a distant memory except for a few discussions in Western states, the historical climate was not tilted toward discussions of federal land management (Dowdle, 1984; Peng, Ahlstrom, Carraher, & Shi, 2017). Likewise, considering John Rohr's methods of considering norms via United States Supreme Court debate, no significant cases related to property or intellectual property were heard. Those that did rise to the federal level, such as Adidas vs. Payless Shoe Source, Inc. did not address topics of administrative concern. Another consideration is methodological: for the authors of the collected Blacksburg volumes (*Refounding*), the purpose was to elaborate a school level perspective on the practice of public administration. For individual authors, advancing a method of thinking through public administration ethics (Rohr) or a description of ideal public administration practice (Goodsell) did not easily include an elaboration on the conceptual bases of their theories, including the concept of property and property ownership. It is within this context that I strive here to reconstruct a Blacksburg concept of property and ethical protections incumbent upon and due to public officials as a result of this concept of property. I do so by referring to the signposts to relevant thinkers who did elaborate on a concept of property from within the writings of scholars in the Blacksburg School of Constitutional Public Administration.

John Locke, the Founders, and the Historical Perspective of the Blacksburg School—Reconstructing a Theory of Property in the Blacksburg Tradition

What does it mean to own something? And what does ownership mean for the executive tasks of the state, such as rights-giving and rights-taking?

The first question was of significant concern to the philosophers and public intellectuals whose work provides the scaffolding for the U.S. Constitution. John Locke, Thomas Hobbes, Montesquieu, Jean-Jacques Rousseau, and their many interlocutors each spent considerable portions of their writings addressing the concepts of property and ownership. For these seventeenth and eighteenth century writers, determining the ownership of land or objects, whether that ownership accrues at the level of the individual or is collective to a family, a firm, or a state, is a fundamental political task. The task was not political only because of the relationship between ownership and law. To the thinkers that informed the founders and to the founders themselves, to have ownership and to exercise rights to property was a fundamental requirement of being a political person.

As is described by multiple scholars of constitutional development in America, John Locke's writings had an exceptional influence on the thinking of the founders. Within the Blacksburg tradition there are strong elements of Locke's writing, and a reconstruction of a theory of property for the Blacksburg School must acknowledge the strains of Locke.

John Locke's theory of property has multiple facets, but the one most essential here is Locke's labor theory of property, captured succinctly in what has been labeled the "Lockean Proviso." In his terms:

> Nor was this appropriation of any parcel of land, by improving it, any prejudice to any other man, since there was still enough and as good left, and more than the yet unprovided could use. So that, in effect, there was never the less left for others because of his enclosure for himself. For he that leaves as much as another can make use of, does as good as take nothing at all. Nobody could think himself injured by the drinking of another man, though he took a good draught, who had a whole river of the same water left him to quench his thirst. And the case of land and water, where there is enough of both, is perfectly the same (*Second treatise on government*, Chapter 5, paragraph 33).

Within Locke's theory of property, ownership is the transformation of a resource that is formerly common, even if only in the hypothetical distant past, into a divided thing through the insertion of an individual's power. The division of the commons is what invites the primary tasks of politics—law, regulation, and policing of rights and claims. For example, Locke's definition of the just distribution of private property requires a concept of sustainability—"there was still enough and as good left"—which, in turn, entails the evaluation of the quantity (enough) and quality (as good left) of the resource by an external actor.

The division of what is common prompts the need for a policing function to maintain those claims. Although the primary coordinator of property in Locke's theory is the law-giving sovereign, Locke wasn't blind to the need for the sovereign to delegate the power to an administrative apparatus. Locke points to the need for an administrative management of the claims to land within subsequent paragraphs of Chapter 5.

> Sect. 45. Thus labour, in the beginning, gave a right of property, wherever any one was pleased to employ it upon what was common, which remained a long while the far greater part, and is yet more than mankind makes use of. Men, at first, for the most part, contented themselves with what unassisted nature offered to their necessities: and though afterwards, in some parts of the world, (where the increase of people and stock, with the use of money, had made land scarce, and so of some value) *the several communities settled the bounds of their distinct territories, and by laws within*

themselves regulated the properties of the private men of their society, and so, by compact and agreement, settled the property which labour and industry began; and the leagues that have been made between several states and kingdoms, either expressly or tacitly disowning all claim and right to the land in the others possession, have, by common consent, given up their pretences to their natural common right, which originally they had to those countries, and so have, by positive agreement, settled a property amongst themselves, in distinct parts and parcels of the earth; yet there are still great tracts of ground to be found, which (the inhabitants thereof not having joined with the rest of mankind, in the consent of the use of their common money) lie waste, and are more than the people who dwell on it do, or can make use of, and so still lie in common; tho' this can scarce happen amongst that part of mankind that have consented to the use of money (*emphasis added*).

Locke's exposition on the relationship between the origin of property and the origin of government is clear. Once there are settlements of property, there is a need for laws, regulations, compacts, agreement, and government. Why, though, does an individual labor theory of property lead Locke to advocate for a liberal constitutional system of government?

Within Locke's work there are indications why a labor theory of property leads to a constitutional system of government. These are salient here to the extent that they help us to understand why effective administration of property claims requires a constitutionally sensitive executive. For Locke, a constitution is a contract, agreed to explicitly or tacitly, between peoples that lays out the basic conditions under which the people can set additional contracts for themselves. The Constitution defines and governs the boundaries between people through a generalized contract, which eliminates the need that individuals fully articulate each element of personal definition and contract themselves before developing a marketplace with their many neighbors. As an expedient, the constitution is a contract to rule contracts. As a political task, a constitution is an agreement to be part of something that is common, though intangibly so: a state.

Within the context of the Blacksburg tradition, the Constitution serves as a contract for contracts and is the backdrop for the implicit contract between administrators and citizens. It articulates the basis of a principal-agent relationship and a relationship of individual versus the state. The articulation of background rights for individuals ensures that there is a basis for them to address the state from their individual perspective, rather than from the perspective of a member of a community, caste, or other group.

The Blacksburg School arguably draws from Locke, but is the Lockean Proviso all that a public administrator needs to know concerning property rights and arrangements? In brief, the Blacksburg concept of property is not strictly Lockean. The Blacksburg School of Property, informed by the changes to the concept of property itself (discussed below), acknowledges that an open horizon of property is no longer a useful fiction. Instead, the Blacksburg School of Property is interventionist and takes as given that virtually all claims of individuals are a matter for state intervention. In contrast to a strictly political theoretic concept of property, a Blacksburg concept of property explicitly acknowledges that property is a mixture of the material and the personal as this is always already defined by the state.

A definition of property that takes the state—constitutions, overlapping administrative offices, administrative discretion to draft and adjudicate contracts within the bounds of agency's delegated power—as given might be specified as follows: *contemporary property is what we own within the bounds of definition by the state and under the understanding that the state may revoke claims of property rights when the quantity or quality of remaining property or opportunities to claim property become prohibitive to expression of the concept of free and equal persons. Any property otherwise unowned by the state or by an individual through the recognition of the state is presumed to be part of the state's remit de facto and will be managed under the terms of the constitution—the contract for contracts—until such time as the claims of an individual compel rearticulation of a specific and narrow contract.*

An example might help to explain this: imagine an enterprising person happens upon an unowned pond, recently opened by an earthquake and filled by rains, now served by a small creek. In this recently opened resource, this enterprising person decides to establish a farm dedicated to growing northern snakehead fish (see Gordon, 1954 for why fisheries is an apt example). Having ensured that the pond is suitable, managed its flow, and stocked it with fish, this enterprising individual is the rightful owner of that pond and the fish within it. This fish farmer may now allow fishing tournaments, have the fish taken for human or animal food, or might have them used as an organic fertilizer: all control of the pond and its content are the property of this farmer under the strict terms of the Lockean Proviso. This enterprising fish farmer has the right to control access to the pond and to the fish within it as they have mixed an open resource with their resources (external and internal) labor to establish ownership.

On a Blacksburg perspective, however, this same enterprising fish farmer would face significant hurdles to establishing their farm. Firstly, regardless of the open nature of the land on which this fissure pond opened, it was already provisionally owned as a common part of the American state. The new owner makes a claim upon it that is always already relevant to others, specifically because it is within the geographical boundaries of the constitutional state. Second, the connection of the water with the remainder of the land, whether through aquifers or streams, or via the wanderings of the fish, connects this property claim to others' property. Although the ownership of this particular pond does not prevent a degradation of the quantity of other ponds, the introduction of a fish species does invite a change to the quality of this and other ponds. Intentional introduction of a species could alter the ecosystem, inviting additional property claims by those whose ponds were effected. Because this fish farmer is part of an ecosystem of contracts governed by the state, this enterprising fish farmer is only allowed to own this enterprise under significant limitations imposed by the state. Thus constrained, a Blacksburg definition of property rights grants permissions rather than rights.

Although this vignette paints the picture that there is a major difference between owning property and having permission to own property—by owning we can do whatever we want; by permission, we can do whatever others allow—in a fully articulated modern state, there is perhaps not so much a difference, but a distinction. The distinction is an important one, however, as there is a background ethics associated with property claims that has not already been articulated.

Property and Ethics

What does property have to do with ethics? What does property have to do with the specific form of applied ethics called public administration ethics? Firstly, ethical problems are situations where there is a choice between two irreconcilable visions of the good. Where both sides to an issue can press a reasoned argument that their alternative for action meets a situation that both sides agree is normatively good (or avoids an agreed upon state of evil), then the situation is one where ethics is involved. Situations where the choice is to do those actions that bring about an agreed upon good, however uncomfortably, rather than bring about an agreed upon evil, however easily, are not ethical decisions. Those decisions are a consequence of living in a society where moral judgments—determination that we can be held liable for failing to do good, however uncomfortably—occur between peers. Likewise, situations where doing actions in a "polite" or "customer service oriented way" are matters for etiquette, not ethics. It is fully possible, and probable, that we can be ethical without being "nice" or "likeable."

Many situations of resource distribution are ethical situations. To wit, the choice between a program to provide funding for a program which gives schoolchildren free access to quality dental care versus a program which gives low-income elderly singles free access to quality dental care results is an agreed upon good: a community in which the least well off and most vulnerable have opportunities to maximize their physical and emotional health. The ethical consideration in this case is whether the right thing to do is to support services for one or another group—the children or the elderly. If one gets the dental services, a divisible good dependent upon discrete allocations of time, personnel, and material resources, the other cannot have the same exact service. In cases involving property, the ethical considerations are often similar: the question is, how can a common good be divided in such a way that awarding the division to one does not irreparably damage the other?

The question of ethical choices under situations of resource constraint have prompted philosophical discussion since the earliest texts of philosophy. General questions on the matter of ethical distribution of property were bothersome to Locke. His assertion that the division of property be sustainable (see above) is one, albeit brief, way of grappling with the question. The American constitutional Founders took a different approach: property is an instrumental good that is only as good as the freedom that its ownership allows. It is not ownership as such that is ethically good, it is the liberty that arises from ownership that is good.

In the context of the American founding, there was a tight coupling between concepts of liberty, personhood, and property. As schoolchildren can well rehearse, the Declaration of Independence sought for American citizens the right to "life, liberty, and the pursuit of happiness." Much ink has been spilled on the fact that property was intended in place of happiness. Without rehearsing these previous explorations extensively, the Founders argued that freedom for an individual required property. Ownership and use of property freed an individual from the misery of debt bondage, shop slavery, and feudal serfdom. In brief, for the Founders, it was obvious that property promoted liberty and happiness.

Intellectual Property as Intellectual Freedom in the U.S. Constitution

For the Founders, to be free meant to have sufficient means to be free from bondage of debt and servitude to others. Given the historical context of the time, the Founders conflated the possession of the means to support oneself off the land or through a self-directed trade with political and intellectual self-possession. An individual could not be free to be himself in the richest sense of the terms—to make his own individually autonomous decisions—if he was in a dependent or heteronomous relationship with others, such as with a feudal lord or a shop boss.

Individual autonomy or the opportunity to self-legislate outside of direct and intentional manipulation by others is a principle common to ethical traditions associated with liberalism, such as consequentialism, and to principles associated with Lockean liberalism, such as commitments to toleration, equality (in both its opportunity and outcome forms), and preservation of life. The work that these systems of ethics does, such as through description of a "right" to liberty, is to determine what peers owe one another when they grant liberty or respect autonomy. Respecting individual autonomy means not coercing an individual to believe or behave in ways that s/he believes will not maximize or honor their good. This includes resisting attempts to coerce individuals to reform their plans to use their labor or their possessions in order to meet the expectations or needs of others. A state that respects individual autonomy is not one that will attempt to coerce individuals to reform their plans to own or dispose of any real or material property unless it is absolutely necessary to prevent a situation wherein one individual's choices actively undermine the opportunity of others to make their choices. Only when an individual's autonomous choice hinders the choices of others can coercion be permitted in a system where respect for individual autonomy is a basic principle. One of the key functions of a constitution is to stipulate when such "liberty preserving coercion" can take place (Rose-Ackerman, 1985).

Property defined as the ability to make up one's own mind also meant the right to use one's body as a form of property. Particularly given the nature of agriculture and artisanship at the time the Founders were writing, meaningful labor meant autonomous choice to follow a trade. The freedom to ply one's self-driven trade was not divorced from the freedom to make one's own mind up about the value of things that supported that trade. Fully free individuals could make up their own minds about the value of the background conditions of society that made the market for things run. For example, a fully free, land owning, person could decide that the value of human dignity and life was greater than the value of profit. They could also decide that abiding by racialist theories of man were abhorrent, and they could thus reject slavery on individual ethical terms as did the early abolitionists. Freed from obligations to behave in ways that traded intellectual freedom for economic freedom, the propertied man could innovate ethically and materially. For the Founders, the freedom from economic servitude opened the door for ideation and innovation.

The freedom to innovate, like the freedom to own land, was not judged by the Founders to arise *ex lex* from some shared sense of mutual accommodation. Just as the freedom to own and operate one's land required law and its implementation, the freedom to create also required the protections of law and regulation. A truly self-possessed inventor required the judgments of a legal apparatus, such as a patent office to certify that his work was original and deserving of the protections of exclusivity. The self-possession of the inventor or the owner would have had limits to recognition by others without such an office. What intellectual property protections ensured is a freedom to create without penalty for foregoing other activities that were safer: trading the time and energy to create a new plow had to be traded for the time and energy to turn the field with existing implements. The freedom to make the choice to innovate rather than re-create with old technology required respect for the freedom to choose which, in turn, requires the freedom to think.

The open horizon to elaborate on controversial ideas with some protection of those ideas is embedded in the earliest concerns of the constitutional Founders. Being able to think and to protect the outputs of thought—copyright of sermons, patent protections for plows, rights against seizure of personal letters—was a value close to the hearts of the earliest colonists and American Founders. Considered by others of the day to be dangerous radicals (whether religious heretics or anti-monarchical revolutionaries), the American Founders were keen to ensure protection of private ideas from government intrusion. They were also keen to protect ideas from one another. Within the Copyright Act of 1790, text was granted protection from direct copying. Over time, the types of ideas protected expanded to industrial designs, plants, music, and recently, software (Fisher, 1997, pp. 3–4). Neither of these types of protected property alone prompted a democratic way of governing, but neither of them could have been excluded and the American democratic experience turn out the way it has. For example, without the copyright of music, protest music would not have moved forward anti-war and Civil Rights movements of the 1960s, and without the protection of software from piracy, the technological tools of contemporary politics—Facebook streaming of debates—could not have arisen in the way they did. What the protection of intellectual property did for the American democracy was to nurture its deliberative nature through proliferation of many types of citizen knowledge and expression.

Just as they did not spend considerable time discussing property rights as these were merely part of the background conditions of rights in the contemporary United States, the Blacksburg authors did not discuss extensively the right to think freely for oneself. That a democratic society requires a plurality of opinions on the arrangements of power that is a result of individuals thinking freely on their own is an assumed background condition. However, within the second volume of the Blacksburg texts, the importance of this background condition received more attention.

Democracy, Open Societies, and the Anti-Federalists in the Blacksburg Tradition of Intellectual Freedom

The authors of the Blacksburg Manifesto and its book length expositions took pains to emphasize that a constitutional perspective on public administration did not connote a legalistic perspective. Likewise, it did not connote a traditionalist or conservative stance; following the Constitution does not create an obligation to strict constructivism over interpretivism (Buchanan, 1988). Instead, the constitutional perspective encouraged by the Blacksburg authors holds up as a value of the spirit of meaningful discourse on the public interest.

Following the spirit of the Founders' discussion in the framing, the Blacksburg style of the public interest is best defined through the practice of democratic discourse between free, equal, and varied persons (Marshall & Choudhury, 1997). Their discursive democratic perspective borrowed key ideas of democracy, civil spiritedness, and a discourse ethic from political and social theorists of the time, to include Herbert Storing (2008) and Karl Popper (2012).

Other observers have pointed out that there is not a coherent theory of democracy, nor a single theory of democratic public administration, expressed in the books of the Blacksburg perspective. Key characteristics of democracy—representativeness, public voice, 1-man/1-vote, and an ongoing project of state legitimation through open and regular procedures—are largely assumed, and each individual author emphasizes one or another component as suits the purposes of their arguments. What is consistent is that democracy is a normative commitment ancillary to the grander value of public interestedness—to the extent that reforms to the practice of public administration fulfill the democratic ideal, then those reforms are normatively laudable.

Although they lamented the trade off between expedient politics and romantic idealism, the Blacksburg authors did not hold an overly rosy view of the practice of democracy. They were keenly aware that democracy invites "winners" and "losers" in political battles, but that the "losers" in political debates hold fast to principles worth revisiting. Chief among the examples of "losing ideas" worth revisiting were the anti-Federalists. Although Federalist centralization of government power eventually won the day, the anti-Federalists' emphasis on close community and deep local connections were not to be discarded as losing ideas (Cornell, 2012). Instead, per the Blacksburg perspective, the communitarian ethos of the anti-Federalists should be revisited as a source for legitimation of administrative activity. Given that administrative action is distinctly local to the citizens asking something of the state and to the state official making a decision that grants or denies permission, the importance of local community influence should not be understated. But, it should not be overstated either: a democracy is intended to be an open society wherein various views are tested as relevant rivals for assertions of public value. No one view takes priority except for the position that democracy and the constitutional rule of law is normatively preferable to the alternatives. If, however, arguments for changing the Constitution or redrawing the boundaries of democratic citizenship are lodged, these are not to be dismissed *a priori*. All arguments that could possibly enhance any one of the essential background conditions for democracy should be entertained. If an idea is entertained and if it "wins" the day, that win should not be interpreted as being permanent. An open democracy requires a provisional attitude toward the superiority of any concept of truth or rightness. The provisional attitude toward what is common or right extended from a faith in the marketplace of ideas, but also a commitment to a common, relatively inclusive, democratic way of governing (Popper, 2012).

The inclusive way of governing entails the commitment to an inclusive way of knowing. There is no explicit theory of knowledge espoused by the Blacksburg authors apart from the commitment to a marketplace of ideas within a democracy. The stipulations of ontological disclosure ask for clarification of the biases and norms that authors imbue into their arguments. But, this demand does not come with a corresponding requirement for the terms of the disclosure. That is, disclosures do not need to be "truthful," although they must be sincere. While it is certainly based on an individualist theory of knowledge—know thyself and disclose—and a predisposition to believe that democratic discourse is a test-bed for individual knowledge, there is no explicit theory or argument for the terms upon which such a disclosure should be accepted. The contestation of disclosure should follow the norms of democracy such as provisionalism, openness, and non-dogmatism. To foster the democratic norms of openness and contestation of knowledge requires some appreciation and protection of the value of thought. Hence, a background condition for democratic discourse, and for such discourse on the public interest, is a system of protections of the outputs of the intellect; public interested democracy requires intellectual property.

Concluding Thoughts

As Overeem defined them, "regime values can be briefly defined, for a start, as collective benefits promoted by a given political order" (Overeem, 2015, p. 47). The idea of property is a benefit that is enjoyed by members of a constitutional, democratic, political order. Although there is no specific exegesis on the importance of property as a regime value in the writings of the authors of the Blacksburg Manifesto, there is good reason to believe that it ought to have made the cut.

It was only for historic and methodological reasons that property did not make the cut. That intellectual property did not find a place in the list of regime values is for similar reasons. In hindsight, however, property plays a critical role in the set of background conditions necessary to make democracy meaningful as the political vehicle for public interest discussions. To own property allows for a degree of self-possession that renders autonomy and autonomous political judgment possible. Ownership of property in material or in oneself allows an individual to take possession of something which must be recognized by others, including the non-self other of the state. As a vehicle to secure recognition of the person, property places individuals on clear footing vis-a-vis the power structures of the state, whether administrative or judicial. In brief, to own is to be recognized, and to be recognized is to be heard. Such are keys to full democratic participation.

Property is important as a background condition for autonomy and democracy. Intellectual property also has a place in the set of background conditions: to be granted ownership claims to an idea further allows persons to situate themselves as visible forces in the discourse on public interest ideas. Holding forth in a conversation on what is good and what is to be done is made easier by being able to wage a warranted claim for having the ideas discussed. To be able to lay a claim to possession of an idea situates the person as demanding a recognizable place in the public.

The opportunity to own material things or intangible ideas is part of the collection of natural rights that John Locke ascribed to the men of his time. Many generations away from the establishment of the contract for contracts that is the Constitution, it can be difficult to grasp how a right to own property is not a right granted by an administrative state. However, the original value of property did not *prime facie* imply a state to administer it. Instead, as he developed the idea of the labor theory of property, John Locke "snuck" a system of property administration into the backdoor. The continued development of the idea over the intervening generations augmented the role of the state in the creation and management of property leaving the contemporary state's relationship to property as one that is deeply intertwined. In contemporary constitutional society, property is an administrative function. Determination of what is property, how one obtains and disposes of property, and when the shrinking common can be divided into property is a complex set of administrative functions. Likewise, with intellectual property—it is an administratively granted right to exclusivity on ideas. Without the state, intellectual property, above other types, would not persist. Finally, without the support of the state as itself a generator of intellectual property or as the sponsor of such generation, key pieces of intellectual property would be lost, thus diminishing the content of public interested discourse and dampening the spirit of a constitutional ethics for the state.

References

Buchanan, J. M. (1988). Contractarian political economy and constitutional interpretation. *The American Economic Review, 78*(2), 135–139.

Cornell, S. (2012). *The other founders: Anti-federalism and the dissenting tradition in America, 1788–1828.* Chapel Hill, NC: UNC Press Books.

Dowdle, B. (1984). Perspectives on the Sagebrush Rebellion. *Policy Studies Journal, 12*(3), 473–482.

Fisher, W. (1997). The growth of intellectual property: A history of the ownership of ideas in the United States. Retrieved from https://cyber.harvard.edu/people/tfisher/iphistory.pdf

Goodsell, C. T. (1985). *The case for bureaucracy: A public administration polemic.* Chatham, NJ: Chatham House Publishers.

Gordon, H. S. (1954). The economic theory of a common-property resource: The fishery. In *Classic papers in natural resource economics* (pp. 178–203). London: Palgrave Macmillan. https://econ.ucsb.edu/~tedb/Courses/Ec100C/Readings/ScottGordonFisheries.pdf

Marshall, G. S., & Choudhury, E. (1997). Public administration and the public interest: Re-presenting a lost concept. *American Behavioral Scientist, 41*(1), 119–131.

Overeem, P. (2015). The concept of regime values: Are revitalization and regime change possible? *The American Review of Public Administration, 45*(1), 46–60. https://doi.org/10.1177/0275074013510771

Peng, M. W., Ahlstrom, D., Carraher, S. M., & Shi, W. S. (2017). History and the debate over intellectual property. *Management and Organization Review, 13*(1), 15–38.

Popper, K. (2012). *The open society and its enemies.* London: Routledge.

Rohr, J. A. (1989). *Ethics for bureaucrats: An essay on law and values* (2nd rev. and expanded ed.). New York, NY: Marcel Dekker.

Rose-Ackerman, S. (1985). Inalienability and the theory of property rights. *Columbia Law Review, 85*(5), 931–969.

Storing, H. J. (2008). *What the anti-Federalists were for: The political thought of the opponents of the Constitution* (Vol. 1). Chicago, IL: University of Chicago Press.

Wamsley, G. L. (1990). *Refounding public administration*. Newbury Park, CA: Sage Publications.

Wamsey, G. L., & Wolf, J. F. (Eds.). (1996). *Refounding democratic public administration*. Thousand Oaks, CA: Sage Publications.

7

PRIVACY AS A SUPRA-REGIME VALUE

The Ethical Argument for a New Evolution of Regime Values to Better Protect Financial Privacy in Local Governments

Mike Potter

Introduction

On March 27, 2018, a ransomware attack targeted the City of Baltimore's computer-aided dispatch system. The system is a significant part of the city's emergency response infrastructure. For 17 hours, the attack delayed emergency medical services throughout the city. The hackers wanted $51,000 in bitcoin to release the system (*Baltimore Sun*, March 27, 2018). The vulnerability of both private and public organizations to external hacking is well publicized and can have widespread policy impacts (Klein, 2015; Libicki, 2018; Pfeifer, 2018).

This chapter aims to better understand how local governments prioritize regime values, often in a resource scarce environment. Scarcity and administrative bandwidth limitations can lead managers to oversimplifying priorities; focusing on explicit guidance. Managers may also ignore more complex issues such as privacy and implied constitutional rights, even when there can be significant economic costs.

While not exclusive to the public sector, governments bear an ethical as well as legal responsibility in protecting data from abuse. Cyber security can be costly, both in training and resources (Henry & Brantly, 2018). These costs can challenge local governments' ability to meet the everyday needs of their constituents. The Ponemon Research Institute (2018a) and Raytheon undertook a widespread survey of information technology professionals at both public and private organizations. Their results show significant and growing concern about the ability of all organizations to effectively prevent unintentional release of private information. Among the organizations they surveyed, only 36 percent of respondents believed their leadership made cyber security an organizational priority (p. 2). The rate for public organizations is most likely even lower.

The costs to customers and citizens can overwhelm local governments. In a separate study, the Ponemon Research Institute (2018b) found that the average total cost of data breaches, globally, was $3.86 million. The average cost, per record of a data breach to the customer/citizen, was $148. On average, it took organizations 196 days to detect a breach. While some localities have cyber attack insurance, many are forced to pay for remediation out of reserves.

Some of the most frequently hacked organizations are state and local governments. These are the primary service providers for citizens, and employ most of the government employees in the United States (Donovan, Smith, Osborn, & Mooney, 2015; Smith, 2019). Some of our most deeply held values are considerable economic cost can be linked to privacy policy (Grant & Bennett, 1999).

According to census data, in 2007, there were 39,044 local governments in the United States. Among these, 90 percent were under 25,000 in population. Small towns have fewer cash reserves or sources of revenue, so a data breach can easily represent a large chunk of expenditures in a year. Remediating a breach can come at the expense of social programs and capital safety expenditures (Bland, 2013). In fact, a data breach in local government exists as a prototypical low-probability, highly impactful event (Taleb & Ochman, 2019).

Rohr (1989) posited that regime values should be statements that reflect cultural norms and core beliefs and should be useful as administrative guidance. This chapter is designed to start a discussion of expanding on John Rohr's work that enables administrators to make decisions guided by his construct of regime values. This chapter is organized to: (1) consider whether or not "privacy" passes Rohr's muster as a "regime value," then (2) it analyzes alternative systems for thinking about the intersection of rights and local government privacy, and finally, (3) it expands upon Rohr's typology and offers an idea of "supra-regime values" as a more workable administrative standard.

Is Privacy as a Regime Value?

A cursory examination of Rohr's seminal work *Ethics for Bureaucrats* reveals that it is relatively silent on the issue of privacy as a regime value. However, tracking two of Rohr's most important contributions to administrative ethics serves to clarify this issue. The first is the idea of "social equity" as the key to unlocking the "high road" of ethics (1989, pp. 64–65). The second is the concept of a "fundamentally just" regime (p. 70).

Rohr's discussion of social equity is a pivot away from the more rights-based legal orientation that colored discussions throughout the 1980s and 1990s (Glendon, 1991). In setting up an administrative and ethical process that mandates striving toward a normative and possibly unattainable end, the "high road" of ethics forces constant re-visitation and improvement. The "low road" of ethics exists as a floor of minimal and legal compliance, while social equity exists as a relative ideal that is not only difficult to attain, but likely impossible.

Social equity as a regime value is a little more complicated. While there is substantial case law that includes spreading the franchise and removing hurdles to civic participation, one need search no further than the significant disparities of financial income to see that our regimes have at best weak commitment to this value. As the trends in our economy lead to higher income disparity, this places more significant stress on enabling individuals to achieve a fair social result (Piketty, 2014).

These concerns beg the question; what does social equity as a value, it's complicated as it is, have to do with financial privacy and local governments? Local governments are the entities that provide the lion's share of services for citizens in the United States (Donovan et al., 2015). These entities also frequently have the fewest resources in our federal system of government. Lacking funds and tasked with frequent consumer interactions with citizens, it is perhaps not surprising that many local governments exist at the frontline of financial privacy as a core concern of their functioning.

The ability to balance privacy and other values is one of the oldest challenges in governance. Parent (1983), defined privacy as being "…the condition of not having personal knowledge of one possessed by others" (p. 269). Raab (2017) documented the considerable variations between American and British balances between privacy and security and argues that "… as individuals, we seek privacy, but as citizens, we seek protection from harm; it is the 'privacy we desire' versus 'the security we need'" (p. 85).

The act of balancing privacy with other values in a regime most often takes the form of "privacy versus security." Kleinig et al. (2011) argued for the importance of liberal, democratic values as a guide to balancing security and privacy. They also contend that as an extension to social contract theory, security represents the value that also the construction of other civic institutions. They also wrote about the balance of security and privacy. Privacy that is most applicable to local government's treatment of financial records is that of "private domain" (p. 186). Private domain relates to the idea that although someone has given their financial information to a public entity, they still consider it their private information, so it must be safeguarded.

Rohr's standard for what constitutes a regime value is clear. He argues that it has to underpin the operation of governments aside from partisan concerns. It also has to have a practical use for administrators. It is interesting to contrast security, an acknowledged regime value, and privacy. In the Articles of Confederation (1781), Article III mentions "security" explicitly in the context of maintaining liberties while both the Articles of Confederation and United States (U.S.) Constitution mention "providing for the common defense," which is a security concern.

Both the Articles of Confederation and the U.S. Constitution are silent regarding explicitly stating privacy. However, the Third Amendment banning the quartering of troops and the Fourth Amendment forbidding illegal search and seizure echo privacy concerns. So, does "Privacy" meet his standard as being "… sufficiently specific to have a practical effect on bureaucratic decision-making…(1989, p. 76)?" Yes, the deeper criticism may be that understanding financial privacy as a regime value narrows the scope too much and is too specific. It would be similar to contending that "fair voting in Mississippi" as a regime value. This is the result of much deeper values regarding equal and fair representation under the law.

So, one is left with the consideration of a particular value and its linkages to another attainable end in government. Like in Goodsell's (1990) discussion of the utility of the term "public interest," there is usefulness in linking daily decisions to an attainable overarching ideal. The daily minutia of administration is fertile ground for divorcing bureaucratic action from the high ideals that underpin it. However, in minimizing the linkages between financial privacy and social equity, one risks reducing the substantial effect on citizens lives that local government can have by failing to safeguard information.

Uplifting this administrative process to the level of regime value allows it to be better prioritized, and by proxy, allocated more resources. We now know that to empower citizens, it takes a legal and financial structure. Citizens racked with debt have little time or consideration for improving their communities in the same way that citizens who face hurdles to voting or are unable to have their voice heard do. This leads us to the next concept that was developed where financial privacy touches on a salient and core idea in Rohr's ethics scheme (Rohr, 1971).

The idea of a "fundamentally just" regime is a caveat rather than a centerpiece of Rohr's ethical argument. By his admission, the concept grew from a somewhat belabored attempt to explain the differences in the ethical context of a civil servant during Nazi Germany and one in the segregation era American South being tasked with carrying out orders. In the shortest form, he argued that the Nazi regime was not fundamentally just, or ever able to become so, so the civil servant was justified in disobeying. Nazi Germany contrasted with the American South which, in his view, was a regime going through an unjust period, but in its essence had the fundamentals of justice. Some scholars would wholeheartedly disagree with this contention (see Grill & Jenkins, 1992). Nevertheless, the concept has some utility overlaid on street-level ethics.

Rohr is arguing for an understanding of the ideas that underpin regimes. Rather than cherry-picking behaviors and results that may not be representative, by understanding the subtotal of the actions of an organization, we can come to a better assessment of it. Once again, we are crossing the bridge that Rohr likely would've never anticipated. Simply by adding the term "financial" to the idea, a fundamental justice brings new relief to this concept (Uhr, 2014).

Owing to the contention that one of the greatest lapses the government can have is to calls at citizens financial ruin, if the ability to do so this systematic an unchangeable, one could argue that government does not meet the standard of being financially fundamentally just. However, if a breach of financial records or lack of internal controls causes a one-time security breach, but that government commits resources to mitigate the effects of and preventing other incidences, the lack of economic justice would not be fundamental.

The Evolving Concept of Privacy

Privacy has been upheld traditionally as property, and therefore, a due process responsibility. We will discuss the evolution of the idea of privacy in the American legal system as a newly evolving right tied to a regime value. Warren and Brandeis wrote the first substantive statement on privacy in American legal scholarship in 1891. Upset by the invasion of someone who dared to take someone else's picture at a cocktail party in Boston, the authors opined upon the evolution. Of a new, only scantly anticipated right in their "modern society" (Mensel, 1991). Warren and Brandies perceived the right to privacy, mainly as the right to "be let alone" (p. 195). They argued that part of a right to privacy is protection against defamation. They also argue that the right to privacy is an extension of the property rights doctrine. They state that privacy does not supersede public interest in releasing materials. They also argue that public proceedings should be treated akin to a privileged communication (such as attorney-client). This is certainly a higher standard for the privacy of public records than is generally now enforced. Finally, they write that the "absence of malice" (p. 218) in the intent of the party that violates privacy is not a defense. Their remedy for such violations is that the aggrieved should be able to sue for all damages incurred. As Mindle (1989), points out, throughout his career, Brandeis's "right to privacy" was not a personal and private right, rather, it was a social right in public spaces.

Surprisingly, there was some change in the intellectual considerations regarding privacy from Warren and Brandeis in 1890 until William Prosser's article in 1960. He criticizes the construct of the right to privacy in the initial article as being too far-reaching. Indeed, he questions whether or not a right existed, even as it was enforced in several states. To Prosser (1960), the critical idea in the understanding of privacy is the concept of intrusion.

Ambrose and Ausloos (2013) articulated the emerging European standard regarding financial privacy; this is the "right to be forgotten." Historically, this has been applied to criminals who paid their debt to society, more progressive consumer advocates now argue it should also apply to one's digital footprint. The crux of their argument is that frequently, privacy rights are reactive and should be more proactive in anticipating potential violations. The authors argue there is a strong history in the United States of individuals being able to protect a reputation and private aspects where there is no compelling public interest. This new perspective, in many ways, mirrors Warren and Brandeis's "right to be left alone."

There is a challenge of comparison when analyzing how the concept of privacy has changed in the United States over time. Kasper (2005) looked at invasions of privacy to understand better how the right to privacy has evolved (or devolved). The significant challenges that the case law mainly focuses on are government intrusions through affirmative action. While protecting consumer information is not an intervention (or "search"), it is still the action of maintaining privacy to record keeping. While *Griswold v. Connecticut*, 381 U.S. 479 (1965) posited that a constitutionally implied right to privacy existed in several amendments to the Constitution, the courts have been reticent to make a requirement for the protection of records that government agencies already hold.

Privacy and Freedom

In his seminal work, MacCallum (2006) argued that there are functionally two types of freedoms; positive and negative. Positive freedom is the ability to do something (vote, own a gun, assembly), while negative freedoms guarantee the government will not interfere with certain activities (religion). The typology is not quite as neat as I have presented it as being. There are overlapping types of freedoms, and it is not always clear whether, in complicated issues, the government is trying to protect freedom by intervening or staying out. For illustrative purposes, let's consider abortion.

Is abortion a positive or negative freedom? Pro-choice advocates would likely argue it is a positive freedom. A woman's ability to have an abortion should be reasonable. This example represents freedom from government intervention. However, what if a state government adds layers of regulations to clinics specifically to inhibit their ability to provide legal abortions? Now pro-choice activists would likely argue it should be his positive freedom, and the federal government should intervene to protect the process.

Privacy exists as both a positive and negative freedom similarly. The positive freedom that underpins privacy relates to affirmatively protecting citizens private lives. When government intervenes to do this, it often protects citizen interests without them being aware. This positive freedom in an assertion of government protection against a neighbor, or even government, releasing information that you do not want in the public domain (Warren & Brandeis, 1891). Protection from release is even more important if the information is damaging or serves to violate the Fifth Amendment's prohibition on self-incrimination.

Privacy as a negative freedom construct is, perhaps, more useful for this analysis. The construct of it being a negative freedom is based on the idea of private information as a property right, and therefore cannot be released by the government without some form of due process, as guaranteed by the Fourteenth Amendment. So, can we treat financial privacy as property, without unduly hampering the consumer nature of local governments?

Perhaps. In *Ethics for Bureaucrats*, Rohr draws a sharp distinction between "old property" (1989, p. 225) as real estate and chattel in its traditional sense, and "new property" (p. 252) as a right to due process when government services are terminated post-*Goldberg v. Kelly*, 397 U.S. 254 (1970). The challenge in applying this doctrine (or its subsequent precedents like *Mathews v. Eldridge*, 424 U.S. 319 [1976]) lies in the positive/negative freedom challenge. Goldberg's doctrine argued that certain government benefits were a new property right and could not be stopped without a pre-termination hearing. So, it is the recipient's process, subject to due process. This is a construct of a new property as a positive freedom guaranteed by the government.

If one accepts the logic that privacy is a property right and that government is tasked with safeguarding it, one could argue, perhaps correctly, that for citizens to be separated from their property, government must meet the standard of due process. Well, admittedly, the legal rules for "due process" are low, indeed, unknowingly releasing information would not fit the bill.

Privacy cannot be guaranteed by the government, even under the best circumstances. This is especially true for financial privacy. There are too many bad actors and emerging technologies. Government, as a good faith protector of property rights, is unable to predict when property will be released, to do so, a timely pre-termination hearing as required by Goldberg and Mathews. So what are we left with to protect?

By treating privacy as a negative freedom, there might be a more useful paradigm. Under this guise, local government should work to protect citizens, within reason, from interference in their private matters. This harkens back to Warren and Brandeis (1891) and elevates privacy in priority, but without the onerous and unworkable aspects of treating personal information as property with Fourteenth Amendment required due process. Once again, one might ask, "why uplift a consumer failure to the level of a constitutional infraction?" The answer is still at the consequences of governmental failure can be so extreme that is order for the safeguarding of financial privacy to prioritize the change of perspective might be necessary.

Developing Practical Guidance for Local Government Using Rohr's Values

While there may not be precise, existing regime values that guide administrative behavior regarding local governments' financial privacy, there are some ethical guidelines that apply. Tenet 2 of the International City Managers Association's Code of Ethics states: "Affirm the dignity and worth of services rendered by government and maintain a constructive, creative, and practical attitude toward local government affairs and deep sense social responsibility as a trusted public servant" (ICMA https://icma.org/icma-code-ethics).

Defending citizens from significant and debilitating financial loss, if practicable, clearly falls under these auspices. So indeed, there is a code of ethics argument regarding how financial information held by the public sector would best be protected, balancing the needs of agencies with the public interest of citizens.

Is There Another Option?

The de-emphasizing of privacy of citizens is something that is particularly American. Martínez and Mecinas (2018) explain the concept of the "right to be forgotten" in the European Union. This right was upheld by the Court of Justice of the European Union, based on the idea that if someone does not want to be found on the Internet, they have that right. If this right were to be applied in the United States, it would have far-reaching effects as an "opt-out" to many public records and financial information management for localities. Perhaps there is something deeper that is occurring regarding public accountability that explains the lack of policymaking priority in privacy protections. Whitaker (2015) writes that many of our modern accountability systems have failed, and the alternative is whistleblowing to make policies accountable. Maybe, if we cannot control our politics, if we shed a light on citizen issues, the sunlight will cleanse (paraphrasing Brandeis)?

Arguing for the elevation of the protection of common consumer information by thousands of local governments is not something one does halfheartedly. The compliance costs for under-resourced localities could be in the billions of dollars. With this comes the opportunity cost of all the essential programs for safety or social welfare that would risk not being resourced at the expense of these protections. However, the cost to individual consumers whose information is compromised is also considerable. So, the negative right based on the criteria of importance to individual citizens might be worth discussion. There may also be an alternative that applies Rohr's "regime values" standard for administrative decision-making in a broader and more generalizable way that still loses little of the practicality of guidance for administrators. This is the concept of "supra-regime values."

Arguing for Supra-Regime Values

Rohr's system of ethical guidance for administration is laid out reasonably completely in *Civil Servants and their Constitutions* (1986) and the second edition of *Ethics for Bureaucrats* in 1989. However, a few years later, he undertook the comparative analysis of constitutional governance between France and the United States called *Founding Republics in France and America: A study in constitutional governance* (1995). This work focused on comparing how administrators operated in similar yet different constitutional regimes.

He contended that these regimes, through tradition, culture, and values inform administrative decision-making in very practical ways. However, he ignored the concept of "supra-national" values as another potential input in decision-making. It shouldn't be a surprise the best functional statement of legally binding rights to which the United States assents is perhaps the International Covenant on Civil and Political Rights (ICCPR, 1966).

The covenant lays out far-reaching protections for citizens of liberal-democratic regimes. The United States failed to ratify the document until June 8, 1992. What American policymakers often ignore is that it does carry the force of law. Article 17 of the International Covenant on Civil and Political Rights directly addresses privacy protections in a way the United States Constitution does not; it states. "(1) No one shall be subjected to arbitrary or unlawful interference with his privacy, family, home or correspondence, nor to unlawful attacks on his honour (sic) and reputation. (2) Everyone has the right to the protection of the law against such interference or attacks." What are you this is a far stronger "supra-regime value" that covers a broader range of local government activity relating to consumer privacy? Developing whether or not this body of laws as an administrative utility is for another time, but it is important to remember that privacy is widely acknowledged as being a fundamental right in regimes other than the United States. Therefore, in the same manner that local governments protect our right to assemble and freedom of speech, privacy should have the highest priority in government behavior.

Conclusion

The late John A. Rohr would likely criticize the advocation of supra-regime values unsound reasoning. He would probably say something to the effect of "if you don't like your regime values do you search for ones that didn't fit your morality?" Moreover, he would be correct to a certain extent. However, it is important to remember that regime values are not static.

The critical aspect of the relevance of the construct of regime values is that there is some inherent flexibility that allows, when necessary, for there to be the creation of new protections. By arguing for supra-regime values, encapsulated in the International Covenant on Civil and Political Rights, it merely simplifies the task of updating values.

One may then say, "but the International regime of laws violates social contract theory of government because I did not assent to be subject to it." However, the reality is, if you are a native-born American, you had no choice in assenting to the United States Constitution. There is a delicate balance that the government must undertake to ensure social equity. Too little intervention and too much freedom can create inequity, too great an intervention, and freedom is truncated. By creating a new and more modern class of supra-regime values, we make this balancing act slightly easier. By working across cultures, it enables values to reflect modern social thought and mitigates cultural or regime biases such as systemic racism or classism. Governing is never perfect and always can be improved, but a good start might be discussing how administrative values, even at the local level, should be shifted.

References

Ambrose, M. L., & Ausloos, J. (2013). The right to be forgotten across the pond. *Journal of Information Policy, 3*, 1–23. https://doi.org/10.5325/jinfopoli.3.2013.0001

Bland, R. L. (2013). *A budgeting guide for local government.* Washington, DC: ICMA Press.

Donovan, T., Smith, D. A., Osborn, T. L., & Mooney, C. Z. (2015). *State and local politics: Institutions and reform.* Stamford, CT: Cengage Learning.

Glendon, M. A. (1991). *Rights talk: The impoverishment of political discourse.* New York, NY: The Free Press of Simon & Schuster.

Goldberg v. Kelly, 397 U.S. 254 (1970).

Goodsell, C. T. (1990). Public administration and the public interest. In G. L. Wamsley, R. N. Bacher, C. T. Goodsell, P. S. Kronenberg, J. A. Rohr, C. M. Stivers, … J. F. Wolf (Eds.), *Refounding public administration* (pp. 96–113). Thousand Oaks, CA: Sage Publications.

Grant, R. A., & Bennett, C. J. (1999). *Visions of privacy: Policy choices for the digital age.* Toronto: University of Toronto Press.

Grill, J., & Jenkins, R. (1992). "The Nazis and the American South in the 1930's: A mirror image?" *The Journal of Southern History, 58*, 668–694.

Griswold V. Connecticut (1965). 381 U.S. 479.

Henry, S., & Brantly, A. (2018). Countering the cyber threat. *The Cyber Defense Review, 3*(1), 47–56. Retrieved from http://www.jstor.org/stable/26427375

International City Manager's Association Code of Ethics (ICMA). Retrieved from https://icma.org/icma-code-ethics

International Covenant on Civil and Political Rights. (1966).

Kasper, D. V. S. (2005). The evolution (or devolution) of privacy. *Sociological Forum, 20*(1), 69–92. Retrieved from http://www.jstor.org/stable/4540882

Klein, J. (2015). Deterring and dissuading cyberterrorism. *Journal of Strategic Security, 8*(4), 23–38. Retrieved from https://www.jstor.org/stable/26465213

Kleinig, J., Mameli, P., Miller, S., Salane, D., Schwartz, A., & Selgelid, M. (2011). The Underlying values and their alignment. In *Security and privacy: Global standards for ethical identity management in contemporary liberal democratic states* (pp. 151–224). ANU Press. Retrieved from http://www.jstor.org/stable/j.ctt24h8h5.13

Libicki, M. (2018). Expectations of cyber deterrence. *Strategic Studies Quarterly, 12*(4), 44–57. Retrieved from https://www.jstor.org/stable/26533614

MacCallum, G. C. (2006). Positive and negative freedom. In D. Miller (Ed.), *The liberty reader.* Boulder, CO: Paradigm.

Martínez, J., & Mecinas, J. (2018). Old wine in a new bottle?: Right of publicity and right to be forgotten in the internet era. *Journal of Information Policy, 8*, 362–380. https://doi.org/10.5325/jinfopoli.8.2018.0362

Mathews v. Eldridge, 424 U.S. 319 (1976).

Mensel, R. (1991). "Kodakers lying in wait": Amateur photography and the right of privacy in New York, 1885–1915. *American Quarterly, 43*(1), 24–45. https://doi.org/10.2307/2712965

Mindle, G. (1989). Liberalism, privacy, and autonomy. *The Journal of Politics, 51*(3), 575–598. Retrieved from http://www.jstor.org/stable/2131496

Parent, W. (1983). Privacy, morality, and the law. *Philosophy & Public Affairs, 12*(4), 269–288. Retrieved from http://www.jstor.org/stable/2265374

Pfeifer, J. (2018). Preparing for cyber incidents with physical effects. *The Cyber Defense Review, 3*(1), 27–34. Retrieved from http://www.jstor.org/stable/26427372

Piketty, T. (2014). *Capital in the twenty-first century.* Cambridge, MA: The Belknap Press of Harvard University Press.

Ponemon Research Institute. (2018a). 2018 Study on global megatrends in cybersecurity. Retrieved April 8, 2019, from https://www.raytheon.com/sites/default/files/2018-02/2018_Global_Cyber_Megatrends.pdf

Ponemon Research Institute. (2018b). 2018 Cost of data breach report. Retrieved April 9, 2019, from https://www.ibm.com/downloads/cas/AEJYBPWA.

Prosser, W. L. (1960). Privacy. *California Law Review, 48*(3), 383–423.

Raab, C. (2017). Security, privacy and oversight. In A. Neal (Ed.), *Security in a small nation: Scotland, democracy, politics* (pp. 77–102). Cambridge: Open Book. Retrieved from http://www.jstor.org/stable/j.ctt1sq5v42.8

Rector, K. (2019, March 27). Baltimore 911 dispatch system hacked, investigation underway, officials confirm. *The Baltimore Sun.* Retrieved from https://www.baltimoresun.com/news/maryland/crime/bs-md-ci-911-hacked-20180327-story.html

Rohr, J. A. (1971). *Prophets without honor: Public policy and the selective conscientious objector.* Nashville, TN: Abingdon Press.

Rohr, J. A. (1986). *To run a constitution: The legitimacy of the administrative state.* Lawrence, KS: University Press of Kansas.

Rohr, J. A. (1989). *Ethics for bureaucrats: An essay on law and values* (2nd ed.). Hong Kong: Marcel Dekker.

Rohr, J. A. (1995). *Founding republics in France and America: A study in Constitutional Governance.* Lawrence, KS: University Press of Kansas.

Smith, K. B. (2019). *State and local government.* Washington, DC: CQ Press.

Taleb, N. N., & Ochman, J. (2019). *The black swan: The impact of the highly improbable* (2nd ed.). New York, NY: Penguin, Random House.

The Articles of Confederation. (1781).

Uhr, J. (2014). John Rohr's concept of regime values: Locating theory in public administration. *Administration and Society, 46*(2), 141–152.

Warren, S., & Brandeis, L. (1891). The right to privacy. *Harvard Law Review, 4*(5), 193–220. https://doi.org/10.2307/1321160

Whitaker, R. (2015). The failure of official accountability and the rise of guerrilla accountability. In M. Geist (Ed.), *Law, privacy and surveillance in Canada in the post-snowden era* (pp. 205–224). University of Ottawa Press. Retrieved from http://www.jstor.org/stable/j.ctt15nmj3c.11

8

PROPERTY AND EMERGING INSTITUTIONAL TYPES

The Challenge of Private Foundations in Public Higher Education

Kathryn E. Webb Farley

Introduction

Fundraising for public universities has been of increasing importance since the 1980s, when some flagships like the Universities of Michigan and Virginia declared themselves to be "state-assisted" schools.[1] Relying on philanthropy rather than state dollars, however, raises questions about accountability and power within the university. Recent headlines ask readers to ponder if donors are gaining too much influence in our universities, as disputes erupt between institutions and philanthropists with different ideas about how very large gifts should be used.

Much of this discussion has left out key underlying elements that contribute to the disputes about control and use of resources. Public universities are operating as a different type of organization than the public bureaucracies we are accustomed to interacting with and "controlling" through appointed officials. Instead, these organizations are now operating as hybrid entities: state organs carrying out their duties to educate and perform some services for the benefit of citizens; nonprofits raising funds to support the public good based on private individual donor interests; and private businesses providing goods and services to paying customers, such as residents of dorms, patrons of dining halls, and customers in coffee shops and bookstores. Operating in this way makes good sense from a "business" perspective. The public university has the opportunity (even if the capacity is lacking) to attract more resources from the environment in a way that many bureaucracies are not afforded (it is hard to imagine a state budget office getting any resources beyond what the legislature deems appropriate, for example).

While more resources seem desirable, the stipulations attached to these resources can cause strife. For example, at the University of Virginia, two gifts of $100 million or more created new schools (akin to colleges at many universities). In doing so, these gifts raised the eyebrows (if not ire) of existing faculty about who sets priorities at the institution, according to reports. These concerns are about accountability: who is the institution beholden to? The state through appointed actors? Donors who can give resources? Faculty who presumably play an important role in institutional governance? Foundation boards who have fiduciary responsibility for the nonprofit?

The normative questions stem from blending organizational types, which results in the challenge of giving multiple types of actors control over the university's resources. These questions of accountability are related to one of Rohr's stated regime values: property. Interestingly, Rohr points out that distinguishing the private from public and thus upholding the value of property has its roots in a court case about a state trying to overtake a private institution of higher education. In particular, donors had given funding to support a private school and government overtake of that institution would not be in keeping with the mission for which philanthropic gifts were made.

Today, we see that what some call the privatization of public higher education raises questions about public institutions and property. If the resources are provided to support the state institution, should those appointed or hired to manage the institution be empowered to oversee all of its resources? Did the donors give the money for the private foundation holding the accounts, and the contracts, or was it entrusted to the foundation for the good of the public university, as decided by those tasked with oversight and administration of the institution?

This normative argument is not academic. Administrators in hybrid organizations rely on different "colors of money" (McCaffrey & Mutty, 1999) or funds that are administered in different ways. The result is tension between being public actors doing their duty to uphold the public good, however that may be defined, while also relying on private resources overseen by nonpublic entities. In one stark example, the University System of Georgia's Board of Regents, along with the university president's employed by them, had public disputes with not one, but two of its' universities' foundations. Court documents, public data, and internal documents made available through a freedom of information request allow us to explore how changes in institutional structures raise issues about regime values, particularly property, in a way that Rohr may not have anticipated. In doing so, questions for administrators operating within these emerging types of hybrid organizations become clearer.

Regime Values and Changing Institutions

As one of the three regime values Rohr (1989) sets forth, property's meaning has evolved over time. To explain "old property," or those things that can actually be possessed, Rohr uses the United States Supreme Court's ruling in *Trustees of Dartmouth v. Woodward*. In this decision, the contracts clause was used to distinguish public from private and thus uphold the value of property.

Specifically, the Court held that the state of New Hampshire had no right to take over administration of Dartmouth, which was established via private charter under colonial rule. In part, the ruling hinged on the compact with donors, who entrusted funds to trustees "to address the interests and purposes of the college" (McGarvie, 1999, p. 554). In effect, the Dartmouth case establishes the legal necessity for organizations seeking philanthropic donations to establish themselves as private entities (McGarvie, 1999).

"New property" relates to entitlements, according to Rohr (1989). Here, he points out, based on the Roth case, that "the origin of new property must be traced to some kind of state law" (Rohr, 1989, p. 270). This precedent has been used to trigger due process questions related to property including employment, benefits, and schooling. He goes on to note that while the courts have not continued to uphold the idea of "new property," administrators can use discretion to uphold the principles of "new property."

Rohr's (1989) discussion of both old and new property does not consider the conflicts that may result from mixing different types of organizational structures under one umbrella. In other words, Rohr's treatise hinges on cases that consider "old" and "new" property within either public or private institutions, but not those that combine both public and private elements, or hybrid organizations. Rohr's analysis of property as a regime value, both old and new property, focuses the discussion on control and responsibility. As such, Rohr's work relates to questions of different dimensions of accountability (Koppell, 2005). These questions are central to organizations that blend types of organizational structures, raising normative questions about control of resources.

Skelcher and Smith (2015) theorize that hybrid organizations follow particular institutional logics, suggesting both practical and theoretical implications of the blending of organizational types. Hybrids are those "in which plural logics and thus actor identities are in play" and thus members "confront multiple identities" (p. 434). The result is organizations that function in different ways, depending on the adherence to normative prescriptions for particular types of organizations, the ways in which actors understand their own roles, and the values to which they adhere, and the stability of the environment. Skelcher and Smith identify five different types of hybrids, which vary along these characteristics, but can be summarized as being somewhat integrated and operational to some extent or being "blocked" and unable to function.

Scott's (2008) widely discussed view of institutions suggests that the regulative framework and resources also matter. While Skelcher and Smith's (2015) theory of hybridity does not explicitly exclude rules and resources, it also does not include them as separate variables which may affect the hybrids form and function. These questions ought to be significant in the minds of public administrators, who in the face of dwindling public resources, might be tempted to turn to hybrid organizational forms. Such forms may be attractive because they could open the door for resource streams, particularly philanthropic donations, that might otherwise be unavailable. It may also, however, give external, nonpublic actors control over resources in a way that raises questions about contracts and due process, two key elements of property.

An Example: The University System of Georgia Board of Regents

Although it is rare for state universities to have high profile, public disputes with their foundations, the Board of Regents that oversees public universities in Georgia has "divorced" two of their universities' foundations. Examining the University System of Georgia raises questions about the ethical and legal implications of state universities functioning as hybrids. Hybrids combine elements of different sectors: public, nonprofit, and for-profit.[2] Combining these organizational forms allows universities to raise and manage philanthropic resources through the foundation. Foundations are separate 501(c)3 organizations with legal roots in the philanthropic law that McGarvie (1999) argues started with the *Dartmouth* case.

Georgia's university system provides an example of the questions about property, both old and new, that might be raised within this operating environment. This chapter proceeds with outlining Georgia's system of higher education followed by a basic explanation of the disputes that arose between two of its' universities, the respective institutional foundations, and the Board of Regents. Facets of the property questions that are raised by this example are provided. A discussion of the implications for administrators follows.

The Operating Environment

Along with the Georgia Public Library Service and Georgia Archives, the University System of Georgia encompasses 26 institutions of higher education. Created in 1931, the System's Board of Regents (BORs) is appointed by the governor and in turn appoints a chancellor. In other words, the Regents, along with the chancellor and chancellor's staff, are responsible for overseeing the 26 public universities and colleges within the state, including appointment and oversight of university presidents (University System of Georgia, n.d.).

Included within those 26 universities are the University of Georgia and what was formerly a stand-alone institution known as the Medical College of Georgia.[3] The University of Georgia Foundation and Medical College of Georgia Foundation were both incorporated as separate nonprofit entities that served as fundraising vehicles for the universities for which they bear a name. Specifically, the University System's policy recognizes these foundations as "cooperative organizations" that exist "primarily … for the purpose of soliciting gifts or assisting a System institution in soliciting gifts … [and] for soliciting grants and contracts or accepting grants or entering into contracts for research or service" (Weber, 2004a, p. 41). As a separate entity, the Foundations have their own trustees and bylaws. Trustees have legal responsibility for overseeing the organizations and "fiduciary obligations to the foundation and its donors" (University System of Georgia, 2010, p. 1).

University fundraisers, including the president and development staff, are state employees. These employees do have close relationships with the Foundation, which may be consulted in the hiring of key individuals (University System of Georgia, 2010). The funds they raise are donated and held by their institution's Foundation, but according to the "Guiding Principles" the Regents guide and approve the "strategic direction of each institution ... [and foundations] support the institution at all times in a cooperative, ethical, and collaborative manner" (Weber, 2004b, p. 46). In some cases, the university employees must seek approval from the Foundation Board to use funds. However, the institution's president, not the Foundation, sets the institutional priorities according to the System's Guiding Principles. For example, the University of Georgia Foundation bylaws allowed for the president to set university funding priorities and then ask the Foundation Finance Committee to review the list of priorities and make funding recommendations to the Foundation Board of Trustees for review.

The implications for property that stem from this complex operating environment are important to think about. Donors may give the money to support the public institution, but the contract is made with a private entity, the Foundation that bears the institution's name. The Foundation has an understanding with the public beneficiary, but still controls the resources. In turn, there is an expectation that in carrying out their fiduciary responsibilities as nonprofit board members, the Foundation Board will make decisions about disbursements of funds after the top public officials have determined priorities. Moreover, the private entities have significant interactions with state employees and may even weigh in on employee job performance, which may raise "new property" questions for administrators.

Dispute with the University of Georgia Foundation

Several accounts exist of why the BORs ultimately decided to dissolve its relationship with the University of Georgia Foundation. Most of these competing narratives center around questions about the university president's leadership and ethics or around the employment of a former football coach-turned-athletic director (Whitt, 2009). Some argue that the president spent funds unethically, possibly illegally, and misrepresented himself. Other interested parties argue that the president was being attacked because he severed the university's employment contract with a much beloved, long-time employed, championship winning football coach. For example, Joel Wooten, BORs chair wrote, "The bully in this matter is not the Board of Regents; it is the small group of [Foundation] trustees that refused to support the mission of the University of Georgia. Despite the foundation's public statements that it would be a 'cooperative organization,' a certain group of trustees never stopped their efforts to frustrate the administration of the University of Georgia" (Email, 2006). Both versions of the story have the same ending: the Board of Regents twice directed the university president to end the relationship with the organization that managed hundreds of millions of dollars for the university.

The first time, there was a last minute effort to reconcile differences. The second time, however, the Foundation trustees refused to sign a new Memorandum of Understanding. The BORs directed employees to implement plans to start a new foundation. There was no reconciliation. Instead, in 2005, a new foundation, the Arch Foundation, was established as the formal fundraising entity of the University of Georgia. It shared some resources, including some board members and staff, with the University of Georgia Foundation, which continued to oversee any funds that had been raised prior to the breakup.[4]

Dispute with the Medical College of Georgia Foundation

In 2008, the Regents decided to create a new foundation, leaving behind the relationship with the Medical College of Georgia (OnlineAthens, October 21, 2009). In October 2009, the BORs filed a lawsuit against the Medical College of Georgia Foundation for continuing to use the college's name. The BOR's suit claimed that using the name Medical College of Georgia was a violation of national and state trademark laws. Furthermore, according to the suit, fiduciary responsibilities were neglected, trustees did not comport with the fundraising priorities of the university, and did not give university officials timely financial information (University System of Georgia, October 20, 2009).

The Medical College of Georgia became the Georgia Health Sciences University with a separate foundation. In September 2010, the Georgia Health Science Foundation trustees and the Medical College of Georgia Foundation board agreed to abide by the new Working Principles-Multiple Foundation (Andrew Newton Email, September 24, 2010). Thus, each foundation played an active role in the private donations made to the university.

Issues of Property Raised by Organizational Form

The University System of Georgia example presents several issues that arise from sharing property among several different organizations with their own lines of accountability. Even when the organizations fall under the same umbrella, the cultures of each may result in what Skelcher and Smith (2015) denote as "blocked" organizations where administrators are mired in their own understandings and ways of doing business. As such, they render the organizational arrangement ineffective. These disputes may in part be steeped in, or at least frustrated by, questions of property, containing elements of both old and new property disputes. Specifically, Georgia provides an example that allows for insights into how money, trademarks, employment issues such as compensation and personnel decisions, and data can become lightning rods for disputes that frustrate organizational actors, resulting in blocked action.

Show Me the Money

Both Foundations held funds that were raised to support the universities, not the Foundations' functions. However, the Foundation trustees do have some discretion in determining the use of some of these funds, particularly those that have not been earmarked by the donor for a specific purpose. Funding organizational priorities is a way of setting the policies of the institution (Rubin, 2013), which according to the Guiding Principles, the BORs noted fell under their purview through their appointee, the president.

The University of Georgia Foundation retained the accounting firm Deloitte & Touche to conduct an audit, part of which was aimed at understanding if the university's president had misused Foundation funds. In particular, the Foundation bylaws have certain stipulations for request and use of unrestricted funds, or funds that have not been designated for a particular purpose by the donor. Both the president and the trustees, through the Finance Committee, have a role to play in determining the use of these funds, according to the bylaws. The Deloitte & Touche audit raised concerns about the auditing process of the president's expenditures, reporting that shortly after taking office, the president had independent audits of the Foundation accounts used for presidential duties. The report specifically notes instances in which these accounts were used to fund activities for which the benefit may have been more personal in nature rather than for professional reasons (Whitt, 2009).[5]

In the Medical College of Georgia dispute, the Regents claimed that the Foundation was withholding funds from the university's (and thus the Regents') stated priorities. Furthermore, the Regents were not forthcoming with financial information needed by the university to budget for its priorities. One major issue seemed to be the development of a dental school. According to OnlineAthens (October 21, 2009), "news reports quoted Medical College of Georgia Foundation Chairman ... saying [the Foundation] turned down a request by then-president ... for $5 million for a new dental school building [saying] it would be irresponsible to spend that much when the foundation only had $8 million in unrestricted money."

In the settlement, the Medical College of Georgia Foundation and the Georgia Health Sciences Foundation were both named cooperating organizations. While fundraising would be undertaken by the university's president and fundraising staff, the Medical College of Georgia Foundation would receive dues and gifts from Medical College of Georgia alumni. The agreement also prohibited the duplication of funds (in other words, fundraising accounts), noting that if there is any overlap in funds between the two foundations, the duplicates would be consolidated into the one that originally created the fund (Working Principles-Multiple Foundations, 2010).

Both of these instances raise interesting property questions. Donors give to support the mission of the university, according to the precedent in the *Dartmouth* case. Although some donors may not even realize funding does not go directly to the university, the gift "contract" is not with the university, but instead with the foundation. In cases where disputes arise, which entity should have control of the funding?

What's in a Name?

Both university-foundation disputes raise naming rights, which are trademarked property. These names presumably help raise resources as people associate the Foundation as at least a supporting organization of the university. For some, who are less knowledgeable about operating structures and laws, may even suggest that the Foundation is a part of the university. Use of the trademarked name can also be lucrative through merchandise sales.

The University of Georgia Foundation was given trademark privileges to use the University of Georgia name. A 1983 memo from the Georgia Attorney General notes that so long as any funds generated from the use of the trademarks are used to benefit the institution, then the Regents could contract the name. In 2004, however, after the dispute with the Foundation, the Regents and university asserted their claim of ownership on the name. The dispute even resulted in a public statement being made by the Regents' Vice Chair that "[i]t is incomprehensible that anyone would seek to appropriate the University of Georgia name for their own use or purposes" (University System of Georgia, 2004a). Similarly, in a dispute with the Medical College of Georgia Foundation, the university's suit states that the Regents own the name and by not ceasing to use the name, the Foundation is violating trademark laws.

In both of these disputes, the Foundations are legally registered and recognized under these trademarked names. Who has the right to use the name? Does the Board of Regents own the names? Or, do these Foundations operating for decades under these names, also have a right to use them?

Employment Issues

Rohr noted that both employment and benefits were considered within new property. The Georgia example presents facets of both of these types of property. Specifically, there are questions raised about who has a say in pay (benefits) and the proper role of foundations in weighing in on personnel decisions (employment).

By some accounts, pay was the issue that acted like the proverbial straw, resulting in the Regents voting to terminate the relationship with the University of Georgia Foundation. Specifically, the Foundation Trustees were reportedly meeting (not for the first time) to reduce the president's pay (Basinger, 2004). A significant portion of the president of the University of Georgia's salary and bonus came from the Foundation. Based on a 2004 draft of a letter from the System Chancellor to the University of Georgia Foundation, it appears that the Foundation based payments on discussions with the chancellor, who represents the Board, at least in part. However, the closing line states, "I hope you and the Foundation will agree that this correspondence is in harmony with our discussions, and that concurrence will be reached and we can move forward," suggesting there may be some dissent among the Foundation Trustees (Meredith, personal communication (FOIA), April 19, 2004). A signed letter from the chancellor to the Foundation about changes to the Foundation's bylaws notes the System's concern that the Foundation wanted some control of employee compensation stating, "it is appropriate for University employees to be of assistance to the Foundation, but decisions regarding their compensation must rest solely with President" (Meredith, personal communication (FOIA), April 16, 2004). Furthermore, a letter from a senior executive of the System to the attorney general's office refers to "the UGA Foundation's failure to meet its compensation commitments to the President" (Cummings, personal communication (FOIA), July 1, 2004). Together, these artifacts suggest that at least in part, the Foundation had the ability to determine pay of a public employee by withholding funding.

Adding to the dispute, some compensation was awarded to the president's wife from the Foundation, which some claimed was a conflict of interest and perhaps even a misuse of funds. Both how the pay amount was determined and the reporting lines were unclear (Whitt, 2009). More concerning, however, was the perception by some that pay to the president's wife would increase the president's compensation without violating an agreement that the Foundation would pay no more than 49 percent of the president's pay (Whitt, 2009). Furthermore, bonuses were paid to another senior staff member of the university, presumably not for work done on behalf of the university, but rather for "good work done for the governor" for his transition team. In a letter, the Georgia Attorney General notes that "The bonus to [the president] and the 'honorarium' for [the senior staff member] appear to violate the spirit of the Georgia Constitution." Regarding the president's pay, the attorney general notes that "*Public office is a public trust* ... By receiving compensation from two separate and distinct sources, [the president] was in fact serving two masters." The attorney general goes on to cite a 1976 attorney general opinion that disallows retroactive compensation, which the senior staff member's bonus appeared to be (Baker, Personal Communication (FOIA), December 5, 2006).

The attorney general's reaction was in part to the 2004 actions of the Board of Regents. In that year, the Board of Regents passed a resolution that the Foundation "leave the determination of the President's compensation and the compensation of his spouse to the Board of Regents ... [and] the Foundation will give good faith consideration to paying any salary supplement that is suggested by the Board of Regents ... [and] that such supplement payment will be made to the ... Regents" (University System of Georgia, 2004b). The Board of Regents updated the policy on presidential compensation "to eliminate any doubt as to where the presidents report and to whom the presidents are responsible" (Weber, 2004b, p. 10). Furthermore, the Board of Regents noted in the minutes that "all compensation will now be paid from state funds. Foundations will be asked to give the same or similar amounts that they would otherwise have been paying for their respective president's supplemental compensation ... to the ... institution's general fund in support of the general mission ... That money will not be directly used or allocated to pay for presidential compensation" (Weber, 2004b, p. 10).

However, the updated Guiding Principles seemingly reopen the door for paying for compensation, stating that no employees or immediate family could be paid from the Foundation without the president's approval (or the chancellor if payment was directed toward president or president's family; or Regents if payment was directed toward chancellor's family). Interestingly, according to meeting minutes, the Regents discussed a draft of these Guiding Principles at the same 2004 meeting as the aforementioned compensation policy changes (Weber, 2004b). These changes are not insignificant to the property discussion because these Principles give a private entity domain over compensation involving a public employee. The attorney general's letter notes, "the Board's own guidelines have institutionalized the 'authorization' of additional compensation ... a common law conflict of interest which jeopardizes the undiluted allegiance [the president] owes to the Board of Regents, and through it, the people of Georgia" (Baker, Personal Communication (FOIA), December 5, 2006).

Furthermore, a Deloitte & Touche audit commissioned by the Foundation (which has its own critics who question the findings) notes that the president entered into a verbal severance agreement with the football coach (Whitt, 2009). Specifically, in trying to recruit the coach, the president offered a $250,000 side agreement without anyone else's knowledge. The university's lawyer allegedly then asked the Athletic Association, also operating as a nonprofit, to pay the severance without notifying its board, which the president chaired. After the matter became public, the Georgia Attorney General questioned "the failure to notify the Association's governing body of a major decision concerning a large amount of money" as a fiduciary and ethical failure on the president's part. Furthermore, it may have constituted a violation of Georgia's Open Records Act (Baker, Personal Communication (FOIA), December 5, 2006).

Although more issues came to light, the University of Georgia dispute seems to largely stem from personnel decisions, particularly as they relate to property matters of contracts and benefits. Multiple outlets reported that the president refused to extend the contract of a much-beloved sports figure. Following this, the Regents seem to believe that some Foundation Trustees contributed to pressure to fire the president, angering the Regents as evidenced by language in an email. Moreover, as an attorney general's (personal communication (FOIA), December 5, 2006) letter notes, the football coaches contract negotiations, and specifically the undisclosed severance package agreement, could be construed to have resulted from "influence by a member of the Foundation's executive committee—external influence by a member of an organization substantially supplementing [the president's] salary, but having no direct responsibility for the contract with the [football] Coach."

One other issue should be noted here. The University of Georgia hired a well known fundraiser to head its campaign. This person also became the Foundation's executive director. For reasons that will not be discussed here, the Foundation Executive Committee decided it no longer believed in the employees' capabilities and relayed this to the president. Not long thereafter, the president offered a severance package to the fundraiser (Whitt, 2009).

In the dispute between the Board and the Medical College of Georgia (MCG) Foundation, the issue was about staff reporting lines. One version of the Regents' proposed resolution included that the Foundation would have "leased non critical staff." The Foundation found this unacceptable (Mayher, Personal Communication [FOIA], 2010), and the final agreement notes that "Employees of each foundation may be leased or hired directly as determined by its Board of Directors" (University System of Georgia, 2010, p. 2). Furthermore, according to the settlement, each Foundation had to employ its own executive director that reported to the Foundation board. Lastly, in the final version of the agreement (2010), the Foundation was one of multiple voices who would have input in filling the university's head of fundraising.

These examples suggest that although an employee may be a state employee, private actors are weighing in on personnel and benefit matters, or new property, according to Rohr. The attorney general's letters in the University of Georgia cases note that based on state law, this raises both constitutional and ethical questions. However, if the person is carrying out work on behalf of the Foundation and Foundation resources are being used to support benefits, should Trustees with the legal responsibility for the organization be given some say in these decisions?

Knowledge Is Power

In fundraising, donor information is a necessary and valuable commodity (Tempel, Seiler, & Burlingame, 2016). In 2006, the Regents and the Medical College of Georgia Foundation Board entered into a cooperating agreement that stipulated that "the Foundation shall maintain ownership of the donor information system including donor records" (University System of Georgia, 2006). In the Regents' first court filing for a request for documents (*Board of Regents of the University System of Georgia for and on behalf of the Medical College of Georgia v. Medical College of Georgia Foundation, Inc.*, 2009), 4 of the 11 requests deal with donor and donor prospect contact information, solicitation, and correspondence. An additional request focuses on correspondence about confusion in making donations following the creation of the Georgia Health Science Foundation.

According to an attorney work product (personal communication (FOIA), n.d.), part of the consideration in the Medical College of Georgia Foundation and Board dispute was about data. In particular, the attorney noted that one consideration of the proposal under consideration was that there was "Still no ready and complete access to [Foundation] data. Availability still subject to [Foundation] discretion. ('appropriate information') ... what is 'appropriate information in database?' Who determines." In the final agreement, this question is still not answered noting that "Each foundation shall own and manage their own record systems. To facilitate successful development, each foundation partner shall provide access to any appropriate information in its database to [Medical College of Georgia's] Development Staff."

Organizations use donor data to raise funds. Beyond contact information, organizations will typically store information on giving history, reports about any contact or known interests, any estimation of ability to give, and other valuable date (Tempel et al., 2016). Therefore, it is an asset to the organization that holds the data. These donors are presumably interested in supporting the university, yet according to these data, the Foundation was keeping their information from the university. Who should own the data, a form of property that enables more fundraising? The university, which the donors and prospective donors presumably have a connection to that has made them prospective donors, or the Foundation, which was created to support the university?

Discussion and Concluding Thoughts

Some argue that public university foundations should be subject to sunshine laws (see, for example, Capeloto, 2015). In fact, Georgia's Attorney General argued as much in his letter to the Board of Regents and suggests that more openness might have disinfected, or even prevented, some of the wounds inflicted in the dispute with the Foundation (Baker, Personal Communication (FOIA), December 5, 2006). Research shows that these laws have limited effect, however, in part because there is little in the way of enforcements (Stewart, 2010). Therefore, the case for ethical administration of these hybrid organizations is still necessary in order to maintain public trust. What might an ethical administration look like? What questions may need to be asked?

First, it appears that understanding that these are questions about property seems to be important. Specifically, if donors make a gift to support a university, what role do the foundation trustees have to play in determining the use of these funds? Alternatively, is it the representatives of the public (either appointees or employees, or both) who have ultimate say over the use of property to support institutional priorities? In the *Dartmouth* case, the Court decided that donors had entrusted their funds to private actors, and therefore, the contract was with a private institution not the state. Given that state employees are generally requesting the philanthropic donation, and that the funds are given to support a state institution's needs, should the administrator consider these resources to be a contract with the public and therefore minimize private influence over them? If so, how would foundation trustees fulfill their fiduciary responsibilities required as the overseers of a nonprofit? Moreover, how much control over personnel decisions, trademarks, and data should a private entity have when these resources have been entrusted to the public institutions?

Second, determining lines and types of accountability may be necessary. Koppell (2005) argues that accountability has multiple dimensions. The tension between these different dimensions can render an organization ineffective as it tries to navigate these tensions. The example presented here suggests that setting out policy may help. In both situations, the Regents amended System policy or made new agreements with the Foundations in order to resolve long-festering disputes over questions of accountability including those highlighted in research: control, responsibility, transparency, liability, and responsiveness (Koppell, 2005). How should administrators approach determining who they are accountable to, however, when property is held by a private entity for a public institution? What should be the guiding principle for an administrator who is tasked with answering to one board appointed by elected representatives and also at least maintaining good relationships with a private board who has control over vital organizational resources?

Third, in the event of a dispute, might competing institutional logics and actors with different ideas render the organization blocked, with public administrators, appointees, and private individuals unable to find ways to work together to carry out the purpose of the organization? What models of interconnectedness and partnership are necessary to understand how these separate, but related boards work together? In other words, returning to the idea of institutionalism, outside of the regulative pillar to use Scott's (2008) term, what normative standards might help administrators of these hybrid organizations know how to act so that property given to fulfill a mission is used in that way? How can administrator's ensure that new property, such as employment and benefit decisions, are protected in such a way that is consistent with personnel policy? For example, at the University of Georgia, the dispute erupted, in part, because of the university president's administrative approach, the Regents view of their roles, and the beliefs of the Foundation Trustees as it related to both old property (funding) and new property (employment and benefits). Together, the actors raised questions about how much power and control each ought to have given the nature of their roles and respective places within the institutional structure. To some extent, rules and laws supported each of their positions, even if these ideas conflicted.

Blending organizational types clearly raises challenges for the regime value of property (and likely other regime values), suggesting that both academics and administrators should focus more on the implications of hybridity. Researchers should devote more attention to studying the roles of different actors within these types of institutions, the relationships between them, and the control of resources. Shedding light on the operating realities of these organizations would help us to develop a shared understanding of the ethical principles, values, and actor roles that should guide those working within these organizations. Practitioners should be educated about hybrid organizations, with a particular emphasis on understanding the legal differences between public and private structures that fall under the umbrella, the duties and roles of public and private actors, and the administrator's responsibility for balancing these stakeholders. To maintain trust and avoid public disputes with foundations and donors, administrators of hybrid organizations must be armed with the knowledge necessary to navigate their operating realities.

Notes

1 Some declare that this is devolving to "state-related" and later "state-located" as public funding continues to decrease and reliance on other resources increases (Duderstadt, 2007).

2 A word of caution is necessary here. Universities also raise revenue through business-like functions. These activities may raise their own questions for administrators. These are beyond the scope of this chapter, however, in which the focus is really on philanthropic donations.

3 The Medical College of Georgia changed its name to Georgia Health Sciences University in 2010 (University System of Georgia, September 15, 2010), later merging with Augusta State University to become Georgia Regents University, at which time the College of Medicine became known as the Medical College of Georgia (University System of Georgia, May 8, 2012; Augusta University Medical College of Georgia, n.d.). Georgia Regents University was later renamed to Augusta University, its current name (Inside HigherEd, September 16, 2015). The Medical College of Georgia is still operating as one of three foundations supporting Augusta University. Since this chapter is focused on understanding the Board of Regents' dispute with the Medical College of Georgia Foundation, the Medical College of Georgia and Georgia Health Sciences names will be referred to.

4 In 2011, The Arch Foundation and the University of Georgia Foundation merged to form a new, consolidated University of Georgia Foundation. This paper focuses on the period after the relationship between the University of Georgia and the original University of Georgia Foundation soured and before the merger and re-establishment of a unified University of Georgia Foundation took place.

5 The Deloitte & Touche Audit was reprinted in Whitt (2009).

References

Basinger, J. (2004, June 11). University of Georgia vies for control of its money and its name. *The Chronicle of Higher Education.*

Capeloto, A. (2015). A case for placing public-university foundations under the existing oversight regime of freedom of information laws. *Communication Law & Policy, 20*(4), 311–342.

Duderstadt, J. (2007). *A view from the helm: Leading the American University during an era of change.* Ann Arbor, MI: The University of Michigan Press.

Koppell, J. (2005). Pathologies of accountability: ICANN and the challenges of "Multiple Accountabilities Disorder". *Public Administration Review, 65*(1), 94–108.

McGarvie, M. D. (1999). Creating roles for religion and philanthropy in a secular nation: The Dartmouth College case and the design of civil society in the early republic. *Journal of College and University Law, 25*(3), 527–568.

McCaffrey, J., & Mutty, J. (1999). The hidden process of budgeting: Execution. *Journal of Public Budgeting, Accounting & Financial Management, 11*(2), 233–257.

Rohr, J. (1989). *Ethics for bureaucrats: An essay on law and values* (2nd ed.). New York, NY: Marcel Dekker.

Rubin, I. (2013). *The politics of budgeting: Getting, spending, borrowing and balancing* (7th ed.). Los Angeles, CA: CQ Press.

Scott, W. R. (2008). *Institutions and organizations: Ideas and interests.* Thousand Oaks, CA: Sage Publications.

Skelcher, C., & Smith, S. R. (2015). Theorizing hybridity: Institutional logics, complex organizations, and actor identities—The case of nonprofits. *Public Administration, 93*(2), 433–448.

Stewart, D. (2010). Let the sunshine in, or else: An examination of the "teeth" of state and federal open meetings and records laws. *Communication Law & Policy, 15*(3), 265–310.

Tempel, E. R., Seiler, T. L., & Burlingame, D. T. (2016). *Achieving excellence in fundraising* (4th ed.). San Francisco, CA: Jossey-Bass.

University System of Georgia. (n.d.). USG Facts. Retrieved from https://www.usg.edu/news/usgfacts

University System of Georgia. (2010). Working Principles-Multiple Foundations. Obtained via Freedom of Information Act request.

University System of Georgia, Office of Media & Publications. (2004a). Statement from Board Vice-Chair Joel Wooten Regarding Trademark Rights to University of Georgia Name [Press Release]. Obtained via Freedom of Information Act request.

University System of Georgia. (2004b). Resolution on the Dispute over the Supplemental Pay for the President of the University of Georgia. Obtained via Freedom of Information Act request.

University System of Georgia. (2006). Affiliation Agreement. Obtained via Freedom of Information Act request.

Weber, G. (2004a, June 8 and 9). *Minutes of the meeting of the board of regents of the University System of Georgia.* Atlanta, GA: Georgia Archives.

Weber, G. (2004b, August 3). *Minutes of the meeting of the board of regents of the University System of Georgia.* Atlanta, GA: Georgia Archives.

Whitt, R. (2009). *Behind the hedges: Big money and power politics at the University of Georgia.* Mongtomery, AL: NewSouth Books.

PART III

Social Equity: The New Frontier of Diversity and Inclusion

9

NON-BINARY GENDER IDENTITY

Challenging Public Values and Reshaping Institutions

Nicole M. Elias and Gwendolyn Saffran

Introduction

In the United States, values of social equity and justice are the foundation of society. The question becomes how are these values defined, and where do these understanding emerge from. America's guiding document, the U.S. Constitution, coupled with decades of U.S. Supreme Court rulings are the basis for understanding our shared values. According to Rohr (1989), *regime values* are "values of [a] political entity that was brought into being by the ratification of the Constitution that created the present American republic" (p. 68). Public administrators and public servants pledge to uphold the U.S. Constitution; this oath is the moral foundation of ethics for bureaucrats (p. 70). The Constitution outlines certain values—"beliefs, passions, and principles that have been held for several generations by the overwhelming majority of the American people" (p. 74)—such as freedom and equality under the law, which has been expanded to include the concept of social equity. Yet, regime values are not always applied consistently to all members of the population (Rohr, 1995; Rohr, 1998). This is especially the case when individuals possess demographic characteristics that do not fit neatly into the structures and norms of society.

Transgender[1] and non-binary[2] individuals are two groups that have been othered for not fitting into the traditional male-female identity categories. In the United States, much of social and economic life is tied to traditional, binary gender roles. Ridgeway (2009) argues that gender is a cultural frame for organizing social relations. Sex and gender serve as categories for defining the self and others, and American society has shared cultural beliefs about men and women that "act as the 'rules' for coordinating public behavior on the basis of gender" (Ridgeway, 2009, p. 149). Gendered "divisions of labor, gender inequalities in income and wealth, gender hierarchies in industrial enterprises, gender differences in rights of ownership, and gender differences in conditions of employment and patterns of unemployment" are pervasive features of the modern American economy (Pearse & Connell, 2016, p. 30). Gendered norms and stereotypes affect the fields in which men and women seek employment; historically, women have been encouraged to stay at home and let their husbands earn a living (Pearse & Connell, 2016), or, if women are to work, they are overrepresented in teaching and other "helping" professions and underrepresented in science, technology, engineering, and mathematics. Sex segregation is also salient in unquestioned symbols of sex and gender such as colors (pink for girls, blue for boys); sex-segregated restrooms and the symbols that denote each (typically a stick figure in pants for the men's restroom and a stick figure in a dress or skirt for the women's restroom); and appropriate behaviors for men and women, such as the expectation that boys will roughhouse or that women will shave their legs.

Over the last several years, transgender individuals have gained both recognition and made strides at the state and local levels legitimizing their identities. However, non-binary people do not necessarily benefit from policies that allow transgender people to transition; a policy allowing a transgender person to change their gender marker from M to F does not have the same effect on a non-binary person who does not identify as male or female. Though some municipalities are incorporating non-binary-specific policies, most approaches to gender equity frequently exclude those who identify outside of the male-female gender binary. The purpose of this chapter is to present a normative argument for non-binary-gender inclusion by building on Rohr's (1989) concept of regime values.

Promoting civil rights for the transgender and non-binary population is consistent with public administrators' oath to uphold the Constitution, because as Gooden (2015) highlights, equity and equality underscore the sentiment of the document. Only recently have "other fields, disciplines, and bodies of professional practice stepped up to consideration of social equity," so public administrators are on the forefront of social equity policy and practice (Frederickson, 2005, p. 32). The regime value framework encourages civil servants to recognize and respect non-binary individuals and identity constructs in both policy and practice. This chapter presents a normative argument for adopting non-binary gender policy and practice based on social equity regime values along with practical recommendations for non-binary gender identity inclusion in identity documents. To do this, non-binary gender identity is contextualized within the framework of social equity regime values. Next, the non-binary gender identity option on state-issued identity documents, a crucial and highly personal form of state recognition, is presented as a timely example underscoring social equity regime values. Lastly, recommendations are offered to improve and promote greater social equity for the non-binary gender population.

Social Equity Regime Values and Gender

Social equity emerges from the equality tradition of justice theory. Equity and equality are both fundamental to American ideals of democracy and share similar concepts of fairness and justice, but there is an important distinction between the two: namely, the sameness vs. difference approach. Gooden (2015) explains, "[i]n terms of public administration, equality means sameness or identical distribution of government services or implementation of public policies. Equity means the fair or just distribution of such services or policies" (p. 372). In public administration, models of equity "are typically guided by an overarching theory of change based on larger societal values and principles" (Gooden, 2017, p. 825). Equity ideals in the United States are rooted in our theoretical approach to democracy, but what constitutes equity has changed over time—for example, "separate but equal," the idea that racially segregated, but "equal" facilities was constitutional, has since been overturned by the Supreme Court and widely recognized as unequal. Instead of the same treatment for all, equity suggests a targeted approach is needed for more disadvantaged groups to achieve equitable outcomes. Social equity in public administration recognizes the importance of public administrators and public organizations in "fulfilling the democratic principle of fairness" (p. 373). Over time, the phrase *social equity* "has come to encompass the many complex issues associated with fairness, justice, and equality in public administration" (Frederickson, 2005, p. 33).

The basis of equity in the United States is rooted in our theoretical approach to democracy. The Declaration of Independence declares that "all men are created equal" and the Pledge of Allegiance ends with the phrase "liberty and justice for all" (Gooden, 2017). Equity was originally understood as a "judicial means of offering relief to people from 'hard bargains' in cases of fraud, accident, mistake, or trust, and as a means of confining the operation of 'unjust and partial laws,' and has since been expanded to offer relief to social classes" (McDowell, 1982, p. 4). Although American politics "has tilted the playing field toward the privileged and away from the under-privileged," were it not for public administrators dedicated to social equity, inequality would be much more severe (Frederickson, 2005, 33). The Civil Rights Act of 1964, for example, marked an important milestone for gender equity; though unequal pay based on gender is still a pervasive problem, it is no longer allowed under the law, and sexual harassment in the workplace is now understood to be discriminatory rather than simply a by-product of a "normal" working environment (Guy & Fenley, 2014). In particular, gender and equity has expanded and diversified. For example, women are now able to vote, hold office, work in any field, and likewise, marriage of same-sex couples is now recognized all 50 states. The Supreme Court treats sex as a "suspect classification," a term that denotes a group vulnerable to discrimination (Schraub, 2016). In recent years, public administrators have worked to promote, or in some cases restrict, the rights of their transgender constituents by passing laws regarding public accommodations as well as requirements for name and gender-marker changes.

Social equity as a regime value in a contemporary context prompts us to rethink how gender fits within the larger regime value framework in several significant ways. In light of the current ethical climate of public service, it is important to situate transgender rights in American Constitutional values. A 2015 Human Rights Campaign survey found that "22 percent of likely voters surveyed reported that they personally know or work with a transgender person, up from 17 percent who said they did in a similar poll" the previous year (Halloran, 2015). A recent global survey of 16 countries including the United States found that 70 percent of respondents believe governments should do more to protect transgender people from discrimination (Vomiero, 2018). In the largest survey of transgender people to date, 35 percent of respondents identified as non-binary—meaning that there may be half a million people in the United States who identify this way (Clarke, 2019, p. 899). Transgender identity is at the forefront of the public consciousness (Clarke, 2019), particularly with the Trump administration's recent redefinition of sex and policies such as the ban on transgender people serving in the military (Elias, Brand, & Federman, 2017). These public values challenge our moral compass as a nation and span some of the most hotly contested social issues in U.S. contemporary history.

Defining gender and situating gender within a Constitutional protection has significant consequences for legal interpretations. Courts are more stringent in interpreting suspect classification equal protection claims where a violation of a person's constitutional rights is brought against a law, regulation, or government action. The legal developments of the last 60 years have implications for public administrators. Public administrators' "liability is such that in order to perform their functions in a fashion acceptable to the judiciary, they must adhere to constitutional values and give them preeminence over administrative values generally" (Rosenbloom, O'Leary, & Chanin, 2010, p. S315). Courts have the power to build on what is outlined in the Constitution and expand rights for subjugated groups. Whether transgender, non-binary, and gender nonconforming people are protected under the term "sex" is disputed; the Obama administration authored a "Dear Colleague" letter in 2016 ordering that transgender students be protected under Title IX of the Education Amendments of 1972 (Lhamon & Gupta, 2016). However, the Trump administration rescinded this guidance and seeks to define gender as "a biological, immutable condition determined by genitalia at birth" (Green, Benner, & Pear, 2018). This definition of gender excludes transgender people entirely from protections based on sex. It is inconsistent with contemporary conceptions of gender equity, which include more gender identities beyond cisgender, traditional males and females.

One of the challenges presented by gender equity policy is that understandings of gender are constantly evolving. Gender is an increasingly complex topic that prompts "new policy and administrative responses within public agencies"

(Elias, 2017, p. 20). As conceptions of gender evolve and change, public administrators must continually ask what constitutes gender equity. Although transgender identity has come to the forefront of the national discussion of gender in recent years, the issue of gender equity extends back centuries. Cisgender women and men have historically been unequal, particularly in the home and at work. Urbanization and industrialization created a dichotomy between the home and work, with different forms of job segregation emerging in both (Guy & Newman, 2004). Women had, and largely still do have, fewer opportunities to move vertically in their jobs, and certain jobs tend to be typed as "for women" or "for men" based on sex stereotypes (Alkadry & Tower, 2006; Guy & Newman, 2004). The lack of women in high-power positions contributes to pay inequality, an issue still persistent today, more than 50 years after the passage of the Equal Pay Act of 1963 (Alkadry & Tower, 2006; Cunningham-Parmeter, 2014). Trans women are even more negatively affected by the pay equity gap, and transgender people in general struggle to find and keep jobs (Bradford, Reisner, Honnold, & Xavier, 2013; Nath, 2018). A modern conception of social equity regime values holds these inequities and disparities as unconstitutional, as has been reflected in legislation and court rulings in the past half century.

The progression of gender equity relies heavily on constitutional regime values. In *Brown v. Board of Education*, the U.S. Supreme Court ruled that the concept of "separate but equal" was unconstitutional. Although *Brown v. Board of Education* specifically addressed racial discrimination, its logic was extended by people who sought to "extend Brown's logic towards a constitutional mandate for gender equality" (McKeown, 2015, p. 815). This principle of anti-discrimination, based on the Equal Protection Clause of the Fourteenth Amendment, as well as women's growing roles in society, "led to the development of Equal Protection jurisprudence that rejects the codification of gender stereotypes" (McKeown, 2015, p. 815). The Supreme Court increasingly began to address the stereotypes and assumptions that undergird sex-based classifications and began to interpret the Equal Protection Clause to mean that women should be given opportunities to prove their capabilities. Based on this clause, Congress passed the Civil Rights Act of 1964, with Title VII prohibiting discrimination based on race, color, religion, sex, and national origin (U.S. Equal Opportunity Employment Commission, n.d.).

Rooted in the constitutional regime value of social equity, Title VII has been interpreted by some courts to include protections based on gender identity and sexual orientation, as well. In *Price Waterhouse v. Hopkins* in 1989, for example, Ann Hopkins claimed that her employer, Price Waterhouse, denied her partnership two years in a row on the basis of her lack of conformity to typical feminine stereotypes (Colvin, 2007; Elias, 2017; Legal Information Institute, n.d.). The court ruled that "'gender stereotyping' cannot be a component of promotion, and such actions violated Title VII of the Civil Rights

Act of 1964" (Legal Information Institute, n.d., p. 341), and opened the door for transgender plaintiffs to make claims that they were discriminated against on the basis of failure to conform to sex stereotyping. Former President Barack Obama also took the position that Title VII of the Civil Rights Act of 1964 applied to claims of discrimination based on gender identity (Elias, 2017; *The New York Times*, 2017). The Obama administration also issued guidance on the responsibilities schools have under Title IX of the Education Amendments of 1972, which state that schools receiving federal funding—including both K-12 schools and higher education institutions—cannot discriminate against their students based on sex (Trumble & Kasai, 2018). This guidance clarified that the law's prohibition of sex-based discrimination protected transgender students in schools and specifically instructed public schools to allow transgender students to use the bathroom that matches their gender identity (Weinhardt et al., 2017).

Not every court understands the "sex" protection as applicable to lesbian, gay, bisexual, trasngender, queer (LGBTQ)+ individuals. In 2016, for example, the Obama administration issued a Dear Colleague letter that included gender identity, and specifically transgender identity, in the sex protections under Title IX of the Education Amendments of 1972 (Whalen & Esquith, 2016). President Donald Trump rolled back the Title IX guidance that protects transgender students, which essentially informs schools that it is no longer necessary to interpret Title IX to protect transgender students in schools (Trumble & Kasai, 2018; Weinhardt et al., 2017). In January 2019, the Supreme Court allowed the Trump administration's ban on transgender individuals serving in the military to go into effect (De Vogue & Cohen, 2019). However, a majority of Americans favor non-discrimination protections being applied to LGBTQ+ individuals, inconsistent with this ruling (Greenberg, Najle, Bola, & Jones, 2019). The social equity regime values that are rooted in the Constitution should be applied to the LGBTQ+ population, just as they are applied to the cisgender population. Yet, these rights are not always affirmed consistently in practice. Examining state-issued identity documents highlights the legal, legislative, and administrative dimensions of defining and enacting gender policy in the current U.S. context.

Toward a More Inclusive Gendered Public: State-Issued Non-binary Gender Identity Documents

Including non-binary gender in public policy promotes social equity regime values. So much of everyday life relies on the gender binary—such as using a public restroom or filling out paperwork at a doctor's office—which effectively excludes non-binary people. Non-binary individuals have always been part of the United States population, but it was not until recently that their identities were legally recognized (Elias and Colvin 2019). Currently, 11 states and the District of Columbia recognize a third non-binary gender.[3] Non-binary gender identity policy provides a rich example of the regime value of social equity in the contemporary context. In recent years, transgender and non-binary people and identities have moved to the forefront of public policy. From the Trump administration's ban on transgender people serving in the military to new policies allowing gender-neutral markers on identification documents, gender identity and non-conformity is being widely considered by public administrators. As non-binary people gain increased visibility and advocacy, new legal arguments become possible (Clarke, 2019). Non-binary individuals, or people whose gender identities fall outside of the male-female binary, face many unique challenges that cisgender and binary transgender people do not (Savoia, 2017).

Non-binary gender identity is extremely limited in the public administration and policy literature; when it comes to legal writing, there have been even fewer pieces on this topic. One article that addresses non-binary gender identity and the law is Clarke (2019), which asks "what the law would look like if it took nonbinary gender seriously" (Clarke, 2019, p. 1). This *Harvard Law Review* article argues that the legal response to non-binary gender "has important implications for a variety of other identity-based legal movements," (p. 6) and presents three models for integrating non-binary identity into policy: recognizing a third gender, creating gender-neutral laws and policies, or integrating non-binary people into binary sex or gender regulation (Clarke, 2019). Non-binary individuals do not always fit neatly into policies that have been constructed to protect or serve other LGBTQ+ or binary transgender individuals.

Considering recent legal arguments for incorporating non-binary identity into law, some jurisdictions have followed suit and crafted policies to include a third gender. The U.S. federal government lags behind in progressive civil rights policies, particularly when it comes to LGBTQ+ issues, and especially in regard to gender identity (Sabharwal, Levine, D'Agostino, & Nguyen, 2019). In response to this lack of policy, some jurisdictions have begun to recognize a third gender by allowing constituents to have an X gender marker on their government-issued identity documents (IDs), as opposed to the traditional M or F. These policies have many benefits; non-binary people who do not identify as male or female may feel that their IDs do not accurately reflect who they are, and this disconnect between gender identity/expression and the marker on an ID may create confusing or unsafe situations (Couch, Pitts, Croy, Mulcare & Mitchell, 2008; Currah & Mulqueen, 2011; Johnson, 2015). In June of 2016, the Oregon Court of Appeals became the first American court to legally recognize a non-binary gender identity (Clarke, 2019). Judge Amy Holmes Hehn of the Oregon Circuit Court granted petitioner Jamie Shupe's request for a legal change of sex from female to non-binary (*State v. Shupe*, 2016). Shupe was the first person in the United States to change their sex to non-binary (Mele, 2016). Since, select jurisdictions in the United States have begun to offer an X gender marker on government-issued identification documents. These policies encompass court orders, legislation, and administrative agency policies; and are available on driver's licenses, non-driver state ID cards, and birth certificates.

Currently, Washington, D.C., Massachusetts, Vermont, Maine, New York, Washington State, Oregon, California, Minnesota, Arkansas, Utah, and Colorado offer the X gender marker on some form of identification. This third-gender option helps not only non-binary people, but intersex people as well.[4] In California in 2016, an intersex individual named Sara Kelly Keenan legally changed her sex from female to intersex on her birth certificate (Levin, 2017). New York City birth certificates can now be amended to list one's gender as X without a doctor's note or requirements for medical transition (Hafner, 2019). In 2018 in Colorado, Anunnaki Ray Marquez, who identifies as gender-non-conforming, androgynous gay man, changed their sex on their birth certificate to intersex (O'Hara, 2018). Individuals who are both intersex and non-binary are integral to non-binary advocacy efforts, as they "may be more sympathetic to the public and judiciary, because intersex traits are regarded as somatic rather than psychological or elective" (Clarke, 2019, pp. 33–34). Intersex people represent the argument that sex is not a strict set of binary traits, and that physical and genetic characteristics do not always "provide a consistent answer to the question of whether a person is male or female" (p. 34). Intersex characteristics also undermine the reliance on medical treatment to "prove" that a person is undergoing physical changes as a requirement for changing one's gender marker.

The requirements for changing one's gender marker to X vary depending on the jurisdiction, but common requirements include an application form, a photograph, monetary fees, court orders, and medical and/or psychological requirements. Recognizing non-binary identity as a third gender lends non-binary people a civil status, affirming their existence and identities (Clarke, 2019, p. 937). Legal recognition may also provide non-binary people with the authority to demand fair treatment from public and private actors. Alternatively, gender neutrality would involve "masking gendered characteristics in certain contexts, eliminating rules that classify by sex, or decoupling certain traits from sex classifications" (pp. 940–941). Instead of adding a third gender to forms, neutrality would eliminate the sex category altogether from documents (p. 942). This option may reduce gender policing and can push back against stereotypes about men and women. Lastly, non-binary people may be grouped in with binary-identifying people; for example, a policy seeking to enhance gender diversity in a workplace may target not only women, but "people who do not identify exclusively as male and LGBT people" (p. 945). As our understandings of gender grow and change over time, so does our understanding of what constitutes gender diversity.

Washington, D.C. serves as a model for comprehensive X gender marker policies. In 2017, Mayor Bowser announced that the District of Columbia's

Department of Motor Vehicles (DMV) would allow residents to choose the gender marker on their driver's licenses, rather than relying on other identification documents such as birth certificates (District of Columbia Department of Motor Vehicles, 2017). The policy that allows residents to choose an X gender marker began as an administrative policy within the DMV and was later crafted into legislation. Changing one's gender marker to X is the same as obtaining a new license: applicants must fill out a Gender Designation form; take a new photograph "as the applicant chooses to present themselves, regardless of requested gender;" and pay a monetary fee (District of Columbia Department of Motor Vehicles, 2017). Applicants are not required to have changed their gender marker on their birth certificates or other forms of identification and are not required to have matching gender designations on all forms of identification. Additionally, the policy notes that DMV staff must respect applicants' privacy and not draw undue attention to them, and that DMV staff have been trained on this process (District of Columbia Department of Motor Vehicles, 2017).

Offering a third gender category has significant benefits for society. Having an identity document that accurately reflects one's gender is associated with feelings of affirmation and civil belonging (Couch et al., 2008). The state recognizing a third gender also lends a level of protection to non-binary people; New York City's anti-discrimination laws, for example, require that correct name and pronouns—including non-binary pronouns such as they/them and ze/zir—be used for transgender people under the penalty of a fine (New York City Commission on Human Rights, 2019). However, recognizing only three genders may not be expansive enough; "non-binary" is an umbrella term that covers numerous and diverse gender identities. There is little room for gender fluidity on state documents. Traditional gender roles have historically been upheld on public identification documents (Newlin, 2008). There are a number of reasons that governments categorize and track gender, including disseminating resources: "Not only does the state have sole authority to legally categorize people by sex, but it also uses those categories as the basis for distributing rights and goods, such as marriage and its associated benefits, over which it maintains a monopoly of power" (Flynn, 2009, p. 467). While gender is an occasionally useful way to categorize people, its evolution has rendered many, if not all, of the reasons why governmental bodies categorize people based on gender.

As gender becomes more fluid and gender norms move further away from traditional male-female binary, it is relevant to consider whether tracking gender is necessary or if there is a benefit to doing away with gender markers altogether. While the X marker has important benefits for non-binary people, it poses certain administrative challenges. For example, if a person with an X marker on their license drives to another state that does not offer the X marker and is pulled over, it is unclear how this person would be processed and treated by law enforcement officers. Likewise, some individuals may also have inconsistent gender markers of different state-issued identity documents—an X on a license, but an M on a passport, for example. These inconsistencies can potentially cause problems for individuals and administrators. There is also concern that the X marker will "out" individuals as non-binary; even though any person, cisgender or transgender, can obtain the X marker, people may have preconceived notions about the X marker and who obtains it. Governments are unlikely to eradicate gender tracking altogether in the near future, so the X marker is still an important and necessary option for many individuals in the United States. Jurisdictions that offer the X marker, as well as the federal government, should, however, provide guidance for processing the marker and incongruent records.

Educational domains have also made significant strides to be more inclusive of non-binary individuals, specifically on college campuses, and public administrators can take note of these efforts. Some college campuses have implemented gender-neutral housing, which allows students of any gender to live together in on-campus housing (Erbentraut, 2015; Willoughby, Larsen, & Carroll, 2012). Sex-segregated housing can be a stressful process for transgender, gender non-conforming, and non-binary students, and can feel exclusive to people who do not conform to the gender binary. This is an issue that affects many transgender college students: nearly one-fifth of the National Transgender Discrimination Survey respondents reported being denied gender-appropriate housing in a higher education setting, and five percent were denied on-campus housing (Grant et al., 2011). Only a small number of colleges and universities offer gender-neutral housing, and sometimes it is offered only on a case-by-case basis or only to transgender and non-binary students (Willoughby et al., 2012). This is problematic because it requires transgender and non-binary students to out themselves as trans in order to obtain appropriate housing. Some students who attend colleges with gender-neutral housing have reported that the housing options are inaccessible or unavailable, or the options that are available are undesirable (Lloyd, 2018). Despite these problems, public administrators can learn from the ways that colleges promote gender equity. Many colleges have also implemented other progressive gender policies, such as allowing students to indicate their preferred names (instead of their legal names) and/or pronouns in the university system, or covering gender-affirming medical procedures in their student healthcare plans (Pérez-Peña, 2013; Scelfo, 2015).

Bolstering Social Equity with Practical Recommendations for Non-binary Gender Identity Policy

Enacting social equity regime values is important for both normative and practical purposes. Policies that exclude transgender and non-binary individuals from any aspect of public life run counter to social equity regime values. One barrier to social equity for transgender and non-binary individuals is obtaining an ID that accurately reflects their gender identities. From a normative perspective, the X marker challenges our most fundamental gendered institution in the current U.S. context. Contextualizing non-binary gender markers within the regime value of social equity provides a normative argument for treating non-binary individuals as equals with their cisgender and binary transgender counterparts. Non-binary people are excluded from so many aspects of public life, from having accurate gender markers on their IDs, to feeling comfortable in a public restroom, to being able to accurately document their gender on paperwork, job applications, etc. There are few other aspects of identity so wholly excluded from public life and accurate representation as non-binary genders; by including non-binary identity in social equity regime values, public administrators demonstrate dedication to gender equity broadly and to promotion of transgender rights.

Key considerations for enacting non-binary gender identity include: granting transgender and non-binary individuals the same rights to have their gender identities reflected in their IDs as cisgender individuals; creating a culture of inclusion and civil belonging in transgender and non-binary individuals; and reducing the burden on transgender and non-binary individuals who wish to change their gender markers. In the United States, there is a heavy reliance on government-issued identification documents: people must show IDs to open a bank account, apply for a job, fly on an airplane, or rent an apartment. A license is required in order to drive a vehicle. On all forms of government-issued IDs, there is a gender marker—typically F or M. For transgender and non-binary people, the gender marker on their ID may not be congruent with their gender identities and/or gender expression. This can present significant challenges, including facing discrimination and violence (Grant et al., 2011). Transgender people are six times more likely to be assaulted by police (Human Rights Campaign & Trans People of Color Coalition, 2017), and an ID with a gender marker that does not match a person's gender presentation can "out" that person as transgender if an officer requests to see their ID (Elias, 2019a). Transgender people have historically been marginalized and discriminated against in the workplace, and while there are initiatives to increase gender diversity, most research and policy focuses on cisgender and binary transgender people (Elias, 2019b). Considering these challenges, municipalities should allow their constituents to change their IDs to accurately reflect their gender identities. This process should not put an undue burden on people who wish to change the gender marker on their IDs, and the application process and public administrators should be mindful to respect applicants' privacy.

Having documentation that reflects a person's gender identity is crucial for one's sense of personal and identity recognition (Couch et al., 2008). Changing one's identity documents to accurately reflect one's gender identity is associated with several benefits, including feelings of affirmation and recognition of one's "civil belonging" (Couch et al., 2008). Conversely, being unable to obtain documentation that reflects one's gender identity can result in feelings of hopelessness, fear, and exclusion, and can put a transgender person in danger by outing them as trans and affecting their ability to "pass" as their gender identity (Couch et al., 2008). This can lead to discrimination, harassment, and even violence (Couch et al., 2008; Grant et al., 2011). The U.S. Constitution guarantees equal protection under the law, so public administrators must grapple with whether this includes the ability for trans people to have their gender identity accurately reflected on their identity documents. Based on social equity regime values, it is the duty of public administrators to serve all of their constituents, regardless of their gender identities, and protect them from discrimination and violence. It can be argued, then, that governments, ethically speaking, must allow their transgender constituents to change their identity documents to accurately reflect their gender identities—including non-binary identities through offering third-gender options like the X marker.

Changing one's gender marker can be a lengthy, complicated, and expensive process and is different in every state in the United States (Mottet, 2013). Some jurisdictions may require applicants to submit documentation showing that they have undergone medical or psychological treatment to "prove" their gender identities; this is problematic because not all transgender people seek medical or psychological intervention to affirm their gender identities (Elias, 2019a). While many trans people transition medically by taking hormone replacement therapy and undergoing surgeries, not every trans person is able to or feels the need to do this to affirm their gender identities. Centering transgender identity on medical procedures focuses gender on physical sex characteristics, even though a person's gender identity is not always connected to their sex characteristics. Medical intervention is also expensive, and trans people are especially vulnerable to discrimination and harassment in medical settings (Elias, 2019a; Grant et al., 2011). Some jurisdictions require a court order for a person to change their gender marker, which can be a lengthy and expensive process. Public administrators should ease the burden on the individual applicant as much as possible; for example, in Washington D.C., applicants who wish to change their gender marker to X on their driver's licenses must only fill out an application form and take a new photograph (Department of Motor Vehicles, 2017). Public administrators should be sensitive, respectful, and discreet when processing an applicant's gender change request.

Important pragmatic questions remain about changing the gender marker on identification documents. What happens if an individual has incongruous IDs, such as an M on a driver's license, but an F on a passport? How will jurisdictions that do not offer the X marker process IDs with the X marker? Are gender markers on IDs even necessary? Jurisdictions can address these questions by offering clear guidance on how to process IDs with all kinds of gender markers, and how to handle incongruous IDs. Jurisdictions should also be mindful of the fact that changing one's gender marker is a stressful and sometimes expensive and extensive process; administrators can mitigate this by keeping requirements for the change to a minimum and by ensuring that employees are respectful of applicants' privacy. Jurisdictions should also allow gender marker changes and, for those jurisdictions that have the X marker, offer the X marker on as many identification documents as possible (e.g., driver's licenses, birth certificates).

Conclusion

Social equity regime values are foundational to American institutions and society in the current U.S. context. The Constitution lays the groundwork for public administrators to promote social equity generally, and gender equity, specifically. Rohr's regime value framework prompts public administrators to consider the relationship between gender and regime values in significant ways. As transgender and non-binary identities become increasingly visible, accepted, and normalized, public administrators in jurisdictions across the country have been promoting gender equity through policy in new and progressive ways. This commitment to social equity regardless of gender is consistent with public administrators' oath to uphold the values of the Constitution. In the spirit of Rohr's work, this chapter serves as a call for public servants and policymakers to craft just and equitable policy that ensures equal rights and protections for people of all genders.

The contemporary civil rights held by residents of the United States are rooted in constitutional regime values of social equity. Yet, in a majority of the United States, non-binary individuals are unable to see their gender identities reflected in their state-issued identity documents and are likewise excluded from some of the most basic aspects of public life, such as access to gender-neutral restrooms. Access to gender markers on IDs that reflect one's gender identity is associated with feelings of civic belonging and has important implications for personal safety as well as emotional well-being. While few jurisdictions have recognized the need for non-binary gender equity and created policies to address the needs of this population, much work needs to be done. Some important questions remain unanswered, particularly concerns regarding incongruent laws resulting from federalism and jurisdictional issues: what happens if a person with an X gender marker travels to a state that does not recognize that marker? Since the X marker is not available at the federal level, how will a person with an X marker on their ID be treated at an airport by Transportation Security Administration (TSA) agents? How do different local and state jurisdictions handle people with incongruent documents, such as people with an X on a license, but an M or F on a passport?

All of these unanswered questions prompt not only administrative concerns, but safety concerns. Presenting inaccurate or incongruous identity documents can trigger abuse and discrimination (Cray & Harrison, 2012). Trans people who "may otherwise move through the world undetected by those who would discriminate against them" that have a gender marker that does not reflect their gender identity and/or presentation can be outed by the inaccurate marker (Crazy & Harrison, 2012). Forty percent of the respondents to the National

Transgender Discrimination Survey reported that presenting an ID that did not match their gender identity resulted in harassment (Grant et al., 2011). It is important that the federal government as well as state and local governments issue guidance on how to handle IDs with the X marker. Ultimately, more support, resources, and clear policy for transgender and non-binary individuals are needed at all levels of government. Rohr's regime value framework provides a normative basis for understanding and articulating a need for greater protections and support of the transgender and non-binary population.

Notes

1 Transgender people are people whose gender identity and sex assigned at birth are not in alignment. The term "transgender" is an umbrella term that covers a large and diverse number of gender identities that are both inside and outside the male-female gender binary.

2 Non-binary people are people whose gender identities fall outside of the male-female gender binary. There are a large and diverse number of gender identities that the term non-binary describes, but what they all share in common is that they are neither strictly male nor strictly female.

3 The states that offer some form of a third gender option are: Arkansas, California, Colorado, Washington, D.C., Maine, Minnesota, New York, Ohio, Oregon, Utah, and Washington State.

4 "Intersex" describes a person whose reproductive and/or sexual anatomy does not fit the typical descriptions of male or female. An intersex person may have a combination of both XX and XY chromosomes. Intersex individuals, like non-intersex individuals, have varying gender identities, including male, female, non-binary, transgender, or another gender.

References

Alkadry, M. G., & Tower, L. E. (2006). Unequal pay: The role of gender. *Public Administration Review, 66*(6), 888–898.

Bradford, J., Reisner, S. L., Honnold, J. A., & Xavier, J. (2013). Experiences of transgender-related discrimination and implications for health: Results from the Virginia transgender health initiative study. *American Journal of Public Health, 103*(10), 1820–1829.

Clarke, J. A. (2019). They, them, and theirs. *Harvard Law Review, 132*, 894.

Colvin, R. A. (2007). The rise of transgender-inclusive laws: How well are municipalities implementing supportive nondiscrimination public employment policies? *Review of Public Personnel Administration, 27*(4), 336–360.

Cray, A., & Harrison, J. (2012). *ID Accurately Reflecting One's Gender Identity Is a Human Right*, Center for American Progress. Retrieved from https://perma.cc/FCR7-ZZUY.

Cunningham-Parmeter, K. (2014). (Un)Equal protection: Why gender equality depends on discrimination. *Northwestern University Law Review, 109*(1), 1–56.

Currah, P., & Mulqueen, T. (2011). Securitizing gender: Identity, biometrics, and transgender bodies at the airport. *Social Research: An International Quarterly, 78*(2), 557–582.

Department of Motor Vehicles. (2017). *Procedure for establishing or changing gender designation on a driver's license or identification card*. Washington, DC: Department of Motor Vehicles.

De Vogue, A., & Cohen, Z. (2019, January 22). Supreme Court allows transgender military ban to go into effect. Retrieved from https://www.cnn.com/2019/01/22/politics/scotus-transgender-ban/index.html

District of Columbia Department of Motor Vehicles. (2017, June 23). Mayor Bowser announces addition of gender neutral identifier to drivers licenses and identification cards. Press Release. Retrieved from https://dmv.dc.gov/release/mayor-bowser-announces-addition-gender-neutral-identifier-drivers-licenses-and

Elias, N., & Colvin, R. (2019). A third option: Understanding and assessing non-binary gender policies in the United States. *Administrative Theory & Praxis*, 1–21.

Elias, N. M. (2019a). Transgender and non-binary gender policy in the public sector. In D. Haider-Markel (Ed.), *Oxford encyclopedia of LGBT politics and policy*. Oxford University Press. https://doi.org/10.1093/acrefore/9780190228637.013.1168

Elias, N. M. (2019b). Lesbian, gay, bisexual, transgender, queer (LGBTQ+) workplace policy. In: A. Farazmand (Ed.), *Global encyclopedia of public administration, public policy, and governance*. Springer International Publishing. https://doi.org/10.1007/978-3-319-31816-5_2396-1.

Elias, N. M. R. (2017). Constructing and implementing transgender policy for public administration. *Administration & Society, 49*(1), 20–47.

Elias, N. M. R., Brand, M. S., & Federman, P. S. (2017, September). Governing by Twitter: Implications of the president's transgender military tweets. *Social Justice Bulletin: ASPA Section on Democracy and Social Justice, 1*(3).

Erbentraut, J. (2015, May 18). College campuses are more trans-inclusive than ever, but still have a long way to go. *The Huffington Post*. Retrieved from https://www.huffingtonpost.com/2015/05/18/trans-friendly-colleges_n_7287702.html

Flynn, T. (2009). Instant (gender) messaging: Expression-based challenges to state enforcement of gender norms. *Temple Political & Civil Rights Law Review, 18*(2), 465–503.

Frederickson, H. G. (2005). The state of social equity in American public administration. *National Civic Review, 94*(4), 31–38.

Gooden, S. (2015). PAR's social equity footprint. *Public Administration Review, 75*(3), 372–381.

Gooden, S. T. (2017). Social equity and evidence: Insights from local government. *Public Administration Review, 77*(6), 822–828.

Grant, J. M., Mottet, L. A., Tanis, J., Harrison, J., Herman, J. L., & Keisling, M. (2011). *Injustice at every turn: A report of the National Transgender Discrimination Survey*. Retrieved from http://www.thetaskforce.org/static_html/downloads/reports/reports/ntds_full.pdf

Green, E. L., Benner, K., & Pear, R. (2018, October 21). "Transgender" could be defined out of existence under Trump administration. *The New York Times*. Retrieved from https://www.nytimes.com/2018/10/21/us/politics/transgender-trump-administration-sex-definition.html

Greenberg, D., Najle, M., Bola, O., & Jones, R. P. (2019). Fifty years after Stonewall: Widespread support for LGBT issues—Findings from American values Atlas 2018. Retrieved from https://www.prri.org/research/fifty-years-after-stonewall-widespread-support-for-lgbt-issues-findings-from-american-values-atlas-2018/

Guy, M. E., & Fenley, V. M. (2014). Inch by inch: Gender equity since the Civil Rights Act of 1964. *Review of Public Personnel Administration, 34*(1), 40–58.

Guy, M. E., & Newman, M. A. (2004). Women's jobs, men's jobs: Sex segregation and emotional labor. *Public administration review, 64*(3), 289–298.

Hafner, J. (2019, January 3). Gender "X": New York City adds gender-neutral option to birth certificates. Retrieved from https://www.usatoday.com/story/news/nation/2019/01/03/new-york-city-birth-certificates-now-feature-third-gender-option-x/2472189002/

Halloran, L. (2015, April 24). Survey shows striking increase in Americans who know and support transgender people. Retrieved from https://www.hrc.org/blog/survey-shows-striking-increase-in-americans-who-know-and-support-transgender

Human Rights Campaign & Trans People of Color Coalition. (2017). A Time to Act: Fatal Violence Against Transgender People in America.

Johnson, J. (2015). Minnesota (trans)gender markers: State statutes and policies on amending identity documents. *William Mitchell Law Review, 41*(1), 213–228.

Legal Information Institute. (n.d.). Price Waterhouse v. Hopkins. Retrieved from https://www.law.cornell.edu/supremecourt/text/490/228

Levin, S. (2017, January 11). First US person to have "intersex" on birth certificate: "There's power in knowing who you are." Retrieved from https://www.theguardian.com/world/2017/jan/11/intersex-rights-gender-sara-kelly-keenan-birth-certificate

Lhamon, C. E., & Gupta, V. (2016, May 13). *Dear colleague letter on transgender students.* Washington, DC: U.S. Department of Education, Office for Civil Rights.

Lloyd, M. (2018, March 22). Gender vs. housing: Room options exclude trans, non-binary students. Retrieved from https://www.huntnewsnu.com/2018/03/gender-vs-housing-room-options-exclude-trans-non-binary-students/

McDowell, G. L. (1982). Introduction: From equitable relief to public policy. In *Equity and the constitution: The Supreme Court, equitable relief, and public policy* (pp. 3–11). Chicago, IL: University of Chicago Press.

McKeown, M. M. (2015). Beginning with *Brown*: Springboard for gender equality and social change. *San Diego Law Review, 52*, 815–824.

Mele, C. (2016, June 13). Oregon court allows a person to choose neither sex. *The New York Times.* Retrieved from https://www.nytimes.com/2016/06/14/us/oregon-non-binary-transgender-sex-gender.html?_r=0

Mottet, L. (2013). Modernizing state vital statistics statutes and policies to ensure accurate gender markers on birth certificates: A good government approach to recognizing the lives on transgender people. *Michigan Journal of Gender and Law, 19*(2), 373–470.

Nath, I. (2018, February 8). For transgender women, the pay equity gap is even wider. Retrieved from https://www.macleans.ca/society/for-transgender-women-the-pay-equity-gap-is-even-wider/

New York City Commission on Human Rights. (2019). NYC commission on human rights legal enforcement guidance on discrimination on the basis of gender identity or expression: Local law no. 3 (2002); N.Y.C. Admin. Code § 8–102. Retrieved from https://www1.nyc.gov/assets/cchr/downloads/pdf/publications/2019.2.15%20Gender%20Guidance-February%202019%20FINAL.pdf

Newlin, A. (2008). Should a trip from Illinois to Tennessee change a woman into a man? Proposal for a uniform interstate sex reassignment recognition act. *Columbia Journal of Gender and Law, 17*(3), 461–503.

O'Hara, M. E. (2018, September 20). Colorado is the first U.S. state to issue an intersex birth certificate. Retrieved from https://www.them.us/story/colorado-intersex-birth-certificate

Pearse, R., & Connell, R. (2016). Gender norms and the economy: Insights from social research. *Feminist Economics, 22*(1), 30–53.

Pérez-Peña, R. (2013, February 12). College health plans respond as transgender students gain visibility. *The New York Times.* Retrieved from https://www.nytimes.com/2013/02/13/education/12sexchange.html

Ridgeway, C. L. (2009). Framed before we know it: How gender shapes social relations. *Gender & Society, 23*(2), 145–160.

Rohr, J. A. (1989). *Ethics for bureaucrats: An essay on law and values* (2nd ed.). New York, NY: Marcel Dekker.

Rohr, J. A. (1995). *Founding republics in France and America: A study in constitutional governance.* Lawrence, KS: University of Kansas Press.

Rohr, J. A. (1998). *Public service, ethics, & constitutional practice.* Lawrence, KS: University of Kansas Press.

Rohr, J. A. (2002). *Civil servants and their constitutions.* Lawrence, KS: University of Kansas Press.

Rosenbloom, D. H., O'Leary, R., & Chanin, J. (2010). The future of public administration and law in 2020. *Public Administration Review, 70*, S314–S316.

Sabharwal, M., Levine, H., D'Agostino, M., & Nguyen, T. (2019). Inclusive work practices: Turnover intentions among LGBT employees of the U.S. federal government. *American Review of Public Administration, 49*(4), 482–494.

Savoia, E. P. (2017). *"Neither of the Boxes": Accounting for non-binary gender identities.* Portland, OR: Portland State University.

Scelfo, J. (2015, February 3). A university recognizes a third gender: Neutral. *The New York Times.* Retrieved from https://www.nytimes.com/2015/02/08/education/edlife/a-university-recognizes-a-third-gender-neutral.html

Schraub, D. (2016). Unsuspecting. *Boston University Law Review, 96*(2), 361–423.

State of Oregon v. Shupe (Multnomah County Circuit Court June 10, 2016).

The New York Times. (2017, February 24). Understanding transgender access laws. *The New York Times.* Retrieved from https://www.nytimes.com/2017/02/24/us/transgender-bathroom-law.html

Trumble, S., & Kasai, N. (2018). Protecting transgender students, and all students, in school. Retrieved from https://www.thirdway.org/memo/protecting-transgender-students-and-all-students-in-school

U.S. Equal Opportunity Employment Commission. (n.d.). Title VII of the Civil Rights Act of 1964. Retrieved from https://www.eeoc.gov/laws/statutes/titlevii.cfm

Vomiero, J. (2018, January 29). Is the world more accepting of transgender people? Yes, but many people still aren't: Ipsos. Retrieved from https://globalnews.ca/news/3991849/transgender-people-world-accepting-ipsos-poll/

Weinhardt, L. S., Stevens, P., Xie, H., Wesp, L. M., John, S. A., Apchemengich, I., … Lambrou, N. H. (2017). Transgender and gender nonconforming youths' public facilities use and psychological well-being: A mixed-method study. *Transgender Health, 2*, 140–150.

Whalen, A., & Esquith, D. (2016). Examples of policies and emerging practices for supporting transgender students. Retrieved from https://www2.ed.gov/about/offices/list/oese/oshs/emergingpractices.pdf

Willoughby, B. J., Larsen, J. K., & Carroll, J. S. (2012). The emergence of gender-neutral housing on American university campuses. *Journal of Adolescent Research, 27*(6), 732–750.

10

SOCIAL EQUITY AND VOTING RIGHTS

A Shrinking Regime

Susan T. Gooden and Brandy S. Faulkner

Introduction

A fundamental legacy of John Rohr's scholarship is the concept of regime values. For Rohr, regime values form the center of bureaucratic ethics. But who constitutes the United States (U.S.) regime, meaning those whose voices are powerful because they have the right to vote? The recent 2013 U.S. Supreme Court decision, *Shelby v. Holder*, 570 U.S. 529 (2013), paves the way for a regime that is shrinking and less inclusive. In particular, the voting rights of African Americans have been a refutation of U.S. democratic principles since our founding and remain so today. Voting rights of African Americans operate on an unbalanced pendulum, which gravitates toward exclusion. Supreme Court decisions are important because they comprise the gravity upon which these rights swing.

While there are many ways to express one's opinion and voice, including via print and social media as well as through advocacy, the power of voice is directly linked to the establishment of citizenship and the right to vote. Voice matters most when it can yield political consequences, which in democratic societies are decided via elections. Who can and cannot vote matters a lot, not only because of their historical record in influencing elections, but most importantly, because of the fear of their *capacity* to do so in future ones.

For Rohr, the manifestation of regime values contained in the U.S. Constitution is best understood by analyzing Supreme Court decisions. This chapter applies this approach to voting in the United States by examining the ruling and subsequent implementation of a landmark 2013 Supreme

Court decision, *Shelby v. Holder*, 570 U.S. 529 (2013), which ruled core aspects of the Voting Rights Act of 1965 unconstitutional. Following the ruling, several states formerly covered under provisions of the Voting Rights Act passed laws removing provisions such as early voting and online voting registration; while some states have also implemented more restrictive voter identification laws and purged voter rolls more aggressively. There are important racial implications of these changes, particularly for African Americans, including the closing of polling locations in predominately African American communities. The aftermath of *Shelby v. Holder*, 570 U.S. 529 (2013) offers a critical social equity paradox by significantly reducing voting protections derived from the original intent of the 15th Amendment. This signals a fundamental shift in regime values relative to voting equity. The U.S. regime is shrinking, and this shrinkage impacts African Americans in particular.

The theoretical grounding for Rohr's concept of regime values is derived from Aristotle. As Uhr (2014) explains,

> The theoretical ambition comes through with Rohr's definition of "regime" as the best word "to suggest what Aristotle means by 'polity,'" with regime values referring to "the values of that political entity" brought into being by the constitutional order "that created the present American republic" (p. 143).

Rohr considers salient values, which are not fixed, but rather evolve over time and within societal context, as shaping and molding the polity. For Rohr, regime values date back much further than the U.S. Constitution, naming the famous political philosopher Aristotle as the "founding father" of the concept.

Relying upon Aristotle as the authoritative basis for both regime values and the advancement of U.S. constitutional principles such as equality is fundamentally problematic. Aristotle was not only a philosopher, but he was also an avowed racist. Namely, he argued through classification and taxonomies that some people are naturally inferior and should be excluded from societal decision-making.

> In the first book of his "*Politics*," written in the 300s B.C., Aristotle uses taxonomies to justify the exclusion of certain people from civic life. While condemning the predominate method of acquiring slaves in his day—capturing prisoners of war—Aristotle argues that some people are by nature (rather than circumstances) fit to be slaves: "For that some should rule and others be ruled is a thing not only necessary, but expedient, from the hour of their birth, some are marked out for subjection, others for rule" (Sears, 2018).

Voting and Social Equity

As Gooden (2015) writes,

> The context for equality in the United States is formal and deeply entrenched. Both the Declaration of Independence and the U.S. Constitution concretely affirm a commitment to equality in the United States. Adopted July 4, 1776 by the thirteen former colonies, these new United States of America proclaimed in their Declaration of Independence: "We hold these truths to be self-evident, that all men are created equal, that they are endowed by their Creator with certain unalienable Rights, that among these are Life, Liberty and the pursuit of Happiness." While this sentence represents a fundamental ideal, the exclusion of women, the enslavement of blacks, and the gross mistreatment of the first Americans— American Indians—left a huge gulf in the implementation of this democratic principle (pp. 211–212).

The equal right to vote is fundamental to an inclusive, democratic society, and as Rohr appropriately acknowledges, the Supreme Court has a dominant role in ultimately deciding democratic principles. Emblematic of this, it was the Taney Court (1836–1864) that decided that even when a slave was free, he would not be counted as a man. "What the Supreme Court did was to take a position that race mattered in public policy, civic life and engagement, and democratic government" (Hopps & Bowles, 2015, p. 3). This has resulted in an enduring legacy impacting public policy in many areas, including voting rights. As Hopps and Bowles continue,

> A much hailed twentieth century achievement and perhaps, the most important and decisive law for advancing the political rights of African Americans since Reconstruction, the Voting Rights Act (VRA), was enacted after a long political struggle that included atrocities and death (p. 1).

The concept of social equity is inextricably linked to John Rawls's *A Theory of Justice*. Rawls developed a principle of justice as "fairness" in which "each person is to have an equal right to the most extensive basic liberty compatible with liberty for all" (1971, p. 250). As Rawls argues, a modern theory of government equalizes the distribution of social and economic advantages (such as voting). He challenges us to put ourselves behind a "veil of ignorance" and to use our innate sense of justice to derive principles of equity without the bias of knowing our own situation. For Rawls, equity includes social primary goods such as power, opportunity, civil rights, and wealth (Stone, 1997, p. 54).

While there have been several Supreme Court decisions specifically related to racial equity (e.g., *Dred Scott v. Sandford* [1857], *Plessy v. Ferguson* [1896],

Brown v. Board of Education [1954]), it was the Civil Rights Act of 1964 and the Voting Rights Act of 1965 that were truly historic steps forward in promoting racial equity. By beginning to reverse dominant racial inequities upheld legally, first by slavery and then the Black Codes, commonly known as Jim Crow laws. Following the ratification of the 15th Amendment in 1870, which specifically forbade the right to deny citizens of the United States the right to vote based on race, color, or previous condition of servitude, the Jim Crow laws systematically disenfranchised African Americans with practices including poll taxes, literacy tests, grandfather clauses, and voter intimidation.

Voting rights were a key focus and long-sought victory of the civil rights movement. Within the national context of the 1960s, which strongly focused on civil rights, racial inequality, and injustice, public administration scholars at Syracuse University's first Minnowbrook Conference in 1968 noted, "A government built on a Constitution claiming the equal protection of the laws had failed in that promise" (Frederickson, 1990, p. 228). Leaders of the civil rights movement fully understood that the realization of equality in America's democracy could not exist without a free and protected right to vote: voting must be fair and equitable in order to realize constitutional equality. The Voting Rights Act of 1965 is "a sacred symbol of American democracy. The act, the most effective civil rights statute ever enacted in the United States, was the last significant stage in the nearly universal formal inclusion of all adult citizens in American democracy" (Epsten, Pildes, de la Garza, & O'Halloran, 2006, p. xi). This meant America's regime had the legal capacity to fundamentally change by becoming more inclusive.

Connection to Rohr's Regime Values

Deciding what a regime promotes as its core values and beliefs is a difficult, yet necessary task. In fact, those core values are directly connected to perceptions of legitimacy. In a democratic regime, for example, legitimacy is directly tied to voting rights, civic participation, and the will of the people. The values of a regime undergird policy decisions, distribution of goods and services, and public discourse. Precisely who or what determines those values is contentious. When groups of people are systematically excluded from the rights and privileges that all others enjoy, legitimacy dissipates. Exclusionary regimes are not democratic ones.

John Rohr (1989) explored the importance of U.S. Supreme Court decisions as a source of ethical instruction for public administrators. He wrote that an analysis of U.S. Supreme Court decisions reveals *regime values*—public values solidified by the ratification of the Constitution and that help to define the American republic. He offered three reasons why understanding regime values was essential for those who work in the public sector. First, ethical standards are derived from the most prominent values of the regime. Second, these values bind public administrators because of the oath each one takes to uphold the Constitution. Third, these values are present in the public law of the regime. In a sense, then, regime values are the core of ethical decision-making.

Rohr's *regime values* approach is a compromise between what he framed as the *low road* approach to ethical decision-making and the *high road* approach. The *low road* approach involves a fairly mundane emphasis on agency rules and regulations. It may lead administrators to conclude that following agency rules is enough to eliminate unethical administrative behavior and they need not consider any other implications of their decisions. While he did not think it was wrong to emphasize following agency rules, he recognized the limitation of this approach. The *low road* conveys a lack of interest in opportunities to promote equity or equality as a value. The *high road* approach is based on the principle of social equity, and Rohr attributed this emphasis to the "new public administration" movement (Rohr, 1989, p. 64). Those who take the *high road* consistently look for opportunities to promote social equity and social justice. They interpret rules in ways that maximize both. The approach is prescriptive in that it encourages administrations to consider how past discrimination and inequality have disadvantaged some and privileged others. Therefore, administrators have an obligation to improve the quality of life for those who have been left behind. He further divided this approach into two sub-approaches: political philosophy and humanistic psychology, rejecting both as too impractical to use in public decision-making. After concluding that neither the *low road* nor the *high road* offered a promising opportunity for ethical decision-making, Rohr presented a third option that he called *regime values*. His approach involves a two-step process of uncovering the values of the U.S. regime, and then considering their significance in administrative decision-making.

How does one uncover the values of a regime? Rohr thought that U.S. Supreme Court decisions were the best source for learning regime values because the dialectic nature of court opinions exposes the reader to multiple perspectives on a single issue and presents conflicting interpretations of American values. Thus, the reader gains an analytical foundation that may not otherwise be available. It is important to note that administrators are bound by constitutional limits placed on administrative actions, however, within these limits most administrators enjoy significant implementation discretion. Regime values may be used to guide an administrator's discretionary decision-making. When choosing among policy alternatives and implementation strategies, the administrator decides which public values to reinforce. In what circumstances should they emphasize liberty or freedom? When should they choose equality or social justice? How these values are identified, internalized, and then applied gives us insight into how decision makers conceptualize their role in democratic institutions.

While Rohr did not provide an exhaustive list of regime values, he mentioned equality as a salient one. In his discussion of race, he stated:

> It is perhaps no exaggeration to say that questions of race, in one form or another, have been the most important issues in American politics. They have certainly been the most abiding—from the troubling compromises in the Constitution itself, through the great debate over slavery in the territories, the Civil War, the postwar amendments, the segregated South of the first half of the present century, the civil rights movement of the 1960s, the "forced busing" controversies of the 1970s, and the tumultuous transformation of the Civil Rights Commission under President Reagan. These are issues that quite literally tried men's souls and at times found them sadly wanting but at other times found them magnificently equal to the most severe moral challenges a society can face (Rohr, 1989, p. 99).

Rohr's assessment is poignant. No doubt, the country has struggled and continues to struggle with questions of equity and equality. Despite the fact that race-based inequality persists, an examination of post-Civil War Supreme Court decisions leans heavily toward the conclusion that it was on the path to recognizing equality as a regime value. As will be shown with *Shelby*, there is far less evidence that social equity has been seriously considered as a value. Further, there has been little consistency in determining what equality looks like in public policy. Does equality require us all to be treated in the same way? How should we consider cultural differences and the lingering effects of race-based disparities? Does equality prohibit corrective policies such as affirmative action? Is any racial discrimination at all acceptable?

Rohr specifically mentioned equality as a regime value and also discussed the problem of conceptualizing social equity in that context. Certainly there are nuances in determining how best to operationalize both equity and equality in governance and civic participation. While equality emphasizes sameness in treatment, equity is conceptualized more broadly in terms of what is fair and just. For example, requiring everyone to pay a poll tax before registering to vote is equality. It requires sameness in treatment regardless of how the tax disadvantages the poor and leads to lower numbers of registered voters among them. Hence, poll taxes are a form of inequity because it disadvantages those who are poor and privileges those who are not. By declaring these taxes unconstitutional, the Supreme Court promoted greater social equity.

Justice Blackmun commented on the difference between equity and equality in *Regents of the University of California v. Bakke*, 438 U.S. 265 (1978), a case in which the Supreme Court upheld affirmative action policies in higher education. These policies were challenged as a violation of the 14th Amendment's equal protection clause, and Bakke argued that this clause required all applicants to be treated the same in the admissions process. Blackmun concluded that so long as racial discrimination was a fundamental feature of society, we must pursue equity, not just equality. He wrote:

> It is somewhat ironic to have us so deeply disturbed over a program where race is an element of consciousness, and yet to be aware of the fact, as we are, that institutions of higher learning, albeit more on the undergraduate than the graduate level, have given conceded preferences up to a point to those possessed of athletic skills, to the children of alumni, to the affluent who may bestow their largess on the institutions, and to those having connections with celebrities, the famous, and the powerful.... In order to get past racism, we must first take account of race. There is no other way. And in order to treat some persons equally, we must treat them differently. We cannot—we dare not—let the Equal Protection Clause perpetuate racial supremacy (pp. 404–407).

Blackmun recognized that while equality may be our legal status, equity remains a social, political, and economic aspiration.

Few would argue that voting as a basic civil right is not germane in a democratic society. However, that right has been restricted based on race, and the Voting Rights Act of 1965 was a critical reinforcement of the 15th Amendment which guaranteed the right to vote to former slaves. The provisions in the Act strengthened protections for non-white voters and provided an avenue for voting participation consistent with the principle of "one person, one vote" as articulated in *Baker v. Carr* (1962) and *Reynolds v. Sims* (1964). However, the Court's decision in *Shelby v. Holder*, 570 U.S. 529 (2013) reveals how fragile the idea of equity is, and individual state voting policies following the case raise important questions about the level of commitment to equality as a regime value.

The *low road* approach requires that all persons be treated the same. No concern for lingering effects of historical discrimination are permissible absent substantial evidence of continued and overt state-imposed discrimination in voting processes. *The high road* approach requires us to investigate the ways in which those who have been historically marginalized still face significant barriers to voter participation. It requires us not only to remove those barriers to access, but also to aggressively confront any practices that interfere with the full participation and value of racially and economically marginalized citizens. Examples of these barriers include gerrymandering or imposing at-large voting instead of district-based voting. In *Shelby v. Holder*, 570 U.S. 529 (2013), the court chose the *low road*.

Shelby v. Holder

The U.S. Supreme Court's decision in *Shelby v. Holder*, 570 U.S. 529 (2013) is instructive when considering how equity as a value affects the legitimacy of a regime. In its opinion, the Court chose state sovereignty over equity as a value even while admitting the country's continued failures regarding racial inclusiveness and participation. Shelby County is a predominantly white, rural county in central Alabama; at the time of the lawsuit, the county was 83 percent white (U.S. Census Bureau, 2010). Although Alabama has a long and tenuous history of voter suppression practices and restrictive voter laws, a state-wide electoral shift in the mid-1990s exacerbated the problem. While the U.S. Supreme Court has consistently upheld the Voting Rights Act of 1965 as constitutional (e.g., *South Carolina v. Katzenbach* [1966], *Allen v. State Board of Election* [1969]), it has also chipped away at the provisions in Section 5, one of the more frequently contested sections (e.g., *Beer v. United States* [1976], *Reno v. Bossier Parish* [2000], *Georgia v. Ashcroft* [2003]). Section 5 held states and localities, referred to as covered jurisdictions, accountable for actions that could adversely affect voters who had historically faced discrimination in those jurisdictions by requiring federal pre-clearance for voting policy changes. Under Section 5, the U.S. Attorney General or D.C. District Court must approve changes to voting laws in these covered jurisdictions. The idea was that if this federal oversight was not included, then states could and would easily circumvent the spirit of the law, which was to ensure that all citizens enjoyed equal protection of their vote. Some covered jurisdictions, however, felt singled out. They argued that their jurisdictions did no worse in ensuring voting rights than some states and localities that were not covered under Section 5. Section 4(b), which sets the formula for determining which jurisdictions will be covered, was also challenged.

In 2010, Shelby County, Alabama, a covered jurisdiction, challenged the constitutionality of Sections 4(b) and 5, arguing that the formula used to determine covered jurisdictions violated the 10th, 14th, and 15th Amendments as well as Article IV of the U.S. Constitution. A majority of the Court determined that Section 4 was unconstitutional, effectively rendering Section 5 also unenforceable. To explain why he thought that the differential treatment of states that had historically discriminated against non-white voters was impermissible, Roberts wrote,

> To serve that purpose, Congress—if it is to divide the States—must identify those jurisdictions to be singled out on a basis that makes sense in light of current conditions. It cannot rely simply on the past. We made that clear in *Northwest Austin*, and we make it clear again today.

Specifically, the court decided: (1) it was unconstitutional for Congress to continue to apply the formula outlined in Section 4(b) because the formula was based on old data, and (2) it was unconstitutional to treat states differently or interfere with their autonomy unless there is direct and compelling evidence that they are still formally engaged in discriminatory practices.

In a stunning opinion, Chief Justice John Roberts lauded the country for being well beyond its racially discriminatory past and reasoned that because we have made such stellar progress in eliminating voter discrimination, it was no longer necessary to retain the key provisions in the Voting Rights Act directly responsible for that progress. His supposition was contrary to social science research which has concluded that while the Voting Rights Act has indeed made voting rights more secure, its provisions are still necessary to ensure that states do not backtrack. A study by Katz, Aisenbrey, Baldwin, Cheuse, and Weisbrodt (2005), determined that covered jurisdictions were more than 5.5 times as likely to be sued for voting rights violations than non-covered jurisdictions. Of the civil rights cases won by non-white voters under the Voting Rights Act, nearly 30 of them occurred in covered jurisdictions for every one that was won in a non-covered jurisdiction. Despite successful implementation of the Voting Rights Act, discrimination still occurs—a fact that Roberts did concede.

Deconstructing Roberts's opinion draws attention to the problem of conceptualizing social equity as a regime value given the country's history of racism. Consider these three points specifically:

1. Roberts's opinion is consistent with a white racial framing of the law as color-blind, a position that has been invidiously used to deny rights and privileges to non-white people.
2. Roberts' opinion is rooted in an inadequate post-racial analysis that gained momentum after the election of President Barack Obama in 2008.
3. Roberts' opinion underscores Derrick Bell's (1987) assertion that the rights of underrepresented groups will be sacrificed when granting them is no longer palatable to the majority.

In his decision, Roberts was less concerned about voting rights violations that could occur absent Section 5 pre-clearance requirements than he was about the stigma of being labeled a covered jurisdiction. He saw Section 5 as an unfair punishment that tarnishes the reputation of nine states based solely on the fact that these states denied voting rights to African Americans prior to the Voting Rights Act of 1965. He mentioned several times that these states have since redeemed themselves by removing barriers to voter participation. He concluded that while pre-clearance may have been necessary in 1965, it was no longer necessary in 2013. He wrote:

> Nearly 50 years later, things have changed dramatically. Largely because of the Voting Rights Act, "voter turnout and registration rates" in covered jurisdictions "now approach parity. Blatantly discriminatory evasions of

federal decrees are rare. And minority candidates hold office at unprecedented levels." *Northwest Austin, supra*, at 202. The tests and devices that blocked ballot access have been forbidden nationwide for over 40 years. Yet the Act has not eased §5's restrictions or narrowed the scope of §4's coverage formula along the way. Instead, those extraordinary and unprecedented features have been reauthorized as if nothing has changed, and they have grown even stronger. Because §5 applies only to those jurisdictions singled out by §4, the Court turns to consider that provision (*Shelby v. Holder*, 570 U.S. 529, 2013, p. 3).

Notice how Roberts overemphasized the progress that has been made since 1965 and underemphasized the inequities that still exist as though those have little to no significance. This is not an equity-based approach, but rather one in which Roberts clearly accepts disparities that are not blatant and obvious. In his majority opinion, he went on to state,

> Regardless of how to look at the record, however, no one can fairly say that it shows anything approaching the "pervasive," "flagrant," "widespread," and "rampant" discrimination that faced Congress in 1965, and that clearly distinguished the covered jurisdictions from the rest of the Nation at that time (*Shelby v. Holder*, 570 U.S. 529, 2013, p. 21).

This statement minimizes the effect of ongoing practices that perpetuate voting discrimination. Justice Ginsberg referred to these persistent inequities as "second generation barriers," and in her dissenting opinion, she explained why these barriers were still important.

Finally, Roberts rejected the argument that it was the deterrent effect of Section 5 that made the most difference in eliminating discriminatory voter practices, and hence Section 5 must remain a critical part of voting rights enforcement. It is a point that Justice Scalia also brought up during oral arguments. Scalia stated,

> You could always say, oh, there has been improvement, but the only reason there has been improvement are these extraordinary procedures that deny the states sovereign powers which the Constitution preserves to them. So, since the only reason it's improved is because of these procedures, we must continue those procedures in perpetuity. (*Shelby v. Holder*, 570 U.S. 529, 2013, Oral Arguments, https://www.c-span.org/video/?311193-1/shelby-county-v-holder-oral-argument.)

Scalia believed that there was a point at which we must simply accept that inequities will always exist, and hence we should not overburden states with having to address them. A majority of the Court agreed. Within the past five years, we have witnessed the effects of the Court's complacency.

Normative Implications for Theory and Practice

The major implication of *Shelby v. Holder*, 570 U.S. 529 (2013) is the legal affirmation of a trend that was beginning to emerge prior to the decision (hence
the need for Supreme Court intervention)—a voting regime with significant
restrictions affecting non-whites. This is being accomplished by two parallel
actions—voter restrictions that disproportionally negatively impact blacks and
voter expansions that disproportionally favor whites.

Relative to voter restrictions, implications of *Shelby v. Holder*, 570 U.S. 529 (2013)
on the American regime began immediately. On the same day of the *Shelby* decision, Texas announced it would implement a strict voter ID law that had previously
failed the pre-clearance process. As Figure 10.1 suggests, in 2016, the first national
election following the *Shelby* decision three years earlier, "counties that were freed
from federal oversight saw minority voter turnout drop more sharply that it had
in decades" (Impacts, 2018). Stricter voting laws impacted voters in 23 states since
2010. "The most common restrictions involve voter ID laws, but they also include
additional burdens on registration, cutbacks to early voting and absentee voting,
and reduced voting access for people with past criminal convictions" (Weiser &
Feldman, 2018, p. 6). Table 10.1 provides a listing of voting restrictions by state.

While much of the focus has appropriately been on voter restrictions affecting
minority communities, particularly in southern states, there is also an expansion
of voting laws permitting ease of registration through mechanisms such as auto-
matic voter registration in a handful of states. With the notable exception of
California, the states that enacted these voting expansions are generally white,
with low percentages of African Americans. These states, include, for example,
Alaska, Colorado, Rhode Island, and Vermont (Weiser & Feldman, 2018, p. 11).
Li, Pomantell, and Schraufnagel (2018) developed a cost of voting index (COVI)

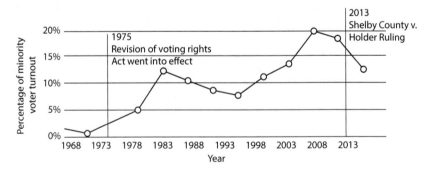

FIGURE 10.1 Impact of the voting rights act and minority voter turnout in presidential elections (From Impacts of the Voting Rights Act and the Supreme
Court's Shelby Ruling, October 26, 2018, https://www.hks.harvard.edu/
research-insights/policy-topics/politics/impacts-voting-rights-act-and-supreme-
courts-shelby-ruling.)

TABLE 10.1 Voting laws since 2011

State	Voting restrictions
Alabama	• Strict voter ID requirement (2011 law) • Documentary proof of citizenship (2011 law; not yet implemented)
Arizona	• Documentary proof of citizenship to register (2004 ballot initiative; currently blocked for registrations using federal form) • Polling place consolidation (2016 law) • Limitations on mail-in ballot collection (2016 law)
Arkansas	• Voter ID requirement (2017 law)
Florida	• Reduced early voting period (2011 law, mitigated by 2012 court ruling and by subsequent 2013 statute restoring some early voting days) • Curbed voter registration drives (2011 law, mitigated by court decisions) • Reduced access to rights restoration for those with past criminal convictions (2011 gubernatorial action)
Georgia	• "No match, no vote" limit on access to voter registration (2017 law) • Reduced early voting period (2010 law) • Documentary proof of citizenship to register (2009 law) • Strict voter ID requirement (2006 law)
Illinois	• Curbed voter registration drives (2011 law)
Indiana	• Aggressive voter purge requirements (2017 law) • Documentary proof of citizenship for certain individuals (2013 law) • Strict voter ID requirement (2006 law)
Iowa	• Voter ID requirement (2017 law; will be partially implemented in 2018) • Restrictions on voter registration drives (2017 law) • Limited access to election-day registration (2017 law) • Limited early and absentee voting (2017 law) • Stricter voting rights restoration policy for the formerly incarcerated (2011 reversed executive action)
Kansas	• Strict voter ID requirement (2011 law) • Documentary proof of citizenship (2011 law; currently blocked for registrations at motor vehicle offices and those using federal voter registration forms)
Mississippi	• Strict voter ID requirement (2011 ballot initiative)
Missouri	• Voter ID requirement (2016 law and ballot initiative)
Nebraska	• Reduced early voting period (2013 law)
New Hampshire	• Restricted student voting and registration (2017 law) • Voter ID requested, but not required (2017 law)
North Dakota	• Voter ID requirement (2017 law, partially halted by court, and less restrictive than earlier law struck down by court)

(*Continued*)

TABLE 10.1 (Continued)

State	Voting restrictions
Ohio	• Reduced early voting period and abolished same-day registration period (2014 law) • Restricted absentee and provisional ballot rules (2014 law)
Rhode Island	• Voter ID requirement (2011 law)
South Carolina	• Voter ID requirement (2011 law, mitigated after lawsuit)
South Dakota	• Stricter voting rights restoration policy for the formerly incarcerated (2012 law)
Tennessee	• Strict voter ID requirement (2011 law) • Reduced early voting period (2011 law) • Proof of citizenship required for certain individuals (2011 law)
Texas	• Voter ID requirement (2017 law, which is less restrictive than 2011 law struck down by court, but more restrictive than the temporary ID requirement in place in 2016) • Curbed voter registration drives (2011 law)
Virginia	• Strict voter ID requirement (2012 law) • Restricted third-party voter registration (2012 law)
West Virginia	• Reduced early voting period (2011 law)
Wisconsin	• Voter ID requirement (2012 law, implemented for the first time in 2016) • Added longer residency requirement before a person could register to vote (2012)

Note: This table itemizes restrictions imposed by each state (Weiser & Feldman, 2018, p. 7).

by examining voter registration factors including voting convenience, identification requirements, poll hours, registration deadlines, registration restrictions, registration-drive restrictions, and pre-registration rules. Using U.S. Census demographic data, Figure 10.2 examines the association between the COVI and race. In general, states with a higher percentage white population also have easier voting requirements. Voting is easiest in Oregon, which allows voters to automatically register and cast ballots by mail. Whites comprise 85.1 percent of Oregon's population and blacks comprise 1.9 percent. In comparison, voting is most difficult in Mississippi which does not permit early voting and voters are required to register 30 days before an election. Blacks comprise 37.5 percent of the population in Mississippi, while whites comprise 59 percent.

The impact of *Shelby v. Holder*, 570 U.S. 529 (2013), is further magnified by the United State's continued record as one of the world's strictest nations in denying voting rights to citizens convicted of crimes.

> As of 2016, an estimated 6.1 million people are disenfranchised due to a felony conviction, a figure that has escalated dramatically in recent decades. There were an estimated 1.17 million people disenfranchised in 1976, 3.34 million in 1996, and 5.85 million in 2010.

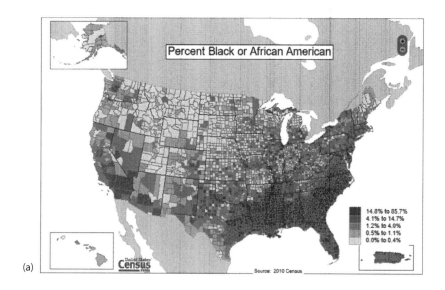

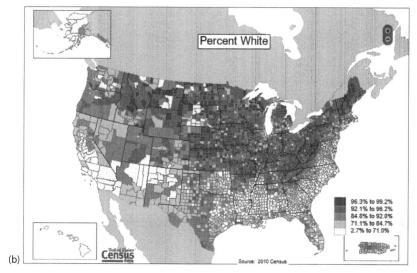

FIGURE 10.2 Maps of the United States by race and COVI: (a) percent black or African American, (b) percent white, and (c) cost of voting index by state

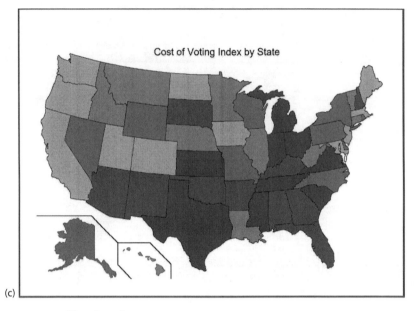

FIGURE 10.2 (Continued)

In fact, "one in 13 African Americans of voting age is disenfranchised, a rate more than four times greater than that of non-African Americans" (The Sentencing Project, 2016, p. 3).

Taken together, these trends suggest a shrinking democratic polity to formulate and determine regime values. Aristotle embraced a hierarchical society, with different people occupying different places in society. Ultimately, Aristotle believed that this would benefit society as a whole, presumably those at the top could be trusted to make decisions of benefit for the remaining collective. In contrast, Rohr did not advocate for a ruling class, "but instead [was] explaining the role-relationship of rulers and citizens by reference to the political regime they both serve" (Uhr, 2014, p. 148). The inherent paradox in both perspectives is very limited evidence suggesting those with political power and voice will work in the best interest of the marginalized and disenfranchised. There is a saturation of racial inequities in a broad spectrum of public policy areas including education, health, environment, criminal justice, employment, drug policy, and economic development, providing compelling evidence that this is indeed not the case.

Conclusion

As Rohr's legacy suggests, regime values are important and Supreme Court decisions are instructive in communicating these values. The Supreme Court also has a decisive voice in defining who constitutes the regime via decisions affecting citizenship and voting rights. *Shelby v. Holder*, 570 U.S. 529 (2013) has paved the way for more restrictive voting, and trends suggest African Americans are being negatively impacted by recent voting requirements at the state level. Fundamentally, the result is a shrinking regime relative to minorities in general and African Americans specifically. Voting rights define the electorate. The electorate chooses leaders. Leaders develop and pass public policies. These public policies impact all facets of social life—housing, criminal justice, education, health, and environment—to name a few. The preamble of U.S. Constitution leads with "We the People." A direct implication of the *Shelby* decision is that the voting "we" enabled by the hard fought Voting Rights Act of 1965 is slowly eroding in ways that directly counter public administration values of social equity.

References

Bell, D. (1987). *And we are not saved: The elusive quest for racial justice.* New York, NY: Basic Books.

Epsten, D. L., Pildes, R. H., de la Garza, R. O., & O'Halloran, S. (Eds.). (2006). *The future of the voting rights act.* New York, NY: Russell Sage Foundation.

Frederickson, H. G. (1990). Public administration and social equity. *Public Administration Review, 50*(2), 228–237.

Gooden, S. T. (2015). From equality to social equity. In M. Guy & M. Rubin (Eds.), *Public administration evolving: From foundations to the future* (pp. 211–232). New York, NY: Routledge.

Hopps, J. G., & Bowles, D. D. (2015). A response to Shelby County, Alabama v. Holder: Energizing, educating and empowering voters. *Phylon, 52*(2), 1–23.

Impacts of the Voting Rights Act and the Supreme Court's Shelby Ruling. (2018, October 26). Retrieved from https://www.hks.harvard.edu/research-insights/policy-topics/politics/impacts-voting-rights-act-and-supreme-courts-shelby-ruling

Katz, E., Aisenbrey, M., Baldwin, A., Cheuse, E., & Weisbrodt, A. (2005). Documenting discrimination in voting: Judicial findings under Section 2 of the Voting Rights Act since 1982. Final Report of the Voting Rights Initiative, University of Michigan Law School.

Li, Q., Pomantell, M., & Schraufnagel, S. (2018). Cost of voting in the American states. *Election Law Journal: Rules, Politics, and Policy, 17*(3), 234–247. https://doi.org/10.1089/elj.2017.0478

Rawls, J. (1971). *A theory of justice.* Cambridge, MA: Harvard University Press.

Rohr, J. A. (1989). *Ethics for bureaucrats: An essay on law and values* (2nd ed.). New York, NY: Marcel Dekker.

Sears, M. A. (2018, April 6). Aristotle, father of scientific racism. *The Washington Post*. Retrieved from https://www.washingtonpost.com/news/made-by-history/wp/2018/04/06/aristotle-father-of-scientific-racism/?utm_term=.81911021dde0

Stone, D. A. (1997). *Policy paradox: The art of political decision making*. New York, NY: W. W. Norton & Company.

Uggen, C., Larson, R., & Shannon, S. (2016). 6 million lost voters: State-level estimates of felony disenfranchisement, 2016. *The Sentencing Project*. Retrieved from: https://www.sentencingproject.org/wp-content/uploads/2016/10/6-Million-Lost-Voters.pdf

Uhr, J. (2014). John Rohr's concept of regime values: Locating theory in public administration. *Administration & Society, 46*(2), 141–152.

U.S. Census Bureau. (2010). *Quick facts*. Shelby County, AL. Retrieved from https://www.census.gov/quickfacts/shelbycountyalabama

Weiser, W. R., & Feldman, M. (2018). The state of voting 2018. Brennan Center for Justice. Retrieved from https://www.brennancenter.org/publication/state-voting-2018

11

A PROPOSAL FOR STRATEGIC CONTROLS TO ENSURE SOCIAL EQUITY IN THE CRIMINAL JUSTICE SYSTEM

Henry Smart III

In this chapter, I offer a response to an important "what if." What if public servants fail to uphold the values that are embedded in the United States (U.S.) Constitution? In some realms of government, the answer to this question is aligned with racially biased outcomes. This is especially true when we examine the outcomes of the criminal justice system—corrections, the courts, and law enforcement. Within the correctional system (i.e., prisons), black and Latinx citizens are overrepresented populations (Alexander, 2011; Burkhardt, 2017). In terms of the courts, previous research has found that blacks and citizens with darker skin color tend to receive harsher sentences (Burch, 2015; Eberhardt, Davies, Purdie-Vaughns, & Johnson, 2006; Fischman & Schanzenbach, 2012; Viglione, Hannon, & DeFina, 2011). Unlike the correctional system and the courts, findings related to racial bias in law enforcement are limited by several factors, such as a lack of data collection standards and the blue wall (Kleinig, 2001; Nolan, 2009). However, the available scholarship and reoccurring news stories do suggest that local policing, in particular, is plagued by similar challenges (Balko, 2018; Epp, Maynard-Moody, & Haider-Markel, 2014).

From the initial point of contact a citizen might have with the criminal justice system to the more advanced processes of justice, there is a consistent theme of racial inequity. Moreover, we should assume that bureaucrats play a fundamental role in the perpetuation of this inequity. Even if the majority of bureaucrats use their afforded administrative discretion to uphold the Constitution, the maladaptive behaviors of a few can create a pattern of civil rights violations and garner distrust from the citizenry. Furthermore, injury from the ill use of administrative discretion is more detrimental when the target is a member of a marginalized group. The following will provide some general context to help guide our thinking away from the normalization of racial inequities in the criminal justice system (CJS). Three proposals are offered with the intent to address divergent administrative behavior within the respective components of CJS—local policing, the courts, and corrections.

Context

In his seminal text, *Ethics for Bureaucrats: An essay on law and values,* Rohr (1978) expressed an aspiration for a "more ethically alert bureaucracy" (p. 8). Rohr's vision is achievable, but to get there, we must address some major roadblocks that are faced by contemporary bureaucrats and their organizations. In fact, it could be said that with the expansion of administrative discretion (Rohr, 1998), bureaucratic behaviors have drifted far from the original intent of our *amended* Constitution (Alexander, 2011). These mal-adaptive behaviors have been defined in a myriad of ways to include terms like dissent (O'Leary, 2010) and conscious/unconscious bias (Downs, 1967; Grafstein, 1948; Kahneman, 2003; Lipsky, 1980; Simon, 1997; Smart, 2019; Tversky & Kahneman, 1981). No matter how bureaucrats exercise their administrative discretion, there is always the potential for their decisions to exacerbate ethical drift (Kleinman, 2006). In terms of public organizations, they currently lack the ability to adequately detect when administrative discretion is abused at a low level. However, most public organizations have a general understanding of overt abuses of administrative discretion. With these two considerations in mind, the following proposals offer controls to reduce ethical drift which should help bureaucrats and their organizations get closer to Rohr's vision. For each proposal, I will: (1) provide some examples of low-level abuse and/or overt abuse of administrative discretion; (2) provide the specifics of the response/proposal; and (3) provide the rationale that motivated the response. It is important to note that the proposals are specifically geared toward practitioners and students of ethics, local policing, the courts, and corrections. However, elements of each proposal can be morphed to fit other contexts.

The Proposals: Strategic Controls to Address Divergent Discretion

Local Policing

Low-Level Abuses of Administrative Discretion

This personal example is offered to illustrate a low-level abuse of administrative discretion within the context of local policing. During my first trip to New York, I found myself lost in Times Squares. I noticed a friendly police officer talking to a family. I moved closer to listen to their conversation. He was giving them directions, but also making recommendations of things to do in New York. Based on what I had witnessed from their interaction, I deemed the officer as approachable, friendly, and willing to help ordinary citizens. When he was done chatting with the family, he slightly turned in my direction, but made no eye contact and his face no longer carried a smile. I asked him if he could help with directions. At first, he pretended to not hear or see me. I asked again. His response was curt and purposefully useless, and not once did he establish eye contact with me. Even with his sour response, I maintained a kind persona. Now, what would make this police officer change his disposition in such a drastic manner? I had experienced this type of passive distain before, and my mind had associated the behavior with bigotry, in a general sense. Each member of the family who he was chatting with were white people, the officer was white, and I am black. I walked away feeling like I had experienced low-level racism.

Overt Abuses of Administrative Discretion

With the growth of social media, more Americans are being exposed to a pre-existing theme of *unarmed black men dying during a law enforcement moment.* Some of the particulars involved with these stories do vary, but the majority of the cases share specific facts. For instance, the suspected criminal behavior was trivial or the law enforcement officer's decisions were informed by false perceptions. The most important shared fact is that these men were unarmed. One of the more complex cases is that of Philando Castile.

On July 6, 2016, Philando and his girlfriend were pulled over by the local police (CNN, 2017). During this traffic stop, Philando disclosed to the officer that he had in his possession a registered firearm and he disclosed the location of the weapon. He was then instructed to retrieve his license. When he followed the officer's instructions, the officer shot and killed him. We can only assume that the officer thought Philando was reaching for his gun instead of his documentation. The officer was charged with second-degree manslaughter, but was acquitted of the charge (CNN, 2017; Silverstein, 2017).

In 2018, Justice Sotomayor issued a dissenting opinion that captures the messaging that stems from these types of cases and the similar outcomes—officers not charged or charged, but not found guilty. Justice Sotomayor expressed her dissent with the U.S. Supreme Court's liberal ruling on the use of deadly force in which she stated that the U.S. Supreme Court's decision sent "an alarming signal to law enforcement officers…shoot first, think later" (Alonso, 2018; *Kisela v. Hughes*, 584 U.S. 15, 2018). She also expressed concern that these types of rulings (e.g., tone deaf) will send a message to the public that "palpably unreasonable [police] conduct will go unpunished" (*Kisela v. Hughes*, 584 U.S. 15, 2018).

Proposal

Screening for individual biases. To reduce the likelihood of bias policing, police departments should screen incoming officers for biases that might hinder their ability to uphold social equity. These screenings should not be used as a mechanism to disqualify incoming candidates for service. Instead, the screening process should be used to develop a training portfolio and a mentoring schema that will support the officer's development. All red flags identified during the screening process should be notated in the officer's record and revisited on a routine basis to ensure that s/he is developing toward a standard of equitable law enforcement. While the primary focus of this discussion is racial equity, the screening process should not be limited to racial bias. Other biases should be taken into account. At minimum, the screening process should include domains for biases related to gender and sexual orientation. When designing the screening process, police departments should consult professionals who are versed in the implementation of strategies to address complex phenomena like *othering, micro-aggressions,* and *implicit bias.*

Universal enhancements to body-worn cameras. Several local police departments have adopted body-worn cameras (BWCs) to help with their policing efforts (Lum, Stoltz, Koper, & Scherer, 2019; White, 2019). While some researchers are steadily working to determine if BWCs are having a positive impact on police behavior (Yokum, Ravishankar, & Coppock, 2017), it may be too early to offer up a conclusive answer. However, as we wait for more data to make this determination, there are a few enhancements that are worthy of immediate consideration. First, policies on how to utilize BWC technology vary across law enforcement departments and agencies (CoS, 2019; NCSL, 2019). Some police departments provide specific instructions on how to use the equipment (CoS, 2019), while others provide limited guidance (NCSL, 2019). In terms of determining the effectiveness of BWCs, this variability in the implementation of the technology has the potential to produce conflicting narratives. Federal legislation could bring about needed organization and increase accountability across the board.

Here are a few considerations that can be addressed via a federal mandate. At no time should a police officer be allowed to turn off a BWC

(IACP, 2014). Humans tend to behave better when they think they are being watched (Farrar, 2013; Pfattheicher & Keller, 2015). If we agree to the general premise that BWCs function as an accountability mechanism, then we must agree that in some instances we are allowing officers to opt out of accountability when they are allowed to power down the camera. This "opting out" can lead to skewed facts and ethical drift. Therefore, Congress should enact funded-legislation that mandates the use of BWCs for all law enforcement agencies and departments who have routine face-to-face contact with the public. Second, the legislation should specifically state that at no time are the devices to be turned off by the law enforcement officer in service. Third, captured footage should be automatically uploaded to a central server—for all agencies and departments—and a local server—for each department/agency. This last condition will enable external reviewers to determine if local police departments have altered footage, and it will provide local leadership (e.g., police chiefs) with access to their unique footage.

Rationale

This proposal is centered on Amendment 14 of the Bill of Rights. Amendment 14, Section 1, of the Bill of Rights (*Rights Guaranteed: Privileges and Immunities of Citizenship, Due Process, and Equal Protection*) states that:

> All persons born or naturalized in the United States, and subject to the jurisdiction thereof, are citizens of the United States and of the State wherein they reside. No State shall make or enforce any law which shall abridge the privileges or immunities of citizens of the United States; nor shall any State deprive any person of life, liberty, or property, without due process of law; nor deny to any person within its jurisdiction the equal protection of the laws (NARAb, 2019).

Prior to BWCs, dash cameras were the only means for recording official police business. If the activities of a traffic stop moved beyond the view of a dash camera, the courts were left to rely on the testimonies of the defendant, the plaintiff, and the witnesses. However, there might be gaps in people's memories and sometimes parties may alter their testimonies for the sake of self-preservation. Altered facts can hinder the courts ability to avoid the deprivation of life, liberty, and property and the ability to provide equal treatment across cases. What happens during a local policing incident and how that story is told in court can contribute to violations of Amendment 14. If we were to put controls (e.g., the inability to turn off BWCs) in place to reduce the influence of ill-motives, we can reduce the likelihood of civil rights violations.

The Courts

Overt Abuses of Administrative Discretion

Viglione et al. (2011) conducted a study in which they reviewed the records of 12,158 female inmates. Each record was coded with skin color notations, "non-light" or "light" (Viglione et al., 2011). The authors found that those coded as having light skin received shorter prison sentences and served shorter stints of their sentence than their "non-light" counterparts (Viglione et al., 2011). What we can surmise from this study is that the inmates skin color played a role in how they were judged by the courts.

Proposal

Physically segregate the defendant. To reduce the likelihood of biased court decisions, we should cloak the physical traits of the defendant from the deciding party (jurors or judges). This can be accomplished by physically segregating the defendant from the decision-maker(s) during court proceedings. The same physical segregation could be applied for all other participants—plaintiff, witnesses, and the judge/jurors.

Rationale

This proposal is centered on the element of impartiality expressed in Amendment 6 of the Bill of Rights. Amendment 6 (*Rights of the Accused in Criminal Prosecutions*) states that:

> In all criminal prosecutions, the accused shall enjoy the right to a speedy and public trial, by an impartial jury of the State and district wherein the crime shall have been committed, which district shall have been previously ascertained by law, and to be informed of the nature and cause of the accusation; to be confronted with the witnesses against him; to have compulsory process for obtaining witnesses in his favor, and to have the Assistance of Counsel for his defense (NARAa, 2019).

Impartiality implies equal treatment (Nagel, 1973), however, it is well documented that individuals are likely to make biased decisions that are based on perceptions of physical traits (Blair, Judd, & Chapleau, 2004; Eberhardt, Goff, Purdie, & Davies, 2004; Eberhardt et al., 2006). The proposed change would reduce this likelihood by removing physical traits from the equation. This idea is inspired by

John Rawl's (1971) conception of the *Veil of Ignorance*. The general premise of the *Veil of Ignorance* is that justice can be achieved by keeping the decision-maker(s) unaware of extraneous factors (Rawls, 1971).

While Rawl's argument has been discussed for several decades, his ideas have not influenced the arrangement of U.S. courtrooms. There could be a multitude of reasons why this is the case, but I will address the two obvious points. First, people may not be motivated to advocate for the rights of the defendant. However, even if a party is guilty of committing a crime, their punishment should not be based on trivial factors such as physicality, ethnicity, skin color, or gender. As expressed in Amendment 6, even the accused party has rights. Second, it could be assumed that the associated cost to implement a "cloaked courtroom" would be a cost suffered by the public. In 2017, it costs approximately $36,299 to incarcerate a federal inmate, which is about $99 per day (FBP, 2018). During the same year, there were approximately 185,617 federal inmates (FBP, 2019). For federal inmates alone, the United States spent approximately $6.73 billion dollars on incarceration (FBP, 2018, 2019). The addressment of biased decisions could help to reduce the current budget for federal imprisonment. Moreover, the cost of cloaking the identity of the defendant would amount to the cost of disguising their voice and having them participate in the court proceedings in a separate room. In terms of budget, these are low-cost changes.

If we take this idea even further, there are some additional benefits for all parties and an important caveat to consider. If the plaintiff, defendant, and the judge/jurors were all in separate rooms, this would minimize the likelihood of biased decisions, and in some cases this arrangement might heighten safety for the plaintiff, the witnesses, and the decision-maker(s)—the judge or the jurors. Granted, the construction of the room would need to prevent the ability for any party to see the other parties. However, some of our established norms can introduce an element of complexity to this frame. In some cases, the identities of the defendant(s) can be figured out based on the stereotypical nature of the crime. For example, it is common knowledge that crack charges are associated with the statuses of "people of color" and the "poor." These types of case details might serve as a signal to some decision-makers. Moreover, the proposed change to the standard courtroom layout and procedures would afford additional protection for victims and increase anonymity for jurors. While the accused has the right to confront their accuser(s), the definition of confrontation can be altered to allow for this proposed reconfiguration. What may come of this are testimonies that are not influenced by intimidation and juror decisions that are based on facts that are void of the influence of extraneous factors such as the defendant's race and/or skin color (see Figure 11.1).

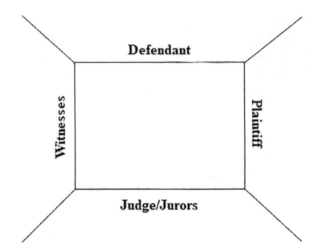

FIGURE 11.1 Depiction of a cloaked courtroom

Corrections

Overt Abuses of Administrative Discretion

The following cases illustrate the need for additional oversight within correctional facilities. In the first case, footage of two correctional officers surfaced in which they physically abused a mentally ill inmate-Terrance Debose who was strapped to a chair and gagged (Ferrise, 2019). Prior to issuing the beating, the officers turned off their body cameras. The incident, however, was captured by the closed-circuit television (Ferrise, 2019). In a second case, an onlooker/inmate captured footage of a fellow inmate—Otis Miller being beaten by three correctional officers (AP, 2019). The onlooker used a cellular phone to capture the incident (AP, 2019). In both cases, the abused inmates were African American males. Had it not been for the leaked video footage, both incidents may have gone unaddressed by the respective facility.

Proposal

Implement two-fold video capture. To reduce the likelihood of mistreatment in correctional facilities, there should be a two-fold video capture. First, all correctional officers (CO) should be equipped with BWCs. Similar to the proposal for local policing, COs should not have the ability to turn off their cameras. Data collected from their cameras should be automatically uploaded to a server and reviewed by supervisors on a routine basis. Second, all correctional facilities should be equipped with an adequate closed-circuit television system. An adequate system would include video coverage in all areas where inmates are the most vulnerable. This should include areas where an inmate can be singled out or find themselves out of the general view of their fellow inmates. Access to television footage and knowledge of the camera locations should be granted to a limited number of supervisors. These measures should be implemented in all state and federal prisons and all local jails.

Implement an annual survey. The American Correctional Association (ACA) provides ethical guidance and training for correctional officers (ACA, 2019). On an annual basis, the ACA should survey COs to gauge the respondents' ethical conduct and that of their fellow COs. For the sake of job security and physical safety, the survey should be implemented in a way that guarantees complete anonymity for the respondents. This mechanism could serve as an opportunity for the ethical authority, the ACA, to enhance its relationship with prison leadership. It would also provide an external avenue to blow the whistle on rogue COs.

Train rotating moles. The ACA, in tandem with the Federal Bureau of Prisons and state equivalent agencies, should make a concerted effort to train COs who rotate in and out of prisons for the sole purpose of identifying and reporting ethical violations. Since the ACA has established the ethical code for COs and it provides CO trainings, they have a clear grasp on what is considered acceptable behavior.

Rationale

This proposal is centered on the current lack of proper supervision within U.S. penal system and Amendment 8 of the Bill of Rights which states that:

> Excessive bail shall not be required, nor excessive fines imposed, nor cruel and unusual punishments inflicted (BRI, 2019).

Amendment 8 is based on the premise of fair treatment. With this principle in mind, the proposed innovations seek to ensure that all prisoners are treated the same and that punishments issued by COs are proportional to inmate behavior. In addition, the innovations are inspired by states that have started to implement BWCs as part of their accountability measures for correctional facilities, which includes New York, South Carolina, Maryland, and North Carolina (Bui, 2016; Fries, 2019; NJE, 2013). Some states are in the process of conducting pilot programs, while others have passed funded legislation to support the innovation (NCSL, 2019). South Carolina has enacted funded legislation that requires BWCs for their police officers, and they have conducted a successful BWC pilot at their Cannon Detention Center in Charleston (NJE, 2013). Without question, BWCs in correctional facilities would provide an extra layer of protection for COs and inmates. For cases when there are conflicting stories, COs can rely on the BWC footage to corroborate their account, and the same surety would apply to inmates.

Concluding Thoughts and the Implications

In general, the constitutional approach to public administration is to overemphasize "positive constitutionalism:" arguing the legitimacy of public administration against its critics...doing so, it has underemphasized, however, the relevance of "negative constitutionalism:" the need for constitutional checks on government power (Overeem, 2015, p. 49).

This passage captures the essence of what is needed to move the U.S. criminal justice system toward Rohr's ideal of a "more ethically alert bureaucracy" (Rohr, 1971, p. 8). To start this shift in paradigm and practice, we must first acknowledge the current conditions surrounding ethical drift and administrative discretion. In terms of ethical drift, the CJS is currently in a reactive mode. Only a few examples of civil rights violations were shared here, but other authors have carefully outlined patterns of violations throughout a reactive system that suffers from disorganization, inequities, and limited compassion (Alexander, 2011; Alonso, 2018; Burkhardt, 2017; FBP, 2018; Fischman & Schanzenbach, 2012; Smart, 2019; Weitzer, 2015). Our preparation to avoid these violations is lackluster, and often these behaviors lead to overspending (e.g., lawsuits) as a response to rogue behavior. If we embrace the proposals presented here, or similar ones, we can start to shift CJS models toward a preventive stance. In terms of administrative discretion, we can no longer give public servants the benefit of the doubt. We should continue to hold them to a high standard, but plan for the likelihood that they may have a fall from grace. In short, let us assume that they are just as human, and flawed, as the citizens they are entrusted to protect and care for. This paradigm should influence our planning strategies, our implementation of justice, and our evaluative methods.

Ethical Drift: Taking a Preventive Stance

As Overeem (2015) has argued, we must consider negative constitutionalism. Without constitutional checks, a defense for the positive aspects of constitutionalism will not withstand the surmounting evidence of failed government. If we set a course to address crime, we must also plan to address the potential crimes of public administrators. This means that every policy and practice manual should take into account that there will be actors who will want to insert a "but" into the established guidance (Kleinman, 2006). Therefore, strict adherence to our values will require structural oversight and prudence. What I mean by structural oversight is the condition of having accountability measures built into our routines (e.g., supervisor reviews), embedded into the physical structures that make up public space (e.g., segregated courtrooms), and captured in our evaluative strategies (e.g., ethics surveys). This is not to say we do not already have such measures in place, but given the current challenges faced by the criminal justice system, there is a need for more structure. To achieve this reality, we must ask questions like "How can this rule be circumvented by public servants?," or more explicitly stated—"How do we control the behaviors of public servants to ensure this task is completed in accordance with the guidance?" Just as we aim to control citizen behavior to prevent fraud, waste, and abuse, we must do the same for public servant behavior. The potential rewards associated with assuming a preventive stance might include an increase in job satisfaction for public servants, improved social equity outcomes, and better trust in government.

Administrative Discretion: Humanizing the Doing of Justice

In the case of vulnerable populations, especially, there are multiple examples of how administrative discretion can be used to perpetuate negative constitutionalism (March, 2016; Weitzer, 2015). Mosher stated that [public] officials should be "regarded and regard themselves as servants, not masters, of the people" (Shafritz & Hyde, 1978, p. 494). In this passage, he was referring to those in the higher ranks of public service, however, this general premise is applicable to all levels of public service. Part of humanizing agents of justice is the process of building in soft- and hard-coded controls that remind bureaucrats of their human nature and that of the general public. We currently issue soft-coded controls by way of methods like oaths and training. Though, if the soft-coded controls fail, then hard-coded controls (e.g., surveillance systems) should be in place to watch over public servant behavior.

The most important point about humanizing justice is related to how agents of justice use their power and authority. When administrative discretion is coupled with power and authority, there is the potential for the bureaucratic actor to forget the purpose of their role or to extend their authority beyond the scope of their charge (March, 2016). In the aforementioned examples of abuse of administrative discretion, the public servants were acting like masters. To prevent these types of abuses from occurring in the future, the power and authority afforded to public servants must be continuously monitored and reproved when necessary. A concerted effort to humanize the role of the public servant, whether it be by way of soft-coded controls or hard-coded controls, has the potential to reduce instances of abuse. There is also the possible benefit of building stronger ties between the criminal justice community and the general public.

References

Alexander, M. (2011). The new Jim Crow. *Ohio State Journal of Criminal Law, 9*, 7.

Alonso, J. A. (2018). How police culture affects the way police departments view and utilize deadly force policies under the fourth amendment. *Arizona Law Review, 60*, 987.

American Correctional Association. (2019). Legacy of care. Retrieved from https://www.aca.org

Associated Press. (2019). 3 guards charged in inmate beating after leaked video. Retrieved from https://www.apnews.com/1ce8adb24bbc4d6abf4696f2f1355269

Balko, R. (2018, September, 18). There's overwhelming evidence that the criminal-justice system is racist. Here's the proof. *Washington Post.*

Bill of Rights Institute. (2019). *Bill of rights of the United States of America (1791).* Retrieved from https://billofrightsinstitute.org/founding-documents/bill-of-rights/

Blair, I. V., Judd, C. M., & Chapleau, K. M. (2004). The influence of Afrocentric facial features in criminal sentencing. *Psychological Science, 15*(10), 674–679. https://doi.org/10.1111/j.0956-7976.2004.00739.x

Bui, L. (2016). Maryland County equips some detention officers with body cameras. Retrieved from http://wapo.st/1PTFOJH?tid=ss_mail&utm_term=.1219252ed873

Burch, T. (2015). Skin color and the criminal justice system: Beyond black-white disparities in sentencing. *Journal of Empirical Legal Studies, 12*(3), 395–420.

Burkhardt, B. C. (2017). Who is in private prisons? Demographic profiles of prisoners and workers in American private prisons. *International Journal of Law, Crime and Justice, 51*, 24–33.

Cable News Network. (2017). Philando castile shooting: Dashcam video shows rapid event. Retrieved from https://www.cnn.com/2017/06/20/us/philando-castile-shooting-dashcam/index.html

City of Sacramento. (2019). Sacramento police department: General orders 525.07-body-work camera. Retrieved from https://www.cityofsacramento.org/-/media/Corporate/Files/Police/Transparency/GO-52507-Body-Worn-Camera-11619.pdf?la=en

Downs, A. (1967). *Inside bureaucracy: A Rand Corporation research study.* Boston, MA: Little, Brown and Company.

Eberhardt, J. L., Davies, P. G., Purdie-Vaughns, V. J., & Johnson, S. L. (2006). Looking deathworthy: Perceived stereotypicality of black defendants predicts capital-sentencing outcomes. *Psychological Science, 17*(5), 383–386. https://doi.org/10.1111/j.1467-9280.2006.01716.x

Eberhardt, J. L., Goff, P. A., Purdie, V. J., & Davies, P. G. (2004). Seeing black: Race, crime, and visual processing. *Journal of Personality and Social Psychology, 87*(6), 876–893. https://doi.org/10.1037/0022-3514.87.6.876

Epp, C. R., Maynard-Moody, S., & Haider-Markel, D. P. (2014). *Pulled over: How police stops define race and citizenship.* Chicago, IL: University of Chicago Press.

Farrar, T. (2013). *Self-awareness to being watched and socially-desirable behavior: A field experiment on the effect of body-worn cameras on police use-of-force.* New Delhi: Police Foundation.

Federal Bureau of Prisons. (2018). Annual determination of average cost of incarceration. Retrieved from https://www.federalregister.gov/documents/2018/04/30/2018-09062/annual-determination-of-average-cost-of-incarceration

Federal Bureau of Prisons. (2019). Past inmate population totals. Retrieved from https://www.bop.gov/about/statistics/population_statistics.jsp

Ferrise, A. (2019). Video shows Cyahoga County jail officer pummel mentally-ill inmate after turning off body camera. Retrieved from https://www.cleveland.com/metro/2019/06/video-shows-cuyahoga-county-jail-officer-pummel-mentally-ill-inmate-after-turning-off-body-camera.html

Fischman, J. B., & Schanzenbach, M. M. (2012). Racial disparities under the federal sentencing guidelines: The role of judicial discretion and mandatory minimums. *Journal of Empirical Legal Studies, 9*(4), 729–764. https://doi.org/10.1111/j.1740-1461.2012.01266.x

Fries, A. (2019). Albany County guards, deputies to get body-warn cameras. Retrieved from https://www.timesunion.com/news/article/Albany-County-correction-officers-to-get-13580957.php

Grafstein, R. (1948). *Institutional realism: Social and political constraints on rational actors.* New Haven, CT: Yale University Press.

International Association of Chiefs of Police. (2014). Body-worn cameras. Retrieved from theiacp.org/model-policy/wp-content/uploads/sites/6/2017/07/BodyWornCamerasPolicy.pdf

Kahneman, D. (2003). A perspective on judgment and choice: mapping bounded rationality. American psychologist, *58*(9), 697.

Kleinig, J. (2001). The blue wall of silence: An ethical analysis. *International Journal of Applied Philosophy, 15*(1), 1–23.

Kleinman, C. S. (2006). Ethical drift: When good people do bad things. *JONA'S Healthcare Law, Ethics and Regulation, 8*(3), 72–76.

Lipsky, M., & Project Muse. (1980). *Street-Level Bureaucracy Dilemmas of the Individual in Public Services.* New York, NY: Russell Sage Foundation.

Lum, C., Stoltz, M., Koper, C. S., & Scherer, J. A. (2019). Research on body-worn cameras: What we know, what we need to know. *Criminology & Public Policy, 18*(1), 93–118.

Nagel, T. (1973). Equal treatment and compensatory discrimination. *Philosophy & Public Affairs, 2*(4), 348–363.

National Archives and Records Administration. (2019a). The Bill of Rights: A transcription. Retrieved from https://www.archives.gov/founding-docs/bill-of-rights-transcript

National Archives and Records Administration. (2019b). The Constitution: Amendments 11–27. Retrieved from https://www.archives.gov/founding-docs/amendments-11-27

National Conference of State Legislatures. (2019). Body-worn camera laws database. Retrieved from http://www.ncsl.org/research/civil-and-criminal-justice/body-worn-cameras-interactive-graphic.aspx

National Jail Exchange. (2013). The technology advantage: Using shoulder mounted cameras within a detention facility. Retrieved from https://www.bja.gov/bwc/pdfs/2870-SACDC-Body-Cameras-Article_275CD995.pdf

Nolan, T. (2009). Behind the blue wall of silence: Essay. *Men and Masculinities, 12*(2), 250–257.

O'Leary, R. (2010). Guerrilla employees: Should managers nurture, tolerate, or terminate them? *Public Administration Review, 70*(1), 8–19.

Overeem, P. (2015). The concept of regime values: Are revitalization and regime change possible? *The American Review of Public Administration, 45*(1), 46–60.

Perry, J. L. (1997). Antecedents of public service motivation. *Journal of Public Administration Research and Theory, 7*(2), 181–197.

Pfattheicher, S., & Keller, J. (2015). The watching eyes phenomenon: The role of a sense of being seen and public self-awareness. *European Journal of Social Psychology, 45*(5), 560–566.

Rawls, J. (1971). *A theory of justice.* Cambridge, MA: Belknap Press of Harvard University Press.

Rohr, J. (1978). *Ethics for bureaucrats: An essay on law and values.* New York, NY: Marcel Dekker.

Rohr, J. A. (1998). *Public service, ethics, and constitutional practice.* Lawrence, KS: University Press of Kansas.

Shafritz, J. M., & Hyde, A. C. (1978). *Classics of public administration.* Chicago, IL: The Dorsey Press.

Silverstein, M. (2017). Rebalancing Harlow: A new approach to qualified immunity in the fourth amendment. *Case Western Reserve Law Review, 68,* 495.

Simon, H. A. (1997). *Administrative behavior: A study of decision-making processes in administrative organizations* (4th ed.). New York, NY: Free Press.

Smart, H. (2019). Operationalizing a conceptual model of colorism in Local policing. *Social Justice Research, 32*(1), 72–115.

Tversky, A., & Kahneman, D. (1981). The framing of decisions and the psychology of choice. *Science, 211*(4481), 453–458. https://doi.org/10.1126/science.7455683

Viglione, J., Hannon, L., & DeFina, R. (2011). The impact of light skin on prison time for black female offenders. *The Social Science Journal, 48*(1), 250–258. https://doi.org/10.1016/j.soscij.2010.08.003

Weitzer, R. (2015). American policing under fire: Misconduct and reform. *Society, 52*(5), 475–480.

White, M. D. (2019). Translating the story on body-worn cameras. *Criminology and Public Policy, 18*(1), 89–91.

Yokum, D., Ravishankar, A., & Coppock, A. (2017). *Evaluating the effects of police body-worn cameras: A randomized controlled trial.* Washington, DC: LAB@ DC.

12

ADVANCING SOCIAL EQUITY THROUGH INCREASED ACCESS TO RESIDENTIAL BROADBAND

Daniel Boden and Roy Kirby

Introduction

Over the past several decades, the Internet has become an increasingly important aspect of American life. Once considered a luxury, high-speed Internet, or broadband,[1] has quickly become a necessity for Americans from all walks of life to engage in educational, professional, and political activities. Modern society has come to rely on digital devices, such as mobile phones and wearable sensor technology like smart watches, to stay connected and to conduct everyday business. These devices, which have become ubiquitous in contemporary life, rely on broadband to function as expected. For many Americans, broadband has become so pervasive that it is often taken for granted. Data sent and received through broadband affect how we receive our paychecks through direct deposit, make purchases from e-commerce entities such as Amazon, interact with others on social media, access continuing and professional education (e.g., apply for jobs, access training, and take classes online), and become informed (e.g., visiting websites, or using apps, as opposed to reading newspapers). Even mundane decisions such as what to wear are often driven by accessing weather reports online. In fact, broadband has pervaded daily life so completely that it has influenced our lexicon; when researching topics, we often refer to it as "Googling" (Merriam-Webster, 2019). As broadband has become an integral component of today's information society, ensuring reliable broadband access for citizens has become an important policy challenge for all levels of government.

Facilitating citizen access to residential broadband is complicated by both individual and community level factors. Individual Internet users can face monetary barriers to accessing the Internet in that they must purchase a digital device, such as a computer, and an Internet connection. Recently, scholars and practitioners have identified community level barriers, such as the lack of broadband information technology (IT) infrastructure as a significant challenge for governments in ensuring citizens have access to broadband (Whitacre & Mills, 2007). Examples of IT infrastructure include fiber optic cables and fixed wireless towers necessary to provide homes and business with broadband service. Individuals in an urban environment are more likely to have fewer IT infrastructure barriers to access broadband, due to advantages such as population density, which typically makes infrastructure cheaper per connection. In urban areas, the number of potential broadband subscribers is higher and the distance to lay fiber optic cables and place fixed wireless towers to provide service is lower. This makes it cheaper to provide broadband; unfortunately, individuals in rural areas may not be as fortunate when it comes to existing broadband infrastructure (Toregas, 2001). The resulting effect of these individual and community level barriers is that some individuals and communities have greater access to broadband than others. Concerns over this "digital divide" are not new (Norris, 2001; van Dijk, 2006; van Dijk & Hacker, 2003); however, in discussing the concept, it is important to acknowledge the challenges in providing broadband service to rural communities. Recognizing this fact highlights the disparate experiences citizens will have with broadband depending whether they live urban or rural locations.

A Tale of Two Virginias

There is a digital divide in the Commonwealth of Virginia. As discussed above, the digital divide is a complex, multidimensional concept that relates to, among other things, access to information technologies (van Dijk & Hacker, 2003). This divide represents those citizens who have access to reliable broadband Internet service and those who do not. Virginia's population centers, known as the "Urban Crescent" are concentrated in counties neighboring Washington D.C., the capital city of Richmond, and the Hampton Roads area that encompass cities like Virginia Beach and Norfolk (Figure 12.1).

Each of these areas generally possesses the necessary IT infrastructure to provide citizens with Internet speed at or above the Federal Communications Commission definition of broadband, which is a speed of 25 mbps download and 3 mbps upload. Compare these regions of the Commonwealth to others where many individuals are either underserved or unserved by broadband Internet service. These underserved and unserved regions of Virginia are typically more rural than those areas with reliable broadband.

For economic development reasons, Virginia has positioned itself as an important location for technology companies, and as a result, approximately 70 percent of the world's Internet traffic, by data volume, flows through data centers housed in Northern Virginia localities such as Loudoun County

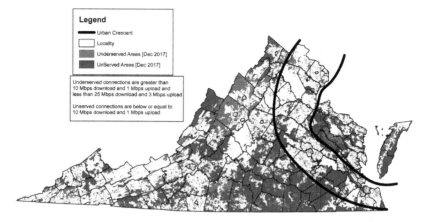

Legend

▬▬ Urban Crescent

☐ Locality

▨ Underserved Areas [Dec 2017]

▩ UnServed Areas [Dec 2017]

Underserved connections are greater than
10 Mbps download and 1 Mbps upload and
less than 25 Mbps download and 3 Mbps upload

Unserved connections are below or equal to
10 Mbps download and 1 Mbps upload

FIGURE 12.1   A Tale of Two Virginias: Broadband access within Virginia's "Urban Crescent" is typically greater than in rural areas (Center for Innovative Technology, 2019)

(Chang & Alcantara, 2017; Commonwealth of Virginia, 2018). Essentially, the Urban Crescent of Virginia has world-class broadband access, whereas other parts of Virginia lag considerably behind; some still have to rely on dial-up Internet connections. As a result, the Commonwealth of Virginia is not ranked highest nationally in most broadband categories. During the first quarter of 2017, Virginia ranked #8 in the United States for broadband adoption[2] with an estimated 660,000 rural Virginians lacking broadband access (Commonwealth of Virginia, 2018).

Understanding the Broadband Landscape

Community Level Barriers

Even as broadband has become more important in modern society, several themes have emerged to explain the difficulties in expanding broadband to rural areas of the country. Population density is a significant barrier to increasing broadband access to rural communities because areas with fewer inhabitants will have fewer subscribers to Internet services. Known as the "take rate," the number of consumers that sign up for service, in comparison with the number of potential residential connections in a service area, is important because a higher take rate decreases infrastructure costs and positively influences private broadband expansion. It is more cost effective for Internet service providers (ISPs) to target areas with high population density, such as urban settings, as this lowers the capital costs associated with broadband infrastructure. Geographic terrain is also an important barrier to expanding broadband services in rural communities. Ironically, the geographic features that attract people to Virginia such as mountains, rivers, lakes, forests, farmland, and beaches make it difficult and costly to provide broadband (Lucas, 2017a). Population density and terrain combine to influence overall capital (infrastructure) and operational (maintenance) broadband costs for ISPs. In many rural areas, the costs are simply too high for many private ISPs to provide broadband. In order to invest in broadband infrastructure, ISPs must ensure the investment will be, and remain, profitable. Enough people must take and keep the broadband service over time to make the business model sustainable. Despite these common barriers to broadband expansion, it is well worth the effort to connect people and businesses. As Kruger (2017) notes, broadband influences a wide variety of daily activities such as streaming video & music, telehealth, telework, financial transactions (banking & shopping), property values, and particularly education.

A Necessity: Public Education

Although the benefits of broadband are expansive, perhaps the most prominent factor associated with the importance of broadband access is the educational benefits. Unfortunately, not all schoolchildren have access to the benefits of broadband in education. Students that attend rural elementary schools, even high performing, award winning schools, suffer when broadband is limited or unavailable in the community. No, or limited, broadband access at home creates what is known as the "homework gap;" that is, children that have insufficient home broadband access find it more difficult to complete homework and projects. Approximately 20 percent of Virginia schoolchildren do not have broadband access at home, 6 percent go to local public libraries to complete homework, and another 5 percent travel back to school property to access the WI-FI network to complete homework (Virginia Department of Education, 2017, p. 14). According to the Virginia Department of Education (2017), this leaves children at a "measurable disadvantage compared to their more affluent peers, resulting in lower test scores, lower grades, and ultimately, lower graduation rates" (p. 16). Homework options are limited, classroom progress slows, communicating with parents is more difficult, and distributing report cards electronically is challenging. In Virginia, approximately 69 percent of school divisions report that lack of broadband access at home creates moderate to severe limitations on teaching and learning opportunities (Virginia Department of Education, 2017). It is a discouraging situation for school administrators, teachers, students, and parents.

Worse yet, burdens from being unserved with broadband at home follow children through life. Students in rural areas unserved by home broadband are at distinct disadvantages when entering middle school, and playing catch-up throughout high school, compared to their peers with home broadband access (Lucas, 2017b). Unfortunately, this difficulty follows these children into adulthood. Dettling, Goodman, and Smith (2015) found that there were significant negative impacts on test scores, college admissions, and other training programs. Online course availability for college degrees and professional development is also limited for those without home broadband access. These education issues all contribute to the "brain drain" occurring in rural areas, in which young people move to urban areas to access employment opportunities and quality of life amenities associated with broadband. Efforts to close the digital divide by elected officials and public administrators at all levels of government highlight the challenges to, and the values of, equality and equity in the United States regime.

Advancing Social Equity through Access to Broadband

In *Ethics for Bureaucrats*, John Rohr (1989) identifies freedom, property, and equality as formative values of the American regime (p. 75). Regime values, by their nature, shape future socio-political action and in so doing are reinforced as foundational to a specific regime (Newswander, Matson, & Newswander, 2017). There is no generally accepted definition or perspective of the philosophical concept of equality (Dworkin, 2000); however, equality has been, and continues to be, an important value of the American regime. The *Declaration of Independence* boldly proclaims the self-evident truth that "all men are created equal." This assertion of equality in one of the country's founding documents has had an important impact on the values of the United States regime. The principle of equality, even when ill defined and contested in practice, is valued because of its relationship with justice (McWilliams, 1986). So much so that many Americans are often troubled by the notion that laws could treat people differently (Barbour & Wright, 2019, p. 148).

Laws by their nature are intended to treat disparate classifications of persons differently from one another. Criminal law, for example, is intended to distinguish between how the government treats law abiding citizens from those who violate society's rules of conduct. The equal protection clause of the Fourteenth Amendment reinforces the value of equality in American public life. It is important to acknowledge that equality does not restrict government from making distinctions between groups of people. Once people are classified and categorized, it does require "that those persons who fall within the classification be treated alike" (Rohr, 1989, p. 114). This idea that those who are "similarly situated" be treated similarly is an important component of equal protection until the law. The United States Supreme Court has provided legislators and administrators guidance in making laws and policies that distinguish between groups (Barbour & Wright, 2019, p. 148). Such classifications must honor procedural equality; that is ensuring that those who are "similarly situated" are treated similarly as well as substantive equality; ensuring that the classifications themselves are not arbitrary in nature and are at the very least relevant to the legitimate goals of the states.

The legal authority of the Constitution is, for most Americans, unquestioned. The Constitution is the supreme law of the land; its legal authority is built on a foundation of moral authority, however. The Constitution's moral authority is not found within the text itself; but rather the shared understanding that "Justice is the end of government" (Cooke, 1961, p. 352). It is the relationship between the American Constitution and the constitution of the American regime (Goldwin, 1986, p. 27); that is, the norms, ideals, and values of the regime. A combination of the legal and moral force of the Constitution is central to John Rohr's (1989, 1998, 2002) investigations into the discretionary decisions of public administrators. For Rohr (1989), the Constitution offers a shared "moral heritage" to the country and, importantly for our purposes, a "standard" by which public administrators can use when faced with ethically challenging circumstances (p. 75). Such a standard is noteworthy for the appearance of social cohesion that it provides to the nation, but is particularly significant for public administrators in that it can be the means of upholding the rule of law and honorable behavior.

The moral authority of the Constitution evoked by Rohr invites public administrators to do more than simply support what is legal, but to support what is right. Rohr's invitation to public administrators is to reflect on and apply the values of the regime as they make decisions relevant to their administrative responsibilities (Stout, 2013, p. 117). Rohr (1989) uses "regime values" derived from the Constitution and significant judicial decisions as a foundation upon which administrators can begin to develop a set of principles to guide discretionary behavior. Rohr's goal is not to offer students and practitioners of public administration a series of the practical guidelines for ethical decision-making; but rather to point them to the values of the very regime they serve as the foundation for administrative decision-making (p. 71).

The values Rohr (1989) identifies as regime values, freedom, property, and equality, were not intended to be exhaustive (p. 285). The concept of equity has been an important aspect of both public administration theory and practice (Frederickson, 1990). Equity has roots in the concept of equality, but is distinguished in that equality is concerned with sameness. Equality demands that government treat those who are similarly situated that same; however, equity acknowledges that treating people the same, even when similarly situated, produces unfair and unjust outcomes (Gooden, 2017). Although Rohr specifically rejected equity as a regime value because of concerns that it is not a universally held value (Overeem, 2015, p. 57), it is undoubtable that equity has become an important value for the field of public administration (Frederickson, 2005; Svara & Brunet, 2004). Equity is concerned with the "fair, just and equitable distribution of public series" and is operationalized through a commitment to procedural fairness where all stakeholders are represented and the fair and just distribution and access to quality public service outcomes (Svara & Brunet, 2005, pp. 256–257).

The value of social equity is consistent with Rohr's (1989) challenge to administrators to do more than simply avoid trouble (pp. 60–64); his is a call for administrators to develop "moral vigor" (p. 67) through "ethical reflection" on the founding principles of the regime (pp. 68–69). This method encourages students and practitioners to reflect on the principles that justify their actions. As administrators consider justifications for their actions, they are forced to identify how their decisions conform to legal and moral norms. From this perspective, the purpose of justifying specific administrative action is not to excuse or defend ethically questionable behavior, but an opportunity to explain—even to oneself—the justness of that action (Walzer, 1972). As administrators compare the principles upon which their discretionary decisions are founded, they can compare them to the legal and moral standard offered by the Constitution and reflected in the values of the regime. This reflection is necessary because it encourages public officials to consider and acknowledge the role and impact their actions have within the system (Rohr, 1989, p. 51). Justifications of administrative action reflective of regime values are not only beneficial to the individual administrator, but perhaps more importantly to the regime itself. Administrative action so justified fosters trust and legitimacy of public action (Carter & Burke, 2010); thus reinforcing the justness and legitimacy of the regime.

For Rohr (1989), the importance of ethical decision-making is not reserved for dramatic moments in the nation's history. Obviously, when faced with extraordinary challenges, it is important for administrators to act in accordance with "regime values"; however, it is the smaller, often mundane, decisions which "influences at least the dominant tone, if not the ultimate fate, of the Republic" (p. 73). To illustrate the importance of such daily decisions, Rohr offers one such example when he recounts a story form the 1970s involving Chester A. Newland, former director of the Federal Executive Institute (FEI). The FEI is tasked with providing leadership development training to senior federal executives and helping them "understand their constitutional role… in serving the American people" (U.S. Office of Personnel Management, n.d.). Rohr explains that at times the FEI invited notable guests to present to attendees. Some of these guests would request to stay at a nearby private resort that had a policy restricting services to African Americans. Rohr continues:

> Part of the training program at FEI was intended to ensure that the executives were made sensitive to the needs and feelings of minority groups. If FEI were to arrange accommodations for some of the top officials in government at an all-white club, the institute would undercut part of its own mission.

The problem was delicate. The racial exclusionary policy of the club broke no laws. An appointed official's choice of where he might want to spend the night was, at least ostensibly, a private matter. FEI was acting merely as a conduit of the very important person's (VIP's) personal choice. Those VIPs unfamiliar with the details of the institute's program—particularly its emphasis on human dignity—might have some difficulty seeing just how the choice of a night's lodging could harm FEI's mission.

Newland's solution was simple, but effective. Whenever a visiting VIP asked for accommodations at the segregated club, Newland instructed his staff to reply along the lines: "Oh, I'm sure the assistant secretary [or whoever] is not aware of the club's racial policies. We wouldn't want to cause him any embarrassment by booking him there." This solved the problem. No one ever replied that he knew perfectly well the club was segregated and wanted to stay there anyway (pp. 72–73).

Rohr's method of using regime values to guide administrative action requires administrators to identify and operationalize the values. In the case above, Rohr identifies equality as a regime value and explains how Newland's actions reflect the affirmative nature of ethical decision-making. That is, Newland was under no legal obligation to alter or refuse the requests of his prominent guests. Newland, however, had a positive obligation to ensure his actions complied with the regime value of equality (Rohr, 1989, pp. 72–73).

The classifications we assign individuals or groups to justify dissimilar treatment often feel natural or obvious, but it is imperative to evaluate and at times revalue these distinctions. As has been seen throughout the nation's history, at times the unequal treatment of individuals and groups has been justified on insubstantial or even dubious reasons. That is, the categorizations used to distinguish one group from another are dependent on the legitimacy granted to them by society itself (McWilliams, 1986, pp. 286–287). As discussed above, there are significant barriers to ensuring broadband infrastructure is available to citizens living in rural areas. Considering the physical and financial challenges to providing broadband to rural communities, it is not surprising that urban areas tend to have greater residential broadband access. Commonwealth's Chief Broadband Advisor, Evan Feinman, has chosen to advance social equity in his effort to promote greater broadband access throughout Virginia.

Advancing Broadband in Virginia

In an effort to expand broadband access to rural Virginia, Governor Ralph Northam appointed Evan Feinman, executive director of the Tobacco Region Revitalization Commission, as the Commonwealth's Chief Broadband Advisor. The Tobacco Region Revitalization Commission (2018) vision statement to "accelerate regional transformation, giving citizens expansive opportunities for education and employment, and providing communities the benefits of economic stability, diversification, and enhanced prosperity" (p. 4) aligns well with the goal of providing a similar education experience for Virginia children throughout the Commonwealth. One of the Tobacco Region Revitalization Commission grants Mr. Feinman oversees as part of that revitalization effort is the Last Mile Broadband Grant Program. This program helps fund "last-mile" or the portion of the Internet that connects end-users (broadband service consumers) to the broader network (Commonwealth of Virginia, 2018).

Mr. Feinman works with a wide cross-section of stakeholders from the public, private, and non-profit sectors to advance community revitalization efforts. These stakeholders include federal and state agencies, local governments, the education community, public utilities, agricultural interests, the business community, healthcare professionals, tourism interests, and elected officials at all levels of government. He is clearly accustomed to collaborating with a wide variety of stakeholders, which proves beneficial to advancing Virginia broadband efforts.

Finding Common Ground

Understanding the broadband landscape helps to connect the diverse stakeholders needed from the public, private, and non-profit sectors. This involves identifying entities engaged in activities such as technology, government, business, healthcare, real estate, and education—just to name a few. These entities have expertise in leveraging broadband to benefit society, while understanding the barriers to broadband expansion. Working together, these entities can overcome previous barriers to benefit society through improved broadband access and adoption.

Messaging: Advancing Social Equity throughout the Commonwealth

To attract stakeholders, there must be a focused message that resonates well, leading to wide-ranging stakeholder buy-in. That messaging topic is equity in the access and distribution of public services. As previously noted, those that lack sufficient broadband in rural areas suffer negative consequences for years to come. Broadband's importance to society is in opportunity. Broadband connects us socially, conveys information, facilitates commerce, leverages conveniences, creates efficiencies, and can improve our quality of life. Those unserved with broadband cannot fully capitalize on these vital opportunities. When announcing his broadband budget recommendation in Bedford (Office of Governor Northam, 2018), Governor Northam summarized the case well. "In the 21st century, broadband is a requirement for opportunity. A moral necessity. Children's educational future should not depend on where they are born. That's just not right" (Governor Ralph Northam, 2018, December 14).

To garner support behind equity of access, as Commonwealth's Chief Broadband Advisor, Mr. Evan Feinman engaged in a continual speaking tour to emphasize the Governor's position on advancing broadband through functionally universal broadband coverage in ten years.[3] At the *Governor's Summit on Rural Prosperity* in Staunton, Mr. Feinman spoke to his target audience—rural localities that lack broadband. He emphasized that the people have spoken; broadband has become a political and social demand.

Broadband is a moral requirement, and I'll tell you why. First, Virginia and American civic life happens online. People, to fully participate in civic life, need [broadband] access. We are saying that "the folks in rural Virginia don't deserve to have the same access, do not deserve to have the same opportunity to have their voices heard" if we don't do this. And beyond that, and even more pressing, children in [school] districts where they do not have access to the internet at home, are put at a significant disadvantage, relative to children that are born in a locality where they can get online all of the time (Feinman, Speech for the Governor's Summit on Rural Prosperity, 2018, October 22).

In concluding that speech, he emphasized that bridging the digital divide will be difficult and expensive—but a problem that we can solve together.

The *Virginia Broadband Summit* in Roanoke held another target audience—local government officials, ISPs, and federal and state funding agencies. These are the primary stakeholders in broadband expansion logistics. During this speech, Mr. Feinman emphasized social equity in education.

Children born into [school] districts that do not have the opportunity to get online, regardless of the quality of their school system, do not have the same opportunities after they graduate from high school as kids who are born in other parts of Virginia do. That is a moral failure. It is a decision we make to say, "these kids get all of the opportunities that they can possibly gather all to themselves. These kids don't." That is not something we can allow to stand! That's not what it means to be an American—and that's not what it means to be a Virginian. Everyone needs to have the same opportunity (Feinman, 2018, October 30).

By reaching out to a wide variety of target audiences, Mr. Feinman is publicly making the case to "do good" to advance social equity throughout the Commonwealth. There were numerous ways Mr. Feinman could have approached advancing broadband. In fact, focus on Virginia broadband originated in advancing economic development. By making the case to enhance broadband, however, Mr. Feinman made the purposeful choice to emphasize social equity—especially for schoolchildren. It can be more difficult to take a moral stand, compared to making an economic argument. Mr. Feinman chose to take this position because it is the right thing to do to ensure that government acts on behalf of all of its citizens. Social equity is an important value in the field of public administration and Mr. Feinman's actions advance that value as he seeks equitable outcomes across the state. Where a child is born, or where a family chooses to live, should not negatively influence lifelong opportunities. By advancing broadband in areas that do not currently have it, all of Virginia benefits.

Reaching out to broadband stakeholders around Virginia consistently with social equity of access messaging provided a focus area around which to coalesce issue network membership. Mr. Feinman successfully led the way in forming an issue network called the Commonwealth Connect Broadband Coalition (CCBC). This coalition currently has approximately 100 members from the public, private, and non-profit sectors that cover many crucial areas such as education, technology, public safety, healthcare, real estate, and more.[4] Household names such as Amazon, Google, Microsoft, and Facebook, are CCBC members.

This CCBC is leveraging knowledge, technology, and resources to build broadband capacity. Based on network interactions, the coalition is helping Mr. Feinman "do good" by advancing social equity throughout the Commonwealth.

Year One Progress

The CCBC was active daily throughout the 2019 Virginia General Assembly session to advance the value of social equity through broadband policy and funding changes.

Policy Changes

Two important broadband bills passed the General Assembly and were signed into law by Governor Northam. First is H 2141. This law empowers local governments to adopt ordinances to create service districts. An annual tax is applied to any property in such service districts subject to local taxation "to pay, either in whole or in part, for expenses" related to service provision, such as broadband infrastructure (Virginia Legislative Information System, 2019a). This is a revenue generating option for localities to ensure they have the funds to address important service needs. In the case of broadband, this can help secure funds to offset capital costs for expanding and/or upgrading infrastructure. Service districts can help "make the math work" for sustainable business models in areas that infrastructure builds were originally too cost prohibitive.

The second law is H 2691. This law establishes "pilot programs under which Dominion Energy and Appalachian Power may submit a petition to provide or make available broadband capacity to non-governmental Internet service providers in areas of the Commonwealth that are unserved by broadband" (Virginia Legislative Information System, 2019b). This law affects "middle mile" infrastructure.[5] As part of ongoing efforts from investor-owned utility companies to improve smart grid technology, these utilities can create pilot projects that enable "last mile" ISPs to access its middle mile infrastructure. This could bring middle mile infrastructure much closer to communities, such as rural localities, that currently lack broadband. This is another way of "making the math work" to achieve business model sustainability for ISPs.

Funding

Policy changes alone are not enough to address a wicked problem such as broadband; funding must be increased. Current broadband funding in Virginia occurs primarily through the Virginia Telecommunications Initiative Grant. During session, the CCBC members actively engaged lawmakers and public administrators associated with broadband policy formulation, implementation, and evaluation. The result was an increase in Virginia Telecommunications Initiative funding from $4 million to $19 million in fiscal year 2020. That is an astounding 475 percent upturn in one year. This funding increase means that much more broadband infrastructure expansion and state sponsored broadband planning assistance to localities can occur.

In the end, progress was made that should connect more Virginians, bringing them the social equity that broadband provides. This progress would not have been possible without Mr. Evan Feinman making a conscious decision to advocate for broadband from a positive perspective that encouraged and advanced the value of social equity. This positive messaging to "do good" rallied a large, powerful, and growing coalition that helped initiate policy and funding change to facilitate broadband infrastructure expansion.

Discussion and Conclusion

In many ways, citizens of the United States have little in common. The vast size of the country ensures a diversity of natural ecosystems, each affecting the daily activities of its inhabitants, altering human interactions and local practices in often subtle, but important ways. Couple the physical diversity of the country with the fact that United States citizens do not share a unified ethnic, religious, or cultural history or identity and it is not hard to imagine why some anti-Federalists worried about the viability of a large republic (Storing, 1981). Of the many things that divide citizens, general respect and support for the Constitution is an important unifying aspect of political life in the United States. The moral authority of the Constitution demands that administrators evaluate actions taken under the color of law. The legal and moral authority of the Constitution invites them to ask two questions: 1. Are my actions legal? and 2. Are my actions consistent with the regime values? While the legal authority of the Constitution contends the first question must be asked; it is the moral authority of the document that insists on the second.

In his analysis of the Supreme Court case *DeShaney v. Winnebago County Department of Social Services*, Rohr (2002) argues that the Constitution "build[s] a floor, not a ceiling" (p. 138). The values embedded within the Constitution serve as a reminder that just because something is legal does not make it right; at times the moral authority of the Constitution demands more than simply obeying the law. In his book, *Dreams from My Father*, former President Barack Obama (2004) states, "the law also records a long-running conversation, a nation arguing with its conscience" (p. 437). The use of case studies, such as the one above, illustrates distinct challenges in which public administrators may find themselves. Additionally, the case study method allows public administrators to develop a principles-based method upon which ethical decisions can be made.

Cases are important to Rohr's method of ethical decision-making in that they elucidate to students and practitioners of public administration how seemingly mundane decisions, such as a decision related to coordinating lodging, can support regime values to aid in the decision-making process. It is in these situations, where the relationship between the legal and ethical obligations of public administrators can be reflected upon. Where public administrators can identify "regime values" which can be used as loadstars in both exceptional and routine situations, such cases offer an opportunity to discuss the obvious "necessity of 'avoiding evil,'" but more importantly the positive responsibility public administrators have "to 'do good'" (p. 73). In the case of Mr. Feinman, he chose to do good by highlighting the value of social equity to ensure that all Virginians, especially children, have access to the opportunities that broadband brings.

In closing, the conscience recognizes when administrative actions have violated the values of the regime. At these times, it is this conversation, the conversation between what is legal and what is right, that is important. In the case of enhancing Virginia broadband, Governor Northam wanted to improve economic development. Commonwealth Chief Broadband Advisor Evan Feinman went a step beyond his legal and political mandate to improve economic development. Like Chester Newland, Mr. Feinman was under no legal obligation to alter or change course, but instead chose to go further to seek social equity—to do good. For it is through this conversation about what is legal and what is right that we recognize that "those words put to paper over two hundred years ago must mean something after all" and as a nation we collectively "choose our better history" (Obama, 2004, p. 439). It is through this conversation that we seek to "Establish a More Perfect Union."

Notes

1 Broadband is defined as a digital connection permitting a large amount of data to be transmitted, generally referenced in terms of download speeds (the speed at which a user's device, used to make a digital connection, receives data) and upload speeds (the speed at which a user's device can send data to a remote server, or website.)

2 The percentage of residential households that subscribe to Internet service.

3 Functionally universal coverage does not mean every structure is connected. It means that every Virginian that wants broadband service should be able to get it (Commonwealth of Virginia, 2018).

4 For an updated CCBC Membership List, please visit https://www.commonwealth connect.virginia.gov/CCBC.
5 Connections between backbone and last-mile connections are referred to as middle mile. Conceptualizing of the Internet as a circulatory system, the middle mile constitutes the large veins and arteries that distribute blood to and from the capillaries (Commonwealth of Virginia, 2018).

References

Barbour, C., & Wright, G. C. (2019). *Keeping the republic: Power and citizenship in American politics* (8th ed.). Thousand Oaks, CA: Sage Publications.

Carter, L. H., & Burke, T. F. (2010). *Reason in law* (8th ed.). New York, NY: Longman.

Center for Innovative Technology. (2019, August 27). *A Tale of Two Virginias: Broadband access within Virginia's "Urban Crescent" is typically greater than in rural areas.* Retrieved from Virginia Broadband Availability Map and Integrated Broadband Planning and Analysis Toolbox: https://broadband.cgit.vt.edu/IntegratedToolbox/

Chang, E., & Alcantara, C. (2017, July 5). Northern Virginia, center of the (data) world. *Washington Post.* Retrieved from https://www.washingtonpost.com/apps/g/page/lifestyle/northern-virginia-center-of-the-data-world/2226/?noredirect=on

Commonwealth of Virginia. (2018). *Commonwealth connect: Governor Northam's plan to connect Virginia.* Herndon, VA: Center for Innovative Technology. Retrieved from https://www.commonwealthconnect.virginia.gov/sites/default/files/CIT%20Documents/Commonwealth%20Connect%20Report.pdf

Cooke, J. E. (Ed.). (1961). *The federalist.* Middletown, CT: Wesleyan University Press.

Dettling, L. J., Goodman, S. F., & Smith, J. (2015). *Every little bit counts: The impact of high-speed internet on the transition to college.* Washington, DC: Federal Reserve Board.

Dworkin, R. (2000). *Sovereign virtue: The theory and practice of equality.* Cambridge, MA: Harvard University Press.

Feinman, E. (2018, October 22). Speech for the Governor's Summit on Rural Prosperity. Staunton, VA.

Feinman, E. (2018, October 30). Speech for the *Virginia* Broadband Summit. Roanoke, VA.

Frederickson, H. G. (1990). Public administration and social equity. *Public Administration Review, 50*(2), 228–237.

Frederickson, H. G. (2005). The state of social equity in American Public Administration. *National Civic Review, 94*(4), 31–38.

Goldwin, R. A. (1986). Of men and angels: A search for morality in the Constitution. In R. H. Horwitz (Ed.), *The moral foundations of the American Republic* (3rd ed., pp. 24–41). Charlottesville, VA: University Press of Virginia.

Gooden, S. T. (2017). Social equity and evidence: Insights from local government. *Public Administration Review, 77*(6), 822–828.

Governor Ralph Northam. (2018, December 14). *Major investment to accelerate Virginia's progress towards universal broadband access.* Bedford, VA.

Kruger, L. (2017). *Defining broadband: Minimum threshold speeds and broadband policy.* Washington, DC: Congressional Research Service.

Lucas, R. (2017a, February 1). Franklin County looks for ways to improve broadband in rural areas. Retrieved from WSLS 10: https://www.wsls.com/news/franklin-county-looks-for-ways-to-improve-broadband-in-rural-areas_20170330135011806

Lucas, R. (2017b, February 24). Limited internet access causes problems for Franklin County students at home. Retrieved from WSLS 10: https://www.wsls.com/news/virginia/franklin/limited-internet-access-causes-problems-for-franklin-county-students-at-home_20170330134934796

McWilliams, W. C. (1986). On equality as the moral foundation for community. In R. H. Horwitz (Ed.), *The moral foundations of the American Republic* (pp. 282–312). Charlottesville, VA: University Press of Virginia.

Merriam-Webster. (2019, March 28). Google. Retrieved from Merriam-Webster: https://www.merriam-webster.com/dictionary/googling

Newswander, C. B., Matson, A., & Newswander, L. K. (2017). The recovery of self-interest well understood as a regime value: What is at stake/why this is important? *Administration & Society, 49*(4), 552–574.

Norris, P. (2001). *Digital divide: Civic engagement, information poverty, and the internet worldwide.* New York, NY: Cambridge University Press.

Obama, B. (2004). *Dreams from my father.* New York, NY: Three Rivers Press.

Office of Governor Northam. (2018, December 14). Governor Northam announces major investment to accelerate Virginia's progress towards universal broadband access. Retrieved from Virginia Governor Ralph S. Northam: https://www.governor.virginia.gov/newsroom/all-releases/2018/december/headline-837222-en.html

Overeem, P. (2015). The concept of regime values: Are revitalization and regime change possible? *American Review of Public Administration, 45*(1), 46–60.

Rohr, J. (2002). *Civil servants and their constitutions.* Lawrence, KS: University Press of Kansas.

Rohr, J. A. (1989). *Ethics for bureaucrats: An essay on law and values* (2nd ed.). New York, NY: Marcel Dekker.

Rohr, J. A. (1998). *Public service, ethics, and constitutional practice.* Lawrence, KS: University Press of Kansas.

Storing, H. J. (1981). *What the anti-federalists were for.* Chicago, IL: University of Chicago Press.

Stout, M. (2013). *Logics of legitimacy: Three traditions of public administration praxis.* New York, NY: CRC Press, Taylor & Francis Groups.

Svara, J. H., & Brunet, J. R. (2004). Filling in the skeletal pillar: Addressing social equity in introductory courses in public administration. *Journal of Public Affairs Education, 10*(2), 99–109.

Svara, J. H., & Brunet, J. R. (2005). Social equity is a pillar of public administration. *Journal of Public Affairs Education, 11*(3), 253–258.

Tobacco Region Revitalization Commission. (2019). Counties & cities eligible for Tobacco Commission funding. Retrieved from Tobacco Region Revitalization Commission: https://www.revitalizeva.org/about-the-commission/areas-served/

Toregas, C. (2001). The politics of E-gov: The upcoming struggle for redefining civic engagement. *National Civic Review, 90*, 235–240. https://doi.org/10.1002/ncr.90304

U.S. Office of Personnel Management. (n.d.). *Center for leadership development: Federal executive institute.* Washington, DC. Retrieved May 16, 2019, from https://www.opm.gov/services-for-agencies/center-for-leadership-development/federal-executive-institute/#url=Overview

Van Dijk, J. A. (2006). Digital divide research, achievements and shortcomings. *Poetics, 34*(4–5), 221–235.

Van Dijk, J., & Hacker, K. (2003). The digital divide as a complex and dynamic phenomenon. *The Information Society, 19*(4), 315–326. https://doi.org/10.1080/01972240309487

Virginia Department of Education. (2017). *Broadband connectivity capability survey report.* Richmond, VA: Virginia Department of Education.

Virginia Legislative Information System. (2019a). HB 2141 Local service districts; broadband and telecommunications services. Retrieved from 2019 Session: https://lis.virginia.gov/cgi-bin/legp604.exe?191+sum+HB2141

Virginia Legislative Information System. (2019b). HB 2691 Electric utilities; provision of broadband services to unserved areas. Retrieved from 2019 Session: https://lis.virginia.gov/cgi-bin/legp604.exe?191+sum+HB2691

Virginia Tobacco Region Revitalization Commission. (2018). *FY 2018–2020 strategic plan.* Richmond, VA: Virginia Tobacco Region Revitalization Commission.

Walzer, M. (1972). Political action: The problem with dirty hands. *Philosophy & Public Affairs, 2*(2), 160–180.

Whitacre, B. E., & Mills, B. F. (2007). Infrastructure and the rural—urban divide in high-speed residential internet access. *International Regional Science Review, 30*(3), 249–273. https://doi.org/10.1177/0160017607301606

CONCLUSION

Where the Constitution Can Lead Us

Nicole M. Elias, Amanda M. Olejarski, and Sue M. Neal

Conclusion

The current United States (U.S.) administrative context and recent disregard for the Constitution, especially at the federal level of government, is incredibly troubling from both a normative and practical perspective. The primary aim of *Ethics for Contemporary Bureaucrats: Navigating Constitutional Crossroads* is to educate students, scholars, and public servants on constitutional values and legal precedent as a basis for understanding ethics in the public sector. This volume brings together classical ethics theory with contemporary public administration and policy challenges in the administrative state. Rooted in the constitutional tradition, each chapter speaks to bureaucrats in the present era of governance. This volume is organized around the three constitutional regime values of freedom, property, and social equity to produce a robust examination of substantive topics, including: financial management, housing policy, environmental regulation, gender identity, property rights, and voting rights.

The crux of the constitutional approach to public administration ethics lies in the values embedded in the Constitution, along with the administrative oath to uphold those values. The Constitution outlines regime values, or "beliefs, passions, and principles that have been held for several generations by the overwhelming majority of the American people" (Rohr, 1989, p. 74). This is not to say that regime values are static or incontestable, if they were, public administration ethics would be easy—we could simply make a list of moral absolutes. Scholars and practitioners, alike, would agree that absolutism in public administration ethics is both impractical and undesirable. Rather, the lived experience makes administrative ethics messy, and this is where the Constitution serves as a compass in guiding ethical decision making. Central to positioning the Constitution's ethical utility is the bureaucratic oath.

Public administrators take a professional oath to uphold the values of the Constitution, which is the moral foundation of ethics for bureaucrats (Rohr, 1989, p. 70). The constitutional approach is not wholly prescriptive in nature and applicable across a wide range of administrative discretion questions beyond the scope of this collection. Administrators must "run a constitution," as Rohr (1998) advocates, by using regime values as their guide. Not only do regime values provide a shared ethics, but the Constitution as the foundation for ethical decision-making in public administration provides stability and fosters public service motivation. This ethical perspective can reinvigorate public administrators in ethical crises by recognizing and valuing the mission and purpose to which they serve. It is worth reviewing what this volume has contributed to understanding Constitutional ethics before positing where to go from here.

Part 1 of this volume explores freedom as a regime value in the contemporary U.S. context. Chapter 1 argues civil servants are on the front lines of greenhouse gas emission regulation and enforcement. This chapter demonstrates how civil servants can stay the course despite leaderships attempts to erode the mission of the EPA. For this to occur, public administrators need latitude to pursue and protect the public interest. The constitutional approach equips public administrators to better weather the perfect storm of constraining court rulings, incalcitrant leadership, and a public that has made bureaucrat bashing a national pastime.

Chapter 2 broaches the question of how regime values can inform preparedness and investment in disaster response. This chapter addresses two key aspects of emergency management: preparation for disasters at the community level and the ability to accelerate the recovery process. Social capital is put forward as a way to balance conflicting regime values of property, liberty, and equity to navigate these priorities.

Transparency in public budgeting is the focus of Chapter 3. Budgeting is used to exemplify a legacy of institutional bias. There are common threads that run throughout the different budgetary models, whether centralized or decentralized in structure. Using a needs-based model provides transparency to the budgetary process and mitigates ongoing bias. Data-driven decision-making likewise promotes transparency and is advanced as a promising solution to the problem of institutional bias in budgeting, despite uncertain financial futures.

In Chapter 4, the interplay of freedom and fairness is contextualized in the housing mortgage crisis. Solutions are put forth that include greater competition in the market and government backing for finance structures. The central argument of this chapter is that when conflict between regime values threatens to gridlock the system, Rohr's balancing wheel metaphor is particularly instructive. This chapter emphasizes the need for mindful oversight and strong enforcement at the same time.

Part 2 of this text delves into the regime value of property. Chapter 5, against the backdrop of Supreme Court rulings, highlights competing priorities between private property rights and the public interest that manifest in private and economic development. This chapter clearly positions the public administrator as policymaker when exercising administrative discretion in cases of eminent domain using the Takings Clause. Despite the Supreme Court's erosion of due process, this chapter argues that regime values persist and provide the groundwork for stable decision-making and maintaining ethical standards.

Chapter 6 contributes a nuanced and contemporary interpretation of property to address intellectual property. In this Chapter, intellectual property is conceptualized as central to the identification of the individual in the public sphere—the penultimate property. From this understanding, the administrative state is both a generator and protector of intellectual property, because it has the right to idea exclusivity. Not only is the state seen as such, the state is uniquely capable of deeming intellectual property a tangible concept. Without this recognition by the state and public administrators, intellectual property becomes an abstraction with the potential to dissipate over time.

The next chapter analyzes alternative systems for considering the intersection of rights and local governance. Chapter 7 details how local governments prioritize regime values, often in scarce resource environments, by ignoring more complex issues such as privacy and constitutional protections, despite the potential for high economic cost. This chapter expands on Rohr's framework and offers the idea of "supra-regime values" as an administrative standard for practice.

The final chapter of the property section explores the non-profit sector and university endowments within the regime values framework. Chapter 8 considers property as donated funds to university endowments and critically evaluates what is due to donors. As public, private, and non-profit sectors continue to blur, the application of regime values becomes central to the role of the public administrator in these complex organizational structures. While no simple solution is feasible in these funding environments, this chapter calls for a greater recognition and purposeful assessment of regime values in hybrid organizations.

Part 3 posits social equity as a regime value, which is a slight, but important, departure from Rohr's original regime value of equality. Chapter 9 distinguishes "social equity" from "equality" and explains the rational for using social equity. Then, the regime value of social equity is applied to gender, specifically non-binary gender identity markers. Calling for an increased awareness of safety and interjurisdictional consistency, this chapter reinforces the need for public administrators to maintain the regime value of social equity as a basis for ethical decision-making in providing non-binary gender state identification markers.

Chapter 10 examines the ruling and subsequent implementation of the 2013 landmark decision, *Shelby v. Holder*. This case ruled sections of the Voting Rights Act of 1965 unconstitutional, and this chapter highlights the implications of of this decision, *Shelby v. Holder* presents a critical social equity paradox by significantly reducing voting protections derived from the original intent of the 15th Amendment. This signals a fundamental shift in the composition of the voting regime and raises compelling social equity concerns.

Chapter 11 applies the regime value of social equity to administrative discretion in the criminal justice system. This chapter addresses concerns that in the absence of structural protections, discretion can depart significantly from regime values and harm vulnerable populations in the criminal justice system. Some of the proposed means of addressing these concerns include screening police officers for biases, universal enhancements to body-worn cameras, physical segregation of defendants during court proceedings, and training correctional officers to report unethical behavior within prisons.

The underlying question posed in Chapter 12 prompts readers to distinguish between "what is legal" and "what is right" in the context of broadband access. This chapter highlights social equity implications that can be realized when administrators use grounded regime values to make decisions. Positioning decision-making within the constitutional framework is a means to move beyond doing what is "legal" to doing what is "right," and in turn, empowering public administrators to foster social equity in the communities they serve.

Each of the chapters in this volume analyzes contemporary issues within Rohr's regime value framework. Yet, challenges to the regime values embedded in the Constitution are not new. Two of the most egregious historical events are the Watergate scandal involving President Nixon in the 1970s and President Truman nationalizing the steel industry during the Korean War in the 1950s. The utility of applying regime values is seen in the interpretation and adherence to constitutional values as time passes and issues evolve. Though the nature of the challenges shift, what remains is the Constitution's resilience in guiding administrative ethics.

At the 30th anniversary of Rohr's seminal work, the question becomes where does constitutionalism lead us. This volume emphasizes the need to bring the Constitution back to the forefront of public administration ethics. Though, we are not suggesting that the constitutional framework should stand alone or in competition with other ethical frameworks in public administration. The crux of administrative ethics is balancing the good with the right, a key, if not the most important normative concern. To be sure, this is no easy position for administrators. As Spicer (2010) explains

> We neither expect nor want our government leaders to act like moral saints because to have them do so would be to rob them of the power to satisfy our desires and hopes... On the other hand, there are real dangers when we seek to rationalize actions that are morally questionable (p. 34).

The constitutional approach presented in this volume serves as a strong basis for ethics in administration, because it provides enough structure to guide public servants, while at the same time, allows rooms for administrative discretion. Regime values are inherently claims of what a society holds as morally good. As part of the Constitution, regime values are interpreted differently as major social, political, and economic shifts likewise impact societal norms and beliefs. In practice, contemporary applications of constitutionalism come down to striking a balance between the responsibility to make the right decision and maintaining moral character in achieving the public good.

References

Rohr, J. A. (1982/1989). *Ethics for bureaucrats: Essay on law and values.* New York, NY: Marcel Dekker.

Rohr, J. A. (1998). *Public service, ethics, & constitutional practice.* Lawrence, KS: University of Kansas Press.

Spicer, M. W. (2010). *In defense of politics in public administration: A value pluralist perspective.* Tuscaloosa, AL: The University of Alabama Press.

INDEX

Note: Page numbers in italic and bold refer to figures and tables, respectively. Page numbers followed by n refer to notes.